W9-CER-755

FINANCIAL STRATEGY FOR PUBLIC MANAGERS

SHARON KIOKO AND JUSTIN MARLOWE

Financial Strategy for Public Managers by Sharon Kioko and Justin Marlowe is licensed under a Creative Commons Attribution 4.0 International License, except where otherwise noted.

This means you can use it, adapt it, and redistribute it as you like, but you must provide attribution to the original authors, by retaining this license notice.

© Sharon Kioko & Justin Marlowe. All authors retain the copyright on their work.

We request that you keep this full notice when you use the book.

You can find free copies of this book in multiple formats (web, PDF, EPUB) at: https://press.rebus.community/financialstrategy/.

Print ISBN: 978-1-927472-59-0

Ebook ISBN: 978-1-927472-60-6

Do you have comments about this book? Please visit https://forum.rebus.community/topic/98/project-summary-financial-strategy-for-public-managers.

Rebus Community

This book was created with support from the Rebus Community for Open Textbook Creation, where we are building new collaborative models for creating & sustaining open textbooks. Would you like to collaborate on an open textbook? Join the Rebus Community at forum.rebus.community.

Are you a faculty member or administrator with questions about this book, or about open textbooks generally? Please get in touch with us at contact@rebus.community.

CONTENTS

FOREWORD

There are many fine textbooks on public financial management. Each does certain things well, but in our view none covers all the concepts, techniques, and analytical tools that today's graduate students of public policy and administration need to put their passion into action. This book is our best attempt to weave that material together in a fresh, robust, concise, and immersive way. We also believe the time is right to bring to the market a free, open source treatment of this critically important subject.

At the University of Washington we use this text for a one quarter (10 week) introductory course titled "Public Financial Management and Budgeting." We believe it's suitable for a similarly-structured semester-long course. Sections of the text might also be suitable for other courses often found in Master of Public Administration, Master of Public Policy, and other programs. Chapters 2 and 3 would be appropriate for courses on governmental accounting, debt management, credit analysis, or non-profit financial management. Chapters 4 and 5 work well for an applied course on public or non-profit budgeting.

The first time we taught "Public Financial Management and Budgeting" together we quickly realized that we approached the course in similar ways. That shared thinking is in part the result of our shared experiences with some exceptional teachers and scholars. They include, in no particular order: the late, great Bill Duncombe, (formerly of Syracuse University); Bart Hildreth, Ross Rubinstein, and Katherine Willoughby (Georgia State); Jerry Miller (Arizona State); and Dwight Denison (Kentucky).

We'd also like to acknowledge the people who helped make this book a reality. It's been a true pleasure to work with the staff at the Rebus Community Project, namely Liz Mays, Zoe Hyde, and Hugh McGuire. They're building a wonderful model for open textbooks, and we're proud to be one of their early products. Chelle Batchelor from the UW Libraries connected us with Rebus and has been a steady supporter and advocate all along. In the autumn 2016 quarter we test drove an early version of this text with our Evans School MPA students. A big thanks to them for their patience and helpful feedback throughout that experience. We're also most grateful to the long list of scholars and practitioners who prepared anonymous reviews of the book for Rebus. We did our best to address all of your invaluable comments.

Finally, we'd also like to publicly thank our boss, Sandra Archibald. Fifteen years ago Sandy took over as Dean of the Evans School. On Day One she committed to making the School a leader in public financial management. This text is a testament to that commitment, and a reflection of our progress so far.

Sharon Kioko and Justin Marlowe
Daniel J. Evans School of Public Policy and Governance
University of Washington
August 2017

INTRODUCTION

In late 2015 Mark Zuckerberg, founder of Facebook, launched a plan to give away most of his $45 billion fortune. Along with his wife Priscilla Chan, he announced the creation of a philanthropic organization known as the "Chan-Zuckerberg Initiative." This "Initiative" defies conventional labels. At one level it's similar to a traditional non-profit organization. It can deliver social services, participate in public policy debates, and partner with other non-profits. It's also like a traditional philanthropic foundation, with plans for grant-making in areas like education reform in the US and clean water in developing countries.

But the Initiative is also decidedly non-traditional. It's organized as a for-profit limited liability corporation. That means when it wants to, it can do many things non-profits and governments can't. It can invest money in other for-profit entities. It can fund election campaigns. It can manage and invest money on behalf of other non-profit and for-profit organizations. So the important question around Chan-Zuckerberg is not what will it do, but rather, what won't it do? With $45 billion at its disposal, and few if any limits on how to spend it, the possibilities are endless.

Some are calling this "philanthro-capitalism." Chan-Zuckerberg is the largest and most visible recent example. But there are many others. If you've ever bought a sweater at Patagonia, worn a pair of TOMS shoes, or used a shot of insulin from by Novo Nordisk, you've participated in philanthro-capitalism. These are all for-profit companies with a social purpose hard-wired into their mission. This also works from the other direction. Strange as it sounds, IKEA – whose founder Ingvar Kamprad was once the wealthiest person in the world – is controlled by a charitable family foundation.

Maybe you didn't think public finance has anything to do with cat videos, Fair Trade Certified™ fleece vests, or the FJÄLKINGE shelving unit. Turns out it does.

Philanthro-capitalism brings the glamour and prestige of big business to the decidedly un-glamorous work of feeding the hungry, housing the homeless, and the other essential efforts of governments and non-profits. That's important. But even more important, it's forced us to re-think what it means to manage "public" money.

Showtime's hit show "Billions" is the story of a hedge fund that operates in the shadowy underworld of finance. That fund – known as Axe Capital, for its founder Bobby Axelrod – will do anything to turn a profit. It's traders buy and sell stocks on inside information, bribe regulators, and spread market-moving rumors, among many other nefarious tactics.

Season 2 features a compelling storyline ripped from the proverbial public finance headlines. Axe learns through a back-channel that the Town of Sandicot, a long-struggling upstate New York community on the verge of bankruptcy, is about to be awarded a state license to open a new casino.

Axe sees an opportunity. When a government is on the verge of bankruptcy investors steer clear of it. As a result, Sandicot's municipal bonds (a form of long-term loan) are available for pennies on the dollar. Axe believes the new casino will drive an economic recovery, and once that recovery is under way, investors will look to buy up Sandicot's bonds. So he decides to get there first. He "goes long" and buys several hundred million of Sandicot municipal bonds.

But then the story takes an unexpected turn. Word of the Sandicot play leaks out, and Axe's opponents persuade the State to locate the casino in another town. At that moment Axe faces a difficult choice: Sell the bonds and lose millions, or force Sandicot to pay back the bonds in full. Unfortunately, Sandicot can repay only if Axe forces it to enact savage cuts to its police, firefighters, schools, and other basic services. Axe is leery of the bad press that will surely follow a group of billionaire hedge fund managers profiting at the expense of a struggling town.

When asked for their opinion, a superstar Axe analyst named Taylor Mason – the first gender non-binary character on a major television show – says:

> "In many ways, a town is like a business. And when a business operates beyond its means, and the numbers don't add up, and the people in charge continue on heedless of that fact, sure that some Sugar Daddy, usually in the form of the federal government will come along and scoop them up and cover the shortfalls, well, that truly offends me. People might say you hurt this Town but in my opinion, the Town put the hurt on itself. Corrections are in order. There's a way to make this work and that way is hard, but necessary…Once we do this the town will face that challenge and come out stronger. Or it will cease being. Either result is absolutely natural."

Governments and non-profits tend to have a "retrospective" view on money. To them, an organization's money is well-managed, if it stayed within its budget, complied with donors' restrictions, and completed its financial audit on time. To them, bigger questions like "is this program working?" or "does this program deliver more benefits than it costs?" are best answered by elected officials and board members. In their view, if we mingle the different sectors' money, taxpayers will never know what they get for their tax dollar, and elected officials and board members won't know if programs they worked so hard to create and fund are delivering on their promises. To public organizations, financial accountability has often meant looking back to ensure that public money was spent according to plan.

Zuckerberg and many others who now operate in the public sector see public money in "prospective" terms. To them, public money is a means to an end. It's how we'll end racial disparities in public education, cure communicable diseases, close the gender pay gap, and pursue other lofty goals. These folks are not particularly concerned with how government tax dollars are different from charitable donations or business profits. If money can move an organization closer to its goals, regardless of where that money comes from, why not add it to the mix? They don't think of financial contributions as a way to divvy up credit for a program's success. They want to know how their money was spent, but far more important, they want to know what their money accomplished.

The opposite is also true. Taylor Mason, and many others who share their views, also sees public money in "prospective" terms. But instead of thinking about what the public sector could accomplish, they also believe no public sector organization is "too big to fail." If a local government like Sandicot is no longer accomplishing its mission, they argue, it should cease to exist.

Both these perspectives – philanto-capitalism and "government is like a business" – are big departure from public financial management's status quo. They're also why public organizations have tended to segregate themselves into "money people" and "everyone else." Money people tend to see the world differently.

And to be clear, both these perspectives illustrate a much broader recent trend: blending the financial lines across the sectors. Many non-profits now operate profitable lines of business that subsidize other services they provide for free. Governments around the world have created for-profit corporations that allow private sector investors to build, operate, and maintain public infrastructure like bridges, subways, and water treatment facilities. Charitable foundations of all sizes now act as "Angel Investors." They buy stock in small start-up companies that develop products to improve the quality of life in the developing world. Many of those investments have turned a handsome profit that in turn subsidized other, far-less-profitable endeavors.

Philanthro-capitalism and "government is like a business" are also animated by pressure on governments to do more with less. For roughly 50 years, taxpayers around the world have said no to new taxes, but yes to a steady expansion of the size and scope of government. They have demanded more spending on health care, education, environmental conservation, and other services, but left unclear how to pay for it. They have allowed their governments to borrow record amounts of money, but denied them the financial means to repay that money. Many governments today are simply maxed out. They have little or no new money to commit to innovate programs of the sort that Zuckerberg and others would like to see.

These trends – blurring of the sectors, emphasis on outcomes, scarce government resources – are redefining what it means to manage public money.

You got into public service because you want to make a difference. Maybe, like Mr. Zuckerberg, you want to tackle big, complex public problems. Maybe you want to make governments and non-profits work just a bit more efficiently. Maybe you think government should do a lot more in areas like health care, education, and transportation. Maybe, like Taylor Mason, you think government should get out of the way and make room for non-profits and for-profits. Regardless of your goals, to make that difference you'll need to speak the language of public financial management. You'll need to translate your aspirations into cost estimates, budgets, and financial reports. You'll need to show how an investment in your program/product/idea/initiative/movement will produce results. You'll need to understand where public money comes from, and where it can and can't go. You probably didn't get into public service to manage money, but in today's rapidly changing public sector, "we're all money people now."

And the opposite is also true. In today's public sector money people must also step outside of their comfort zone. They must be able to communicate with program managers, board members, and many other stakeholders from whom they don't traditionally interact. They must help others translate their ideas into the language of finance. As a public manager, a big part of your job will be learning to inspire your money people to step far outside of their comfort zone in the name of accomplishing your organization's goals.

WHAT IS FINANCIAL STRATEGY?

Money is to public organizations what canvas is to painting. The painter wants to bring his or her artistic vision to life on the canvas. But to do this they must work within the confines of that canvas. If the canvas is too small, too rough, or the wrong shape, the painter must adapt their vision. If they stray too far from their vision, they must know when to find a different canvas.

As a public servant, you are like a painter. You know what you want your organization to accomplish, but you must bring those accomplishments to life on its financial canvas. Every organization's financial canvas is a bit different. Some have many revenue streams that produce more than enough money, where others depend on a single revenue source to generate just enough money to keep the organization running. Some have broad legal authority to raise new revenue and borrow money, where others must get permission at every step from their board, taxpayers, or other stakeholders. Some have sophisticated financial experts to produce their budgets and manage their money, where others have no such expertise.

It's not a problem that each public organization's financial canvas is different from the rest. In fact, those differences are an important part of what makes public financial management an exciting and dynamic field of study. The problem, however, is that many great policies and programs fail because they're painted on the wrong financial canvas. Public organizations often take on policy challenges without the right financial tools, authority, and capacity. By contrast, some organizations are too modest. They have the tools, authority, and capacity to take on big challenges, but for a variety of reasons they don't. Financial strategy is how public organizations use their financial resources to accomplish their objectives. It's how they put their organization's vision to its financial canvas.

All public organizations must confront limits on the amount and scope of financial resources they can access. So in practical terms, financial strategy is often about tempering our expectations to match what our financial canvas can support. It's about analyzing a program's cost structure to make it more efficient, scaling back its goals and objectives, or finding partner organizations to help launch it. Sometimes strategy means finding a new canvas. That might mean forming a new organization, re-purposing an existing program, or recruiting a new foundation or venture capitalist to invest. This book tells you how to understand the many different types of canvases available to you, and the many different ways to put your organization's vision to one of those canvases.

TECHNIQUE SUPPORTS STRATEGY

This book is organized around a simple idea: technique supports strategy. There are many fine textbooks on public financial management, and almost all of them focus on technical skills. For more than a generation students of this subject have learned how to forecast revenues, build budgets, record basic transactions in an organization's financial books, and many other useful skills. At the same time, students have rarely been asked a far more important question: Where and how should they apply those skills? We believe technical skill is useful only if it informs actual management decisions. A cost analysis is useful only if tells us whether and how to launch a new program. Financial statement analysis is a powerful tool because it can inform when to build a new building, start a capital campaign, or invest unused cash. Budget variance analysis is important because it tells program managers where to focus their attention. And so forth. We present these and other techniques, but more important, we try to explain how those techniques can and should inform crucial management, strategy, and policy decisions.

Strategic thinking is at some level about "knowing what you don't know." It's about stepping outside of your own experience. It's about looking into your organization's future. It's about putting yourself in your stakeholders' shoes. That's why one of the most valuable tools in financial strategy is asking the right questions. No one can be an expert on all things financial. But if you can ask the right questions and access the right expertise, you can know enough to drive your strategy.

That's why one of the most important techniques in public financial management is asking good questions. This book is littered with questions. In fact, each chapter begins not with learning objectives, but with the kinds of questions managers ask, and how the information, conceptual frameworks, and analytical tools from financial management can help answer those questions. It includes exercises to help you refine your financial management technique. But more important, it includes cases and other opportunities for you to apply that technique in support of a genuine financial strategy. In fact, the centerpiece case at the end of the book – "The Cascadia Hearing School" – offers several opportunities to develop a financial strategy for a real public organization.

Strategy is not entirely sector-specific. What works in the for-profit sector might work in non-profits or governments, and vice versa. And as sector distinctions matter less, the origins of financial management strategy also matter less. That's why most of the discussion in this book is predicated on the idea that all governments, non-profits, and "for benefit" organizations (i.e. for-profit organizations with an explicit social purpose) are mostly alike. You'll see "public organization" and "public manager" used often. These are generic terms to describe people who interact with the financial strategy of any of these types of organizations. To be clear, "public manager" includes policy analysts, community organizers, for-profit contractors, and anyone else who has a stake in a public organization's finances. Where necessary and appropriate, you'll see discussions that highlight how each sector's technical information, legal environment, and strategic directions are different. But for the most part, this text assumes that public organizations have a lot in common.

HOW THIS BOOK IS ORGANIZED

First and foremost, this is a book about people and organizations. To many of us finance and budgeting are abstract subjects. They're numbers in a spreadsheet, but not much more.

In reality public financial management is how real public servants in real public organizations bring their passions to life. That's why all of the technical information is presented in the context of specific people, organizations, and strategies. Throughout this book you'll also find lots of illustrations and examples drawn from real public organizations.

The first chapter is titled "How we Pay for the Public Sector." It covers where public organizations' money comes from, and where it goes. It also highlights some of the pressing challenges now facing public organizations – namely shrinking public resources, debt, and entitlements – and how those challenges present tremendous opportunities for entrepreneurial public managers.

Each of the subsequent chapters covers a bundle of tools that public financial managers use to inform financial strategy. The second chapter covers the basic financial statements. Financial statements are an essential and often overlooked tool to understand an organization's financial story. This chapter introduces those statements, the information they contain, and the questions they help public sector managers ask and answer.

Chapter 3 is about financial statement analysis. If financial statements tell an organization's financial story, financial statement analysis is the annotated bibliography of that story. It's a tool to understand the specific dimensions of an organization's financial position, to place that position in an appropriately nuanced context, and to identify strategies to improve that financial position in both the near and long term.

To truly understand the numbers in the financial statements, and how those numbers might change as an organization pursues different financial strategies, you must also understand the core concepts of accounting. To that end, the fourth chapter is an applied primer on core accounting concepts like accruals, revenue and expense recognition, depreciation and amortization, and encumbrances. These concepts and their application to actual financial activity are collectively known as "transaction analysis."

Chapter 5 is about cost analysis. Many public organizations struggle to meaningfully answer a simple question: What do your programs and services cost? They struggle not because they're lazy or inept, but because it's challenging to measure all the different costs incurred to produce public services, and then express those costs in an intuitive way. It's even more challenging to think about how those costs change as the amount of service changes, or as the scope of a service expands or contracts. It's challenging, but it's also essential. Every successful public program ever devised was designed with a careful eye toward its cost structure. In this chapter you'll learn the different types of costs, the core concepts of cost behavior, and how to think about ways to improve an organization's financial position given its cost behavior.

Chapter 6 covers budgeting. A public organization's budget is its most important policy statement. It's where the mission and the money connect. Budgeting is at one level a technical process. It demands solid cost analysis, revenue and expense forecasting, and clear technical communication. But more important, it's a political process. It's how policymakers bring their political priorities to life, and shut down their opponents priorities. It's how the media and taxpayers hold public organizations accountable. It's where sophisticated public managers can advance their own priorities. This chapter focuses on budgeting as a technical process, with particular emphasis on the different types of budgets and the legal processes by which budgets are made. But it also covers some of the common political strategies that play out in the budget process, and how public managers do and do not engage those strategies. The discussion of those strategies is loosely organized around concepts borrowed from the burgeoning field of behavioral economics, such as loss aversion and the "endowment effect."

At the outset it's also worth highlighting what this book does not cover:

- Unlike other textbooks in this space, we do not give special attention to healthcare financial management. Health care financial management has much in common with public financial management. But recent trends in the former – especially the Medicare Modernization Act, the Affordable Care Act (i.e. "Obamacare"), and the collapse of the municipal bond insurance market – have made it too distinct to cover in a coherent way within the framework of this book.

- We gloss over government budgeting systems and processes. We cover the steps outlined in law that governments are supposed to follow to arrive at a budget. But for roughly a decade now the actual budget processes in Washington, DC and many state governments have been quite different from what's prescribed in law. Terms that used to describe deviations from that process, like "continuing resolution," "sequestration," "sweeps" and "recissions" now seem like parts of that process. That's why it seems silly to devote much attention to the budget process. Instead, we treat budgeting as the place where money, politics, and priorities come together in predictable and unpredictable ways.

- Financial managers find themselves in the throes of some transformational changes in public organizations. They are asked to push the boundaries of what traditional procurement and contracting processes will allow. They are often asked to implement massive new information technology projects. They find themselves leading new initiatives around "evidence-based decision-making," "lean management", and "performance benchmarking," among others. Woefully, we do not have time or space to devote to these processes. We hope to cover these topics in future iterations of this text.

CHAPTER 1.

HOW WE PAY FOR THE PUBLIC SECTOR

WHERE THE MONEY COMES FROM, AND WHERE IT GOES

Managers need to know where public money comes from, and where it goes. That information can answer important questions like:

- What revenue options are available to governments? Non-profits?

- What are the advantages and disadvantages of various revenue sources with respect to efficiency, equity, fairness, and other goals?

- How will the US federal government's financial challenges shape the financial future of state governments, local governments, non-profits, and other public organizations?

- What is the optimal "capital structure" for a non-profit?

- How, if at all, can governments address the challenges of entitlements and legacy costs?

In January of 2010 the United States Department of Justice (DOJ) received a formal civil rights complaint from a local community organization in the City of Ferguson, MO. In their complaint they accused the Ferguson Police Department of aggressive and biased policing tactics, including large numbers of traffic stops, searches, seizures, and arrests in the city's African-American communities. DOJ officials corroborated the report with the Missouri Attorney General's office, who had also received several similar complaints throughout the previous five years. Both offices agreed to monitor the situation.

On August 9, 2014, Michael Brown, a teenager and resident of Ferguson, was shot and killed by a Ferguson police officer who was investigating a nearby robbery. Ferguson police officials drew sharp criticism for the incident and for their management of the subsequent investigation into potential police misconduct. Several weeks later a grand jury later declined to indict the police officer. In their view the evidence suggested the police officer had reason enough to consider Brown a potentially dangerous suspect.

The shooting sparked violent protests across the US. Ferguson residents said the shooting was just the most recent example of the racist policing they had pointed out to federal and state officials years earlier. They implored Attorney General Eric Holder to immediately open a DOJ civil rights investigation into the Ferguson Police Department. Holder said his office would gather as much information as possible, but cautioned everyone that anecdotes and demographics are not sufficient to prove an accusation of biased policing. For several weeks, the country anxiously awaited word on what DOJ would do next.

On September 20, 2014 DOJ opened a formal civil rights investigation. The report from that investigation was released in March 2015. It excoriated the Ferguson Police Department and the Ferguson City Council for encouraging, both actively and passively, the sort of aggressive policing that Ferguson residents had decried. But perhaps even more important, it explained that the most compelling evidence of biased policing was not arrest records or police reports. It was Ferguson's budget. The report said "Ferguson's law enforcement practices are shaped by the City's focus on revenue rather than on public safety needs." It documented a recent trend toward raising new city revenues through aggressive enforcement of fines and fees. Ferguson generated more than $2.5 million in municipal court revenue in fiscal year 2013, an 80 percent increase from only two years prior. In all, fines and forfeitures comprised 20 percent of the city's operating revenue in fiscal year 2013, up from about 13 percent in 2011. By comparison, other St. Louis suburbs relied on fines and fees for no more than six percent of operating revenue. This budget strategy legitimized and even encouraged Ferguson's law enforcement and court officials, most of whom were not racists, to pursue such aggressive policing against Ferguson's majority African-American community.

The take away here is clear: Where a public organization gets its money says a lot about its priorities. In Ferguson's case, choices about where to get revenue led to a nationwide social movement.

Learning Objectives

After reading this chapter you should be able to:

- Identify the revenue sources used by the federal, state, and local governments.
- Contrast government revenue sources with non-profit revenue sources like donations and earned income.
- Identify public organizations' main spending areas, and the division of that spending across the government, non-profit, and for-profit sector.
- Show how similar governments pay for similar services in quite different ways.
- Identify some of the "macro-challenges" that will shape public organizations' finances well into the future.

Governments across the United States do the same basic things. Cities and towns mostly maintain roads, plow snow, keep neighborhoods safe, prevent and fight fires, and educate children. County governments run elections, care for the mentally ill, and prevent infectious diseases. State governments coordinate health care for the poor, incarcerate prisoners, and operate universities. The national – or "federal" – government regulates trade and commerce, defends our borders, and pays for health care for the elderly.

At the same time, governments are remarkably dis-similar in how they pay for and deliver these services. Some rely on a single tax source for most or all of their revenue. Others draw on many different revenue sources. Some deliver their services with the help of non-profits, health care organizations, private sector contractors, and other stakeholders. Others engage outside entities infrequently, if at all. Some citizens want their government to deliver many different high-quality services. Others want their government to do as little as possible.

These choices, about how governments pay for their services, how much they provide, and how they ultimately deliver those services, matter a lot to citizens. For instance, if a city government depends mostly on property taxes, its leaders might have an incentive to emphasize services that benefit property owners, such as public safety and sidewalks, and to worry less about services more likely to benefit those who do not own property, like public parks or housing the homeless. In some regions governments pay non-profit organizations to deliver most or all of the basic services in areas like foster care, child immunizations, and assisted living for seniors. For those who use those services, the quality of service they receive can depend a lot on which non-profit manages their case.

So at a high level, governments look the same. But if we examine them more carefully, we see they vary a lot on where their money comes from, and where it goes. That variation, and its implications for citizens, is a key part of the study of public finance. This chapter is a basic overview of where governments get their money, where they spend it, and some of the financial challenges they're likely to face in the future.

THE FEDERAL GOVERNMENT

The national government – also known as the "federal government" – is one of the largest and most important employers in the United States. Every soldier in the military, customs agent at an airport, and astronaut at NASA (the "National Aeronautics and Space Administration") works for the federal government. And so do many, many others. In 2015 the federal government spent just under $4 trillion and employed an estimated five million people, both directly and as contractors. For the past decade or so, federal government spending has accounted for roughly one-quarter of the entire economic output of the US.

The chart below shows where the federal government has received and spent its money since just before World War II. Areas shaded blue represent *revenue*, or money that comes into the government. Areas shaded red are spending items. Spending is called many different things in public finance, including *expenses, expenditures,* and *outlays.* These different labels have slightly different meanings that you'll learn throughout this text. All the figures shown here are in per capita constant 2015 dollars. In other words, they've been adjusted for inflation, and they're expressed as an amount for every person in the US.

Roughly 80% of the federal government's revenue is from two sources: the *individual income tax* and *social insurance receipts.*[1]

- In 2015 the federal government collected just over $3,500 per capita from individual income taxes. The income tax an individual pays is determined by their taxable income, tax rate, and any

1. Portions of the following discussion are quoted and adapted from the *Governing Guide to Financial Literacy, Volume 1*

applicable tax preferences. *Taxable income* is an individual's income minus any *tax preferences*. The federal government offers a *standard exemption,* or a reduction of an individual's taxable income, that all taxpayers can claim. Beyond that standard deduction, eligible taxpayers can claim hundreds of other exemptions and other tax benefits related to homeownership, retirement savings, health insurance, investments in equipment and technology, and dozens of other areas. Why does the federal government offer these preferences? To encourage taxpayers to save for retirement, buy a home, invest in a business, or participate in many other types of economic activity. Whether tax preferences actually encourage those behaviors is the subject of substantial debate and analysis (see the discussion later on *tax efficiency* and *market distortions*). The *tax rate* is the amount of tax paid per dollar of taxable income. In 2015 the federal tax code had seven different rates that applied across levels of taxable income (also known as *"tax brackets"*). Those *statutory* rates ranged from a 10% on individual annual income up to $9,225, to 39.6% on annual income over $413,201. An individual's *effective tax rate* is their tax liability divided by their total income. If an individual claims a variety of tax preferences, their effective tax rate might be much lower than the *statutory tax rate* listed here.

- Social insurance receipts are taxes levied on individuals' wages. Employers take these taxes out of workers' wages and send them to the federal government on their behalf. That's why they're often called *payroll taxes* or *withholding taxes.* Social insurance receipts are the main funding source for social insurance programs like Social Security and Medicare (see below).

- The remaining 20% or so of federal revenue is from a variety of sources including the *corporate income tax* (taxes on business income, rather than individual income), *excise taxes* (taxes on the purchase of specific goods like gasoline, cigarettes, airline tickets, etc.), and *estate taxes* (a tax imposed when a family's wealth is transferred from one generation to the next). As shown in the figure, these revenues as a share of total revenues have not changed much in the past several decades.

Tax Preferences: Spending by Another Name

Tax preferences – sometimes called tax expenditures – are provisions in tax law that allow preferential treatment for certain taxpayers. They include credits, waivers, exemptions, deductions, differential rates, and anything else to reduce a person's or business' tax liability. Many are quite specific. For example, some states have reduced tax rates that apply only to particular employers, industries, or geographic areas. Tax expenditures are, in effect, a form of spending. They require the government to collect less revenue than it would otherwise collect. Some think they're unfair because they offer targeted benefits but without the transparency of the traditional budget process. Proponents say that despite these drawbacks, tax preferences are essential to promote important behaviors, like buying a home or starting a business. At the state and local level they're an especially important tool to attract and retain businesses in today's competitive economic development environment.

Federal government spending is divided roughly equally across six main areas:

- National defense includes pay and benefits for all members of the US Army, Navy, Air Force, and

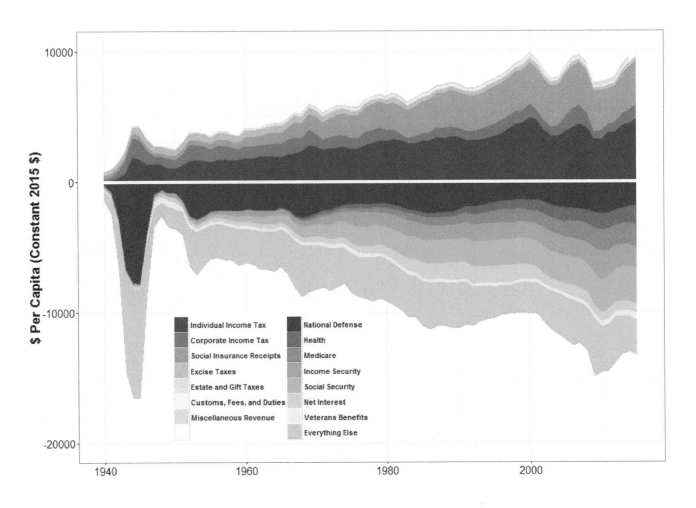

Federal Government Revenues and Outlays since 1940; source: authors' calculations based on data from the Congressional Budget Office, the Office of Management and Budgeting, and the US Department of Commerce

Marines, and all civilian support services. It also includes *capital outlays* – or spending on items with long useful lives – for military bases, planes, tanks, and other military hardware. Note the large spike in national defense spending during World War II (1939-1945) and the Korean War (1950-1953).

- *Medicare* is the federal government's health insurance program for the elderly. It was established in 1965. By some estimates, Medicare paid for nearly one-quarter of all the health care delivered in the US, a total of nearly $750 billion in 2015. Medicare has three main components. "Part A" pays for hospital stays, surgery, and other medical procedures that require admission to a hospital. "Part B" covers supplementary medical services like physician visits and procedures that do not require hospital admission. "Part D" pays for prescription drugs. Part A is funded through payroll taxes and through premiums paid by individual beneficiaries. Part B and Part D are funded mostly through payroll taxes. Medicare does not employ physicians or other health care providers. It is, in effect, a health insurance company funded by the federal government. In 2015 it served more than 55 million beneficiaries and spent an average of $18,500 per beneficiary.

- *Health* is a broad category that covers health-related spending outside of Medicare. The largest segment of this spending is the federal government's contribution to state Medicaid programs. It includes funding for public health and population health agencies like the National Institutes of Health (NIH) and the Centers for Disease Control and Prevention, and for health-focused regulatory agencies like the Food and Drug Administration.

- *Social Security* is an income assistance program for retirees. In 2015, over 59 million Americans received nearly $900 billion in Social Security benefits. Social Security is simple. Individuals contribute payroll taxes while they are working, those taxes are deposited into a fund, and when they retire, they are paid from that fund. In 2015, the average Social Security benefit was around $1,300 per month. Social Security also distributes benefits to disabled individuals who are not able to work.

- *Income security* is cash and cash-like assistance programs outside of Social Security. Most of these programs help individuals pay for specific, basic necessities. It includes unemployment insurance, food stamps, foster care etc.

- The federal government borrows a lot of money. Some of that borrowing is to pay for "big ticket" or *capital outlays* like aircraft carriers or refurbishing national parks. Like most consumers, the federal government does not have the money "saved up" to purchase these items, so it borrows money and pays it back over time. It also borrows when revenue collections fall short of spending needs. This is known as *deficit spending*. The federal government borrows money by issuing three types of *Treasury Obligations*: *Treasury bills, Treasury notes, and Treasury bonds.* Much like loans, obligations are bought by investors and the government agrees to pay them back, with interest, over time. Treasury bills come due – i.e. they have a *maturity* – of three months to one year. Treasury notes have maturities of two years to ten years. Treasury bonds mature in ten years upto 30 years. Each year the government pays the annual portion of the interest it owes on its Treasury obligations, and that payment is known as *net interest.*

- "Everything Else" is just as it sounds. This includes federal government programs for transportation, student loans, affordable housing, the arts and humanities, and thousands of other programs.

Who Owns Treasury Bonds?

At the end of 2015, the US Treasury had $19 trillion of outstanding Treasury bonds. About $12 trillion is owned by US investors. The remaining $7 trillion are held by investors outside the US, including nearly $1.5 trillion in China, and just over $1 trillion in Japan. The remaining $3.8 trillion is held by nearly 100 other countries. Why are US Treasury bonds so attractive to foreign investors? Because the US government is seen as the safest investment in the world. Investors across the globe believe the US government will pay back those bonds, with interest, no matter what.

We often divide federal government spending into two categories: *discretionary* spending and *non-discretionary* or *mandatory* spending. Non-discretionary spending is controlled by law. Social Security is a good example. A person becomes eligible for "full" Social Security benefits once they are over age 65 and have paid payroll taxes for almost four years. Once they become eligible, the benefit they receive is determined by a formula that is linked to the total wages they earned during their last 35 years of working. That formula is written into the law that created Social Security. Once a person becomes eligible they are "entitled" to the benefits determined by that formula. Other federal programs like Medicare, food stamps, Supplemental Security Income, and many others follow a formula-based structure. If Congress and the President want to change how much is spent on these programs, they must change the relevant laws. By some estimates, non-discretionary spending is more than 65% of all federal spending. Add to that the roughly 7-8% for interest on the debt, and we see that nearly three-quarters of federal spending is "locked in."

The remaining one-quarter is discretionary spending. This is spending that Congress and the President can adjust in the annual budget. It includes national defense, most of the "health" spending category, and virtually all of the "everything else" category. There is considerable debate on whether national defense is, in fact, discretionary spending. Legislators are not eager to cut funding to troops in harm's way. So keep in mind that when Congress debates its annual budget, in effect, it's debating about 10-25% of what it will eventually spend. The vast majority of federal spending is driven by laws, rules, and priorities that originate outside the budget.

This discussion about entitlements raises another absolutely essential point: the Federal Government has a substantial structural deficit. A *structural deficit* is when a government's long-term spending exceeds its long-term revenues. The figure below illustrates this point. It shows that in 2016, the federal government has a projected budget deficit of 2.9% of the US Gross Domestic Product (GDP; the county's total economic output), or around $1.5 trillion. By the year 2046, assuming no major changes in spending or revenue policies, that annual budget deficit will grow to 8.8% of GDP. Why is the deficit expected to grow so quickly? In part because federal non-discretionary spending is going to grow. More and more of the "Baby Boomer" population will become eligible for Medicare, Social Security, and other programs. As the eligible population grows, so too will spending. Moreover, the cost of health care services has increased three to four times faster than all other costs across the economy. That's why health-related non-discretionary spending is the proverbial "double whammy" – the number of people who need those services will increase, and so will the rate of spending per person to deliver those services. At the same time, most economists are projecting slower economic growth for the next several decades. Given the federal government's current revenue policies, that will mean slower revenue growth over time. Those two main factors, growth in non-discretionary spending and slower revenue growth, will lead to much larger deficits over time.

You're probably asking yourself how will the federal government finance those deficits? If it does not collect enough revenue to cover its spending needs, it will borrow. The figure below shows how the federal government's debt will increase in response. In 2016, federal government debt was around 72% of GDP. The Congressional Budget Office estimates it will grow to just under 150% of GDP by 2046. For context, consider that in 2015 Greece, long considered the "fiscal problem child" of the European Union, had a debt-to-GDP ratio of 158%.

This rapid growth in debt is concerning for many reasons. First, federal government borrowing "crowds out" borrowing by small businesses, homeowners, state and local governments, and others who need to borrow to invest in their own projects. Since there are only so many investors with money to invest, if the federal government takes a larger share of that money, there's less for everyone else. Many economists and finance experts have also warned that if the federal government's debt

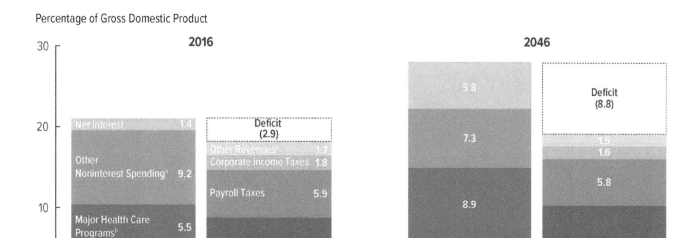

Percentage of Gross Domestic Product

2016

Net Interest 1.4

Other Noninterest Spending 9.2

Major Health Care Programs 5.5

Social Security 4.9

Deficit (2.9)

Other Revenues 1.7
Corporate Income Taxes 1.8

Payroll Taxes 5.9

Individual Income Taxes 8.8

Spending   Revenues

2046

5.8

7.3

8.9

6.3

Deficit (8.8)

1.5
1.6

5.8

10.5

Spending   Revenues

Components of the Federal Government's Structural Deficit; Source: Congressional Budget Office

grows too high, then investors might be less willing to loan it money in the future. If investors are less willing to loan the government money, the government must offer higher interest rates to increase investors' return on investment. As the federal government's interest rates rise, interest rates rise for everyone else. Occasional increases to interest rates are not necessarily a bad thing, but prolonged high interest rates mean less investment by people and business, and that leads to lower productivity and slower economic growth.

The federal government's structural deficit is the single most important trend in public budgeting and finance today. Without major changes in federal government policy, especially in areas like Medicare and Social Security, the federal government will have no choice but to run enormous deficits and cut non-discretionary spending. Those cuts will mean less money for many of the key programs that you probably care about the most: basic scientific research, student loans, highways, transit systems, national parks, and every other discretionary program. In fact, some cynics have said that in the future, "the federal government will be an army with a health care system." State and local governments will be forced to take on many of the services the federal government used to provide in areas like affordable housing, environmental protection, international trade promotion etc. At the same time, some optimists say this is a welcome change. Without the rigidity and uniformity of the federal government, local communities will have the latitude and flexibility to experiment with new approaches to social problems. What's not debatable is that absent major changes in policy, especially for non-discretionary spending, federal government spending will look quite different in the not-too-distant future.

Percentage of Gross Domestic Product

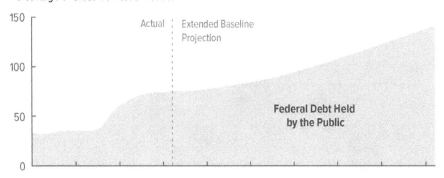

In CBO's extended baseline, **debt held by the public** rises . . .

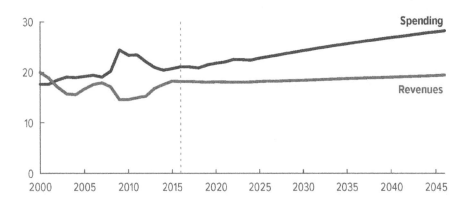

. . . because growth in **total spending** outpaces growth in **total revenues**, resulting in larger budget deficits.

Projected Growth in Federal Debt and the Structural Deficit; *Source: Congressional Budget Office*

What Moves Interest Rates?

Interest rates are one of the most important numbers in public budgeting and finance. *Interest* is what it costs to use someone else's money. Banks and other financial institutions lend consumers and governments money at "market interest rates" like the *annual percentage rate* (APR). Small changes in interest rates can mean big differences in the cost to deliver public projects. That's why it behooves public managers to know what drives interest rates.

Interest rates fluctuate for a variety of macroeconomic reasons. If inflation is on the rise, then businesses will be less willing to spend money on new buildings, equipment, and other capital investments. If demand for capital investments is down, then so is demand for borrowed money to finance those investments. In those market conditions banks and other financial institutions will lower the interest rates they offer on loans to entice businesses to make those investments. The opposite is also true. Businesses will seek to invest during periods of low inflation, and that drives up demand for borrowed money, and that drives interest rates up. Government borrowing and capital investment can also drive demand for borrowed money. Macroeconomists have complex models that explain and predict these interrelationships between consumer spending, investments, and government spending.

The *Federal Reserve Bank of the US* – i.e. "The Fed" – is also a crucial and closely-watched player. The Fed is the central bank. It lends money to banks and holds deposits from banks throughout the US. Its mission is to fight inflation and keep unemployment to a minimum. In finance circles, this is called the *Dual Mandate*.

The Fed has many tools to achieve that mission, and most of those tools involve interest rates. It can raise or lower the *Federal Funds Rate*, or the interest rates at which banks lend money to each other. It can demand that banks keep more money on deposit at the Fed. Increases in either will reduce the amount of money banks have available to lend, and that drives up interest rates. It's most powerful tool is called *open market operations* (OMO). If the Fed wishes to lower interest rates it buys short-term Treasury bonds and other financial securities from investors. This increases the money available for lending and reduces interest rates. When it wishes to raise rates it sells securities to banks. When banks buy those securities they have less money available to lend, and that increases interest rates.

STATE GOVERNMENTS

There's an old adage that state governments are in charge of "medication, education, and incarceration." That saying is both pithy and true. In 2015 state governments spent $1.6 trillion, and most of it was spent on schools, Medicaid, and corrections. That said, they vary a lot in how much of those services they deliver, and how they pay for those services. In some regions, the state is one of the largest employers. This is especially true in rural areas with state universities or state prisons. In other regions state government has a limited presence.

The figure below shows the trends in state government revenues and spending since the late 1970s. All the shaded areas above 0 are revenues, and all the area below 0 is spending. All figures are expressed in 2015 per capita dollars.

Three trends stand out from this chart. First, the size and scope of state governments varies a lot. Today Nevada, for example, spends just under $5,000 per capita. On a per capita basis it's one of the smallest state governments. Vermont, by contrast, spends more than $9,000. Both states have roughly the same population, but one state's government spends almost twice as much per capita. There are several reasons for this. One is that much of Nevada's land is managed by the federal Department of Interior and by Native American Tribes. Those governments deliver many of the basic services that state governments deliver in other states. Citizens in Nevada have also historically preferred less government overall. In Vermont, the state government is largely responsible for roads, public health, primary and secondary education, and many other services that local governments deliver in most other states. That's why state government spending in Vermont is roughly equivalent to state government spending plus total local government spending in most other states.

A second key trend is that overall state spending grew substantially over the past few decades. In 1977, the average state per capita spending was around $2,800. In 2012 it was $5,100. Revenues have grown on a similar trajectory. But note that growth was not uniform. Spending in states like Arizona, California, Colorado, and Washington grew far slower than the average. This is not a coincidence. These states have passed strict laws, broadly known as *tax and expenditure limitations*, that restrict how quickly their revenues and spending can grow. States without those limits, like Connecticut, Delaware, New York, and Massachusetts, have seen much faster growth in both revenues and

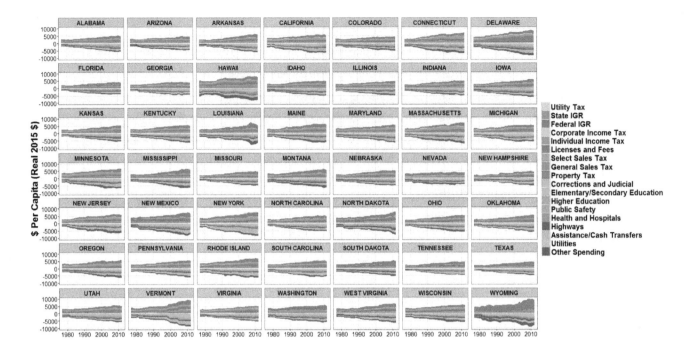

State Government Revenues and Spending, 1977-2012; Source: Authors' Calculations Based on US Census of Governments Data; Note that Alaska is excluded because it is an outlier. In 2015 it spent more than $22,000 per capita.

spending. North Dakota, Wyoming, and New Mexico saw large jumps in revenues and spending in the past decade or so, due mostly to growth of their respective shale oil industries (more commonly known as fracking).

Tax and Expenditure Limitations

Tax and expenditure limits (or *TELs*) restrict the growth of government revenues or spending. While there are no two TELs that are alike, they all share key elements. At the state-level, TELs are either dollar limits on tax revenues or procedural limits that mandate either voter approval or a legislative super-majority vote for new or higher taxes. In estimating the dollar limits, the state is required to establish base year revenues or appropriations subject to the limit and adjust for a factor of growth that is equal to changes in population, inflation, or personal income. States can only exceed the TEL revenue or appropriation caps if they exercise their override provision (e.g., legislative majority or super-majority vote). Funds in excess of the limitation are refunded to taxpayers, deposited in a reserve fund (commonly referred to as a rainy day fund), or used for purposes as provided by law (e.g., capital improvements, K-12 spending). Procedural limits are unique in that they are not part of the budgeting processes and apply only if the Governor seeks to levy new or higher taxes.

At the local level, TELs are either a limit on property tax rates, the taxable base (or assessed value of taxable property), property tax levy, or on the aggregate of local government taxing or spending authority. The limits on tax rates apply to either all municipal governments (an overall property tax rate limit) or specific municipalities (e.g., city, county, or a school district). Limits on assessed valuation are limits on annual growth in the valuation of property (e.g., 2 percent) while limits on property tax revenues are dollar limits on the total amount of revenue that can be raised from the property tax. Caps on the aggregate of local government taxing or spending authority are dollar limits on overall spending authority.

While these revenue suppression measures remain popular, they have had unintended and perhaps detrimental effects, especially at the local level. For example, data from 1977 through 2007 shows the precipitous decline in property tax revenues as a share of own-source revenues. In California, Massachusetts, and Oregon, revenues from the property tax revenues fell more than 15 percent. In response, local governments have come to rely more on intergovernmental transfers and user charges and fees. They have also adopted local-option sales and/or income taxes to make up for lost property tax revenues. As a result of changes, revenues are more volatile and local governments have less control over their budgets than they did prior to the tax-revolt movement. TELs have also altered how local governments are willing to borrow, market perceptions of their credit quality (or default risk), and their ability to manage their other long-term obligations and legacy costs.

A third important trend is that state revenues roughly equal state spending. Virtually every state's constitution requires that its legislature and governor pass a *balanced budget*. As you'll see later, "balanced budget" can mean rather different things in different places. But overall, states don't spend more money than they collect. This is in sharp contrast to the federal government. As you saw above, throughout the past several decades the federal government's spending has routinely exceeded its revenues. Unlike the federal government, the states cannot borrow money to finance budget deficit. In a number of states, restrictions on deficit spending are enshrined in law.

What is a "Fair" Tax?

Governments tax many different types of activity with many different types of *revenue instruments* (i.e. taxes, fees, charges, etc.). Each instrument is fair in some ways, but less fair in other ways. In public finance we typically define fairness along several dimensions:

- *Efficiency*. Basic economics tells us that if a good or service is taxed, then consumers will purchase or produce less of it. An efficient tax minimizes these market *distortions*. For instance, most tax experts agree the corporate income tax is one of the least efficient. Most large corporations are willing and able to move to the state or country where they face the lowest possible corporate income tax burden. When they move they take jobs, capital investments, and tax revenue with them. Property taxes, by contrast, are one of the most efficient. The quantity of land available for purchase is fixed, so taxing it cannot distort supply the same way that taxing income might discourage work, or that taxing investment might encourage near-term consumption.

- *Vertical Equity*. Vertical equity means the amount of tax someone pays increases with their ability to pay. Most income tax systems impose higher tax rates on individuals and businesses with higher incomes. This is meant to ensure taxpayers who have greater ability to pay will contribute a higher share of their income through taxes. A tax with a high degree of vertical equity, like the income tax, is known as a *progressive* tax. A *regressive* tax is a tax where those who have less ability to pay ultimately pay a higher share of their income in taxes.

- *Horizontal Equity. Horizontal equity – sometimes called "tax neutrality" – means that people with similar ability to pay contribute a similar amount of taxes. The property tax is a good example of a tax that promotes horizontal equity. With a properly administered property tax system, homeowners or business owners with similar properties will pay similar amounts of property taxes. Income taxes are quite different. Because of tax preferences, it's entirely possible for two people with the same income to pay very different amounts of income tax.Elasticity.* An elastic tax responds quickly to changes in the broader economy. If the economy is growing and consumers are spending money, collections of elastic taxes increase and overall revenue grows. This is quite attractive to policymakers. With elastic taxes, they can see growth in tax collections without increasing the tax rate. Of course, the opposite is also true. If the economy is in recession, consumer spending decreases, and so do revenue collections. Sales taxes and income taxes are the most elastic revenues.

- *Stability.* A stable – or "inelastic" – tax does not respond quickly to changes in the economy. Property taxes are among the most inelastic taxes. Property values don't typically fluctuate as much as prices of other goods, so property tax collections don't increase or decrease nearly as fast as sales or income taxes. They're more predictable, but they can only grow so fast.

- *Administrative Costs.* Some taxes require a lot of time and resources to administer. Property taxes are a good example. Tax assessors go to great lengths to make certain the *appraised value* they assign to a home or business is as close as possible to its actual *market value*. To do this they perform a lot of spatial analysis. That analysis demands time and expertise.

The chart below illustrates a basic fact about taxation: all taxes come with trade-offs. For instance, the property tax is stable and promotes horizontal equity, but it's costly to administer and generally non-responsive to broader trends in the economy. The sales tax is cheap to administer and produces more revenue during good economic times, but it's also quite regressive. Also note that for many of these instruments the evidence is mixed. That is, tax policy experts disagree on whether that characteristic is a strength or weakness for that particular revenue instrument.

States rely on a few key revenue sources:

- About one-third of state government revenues are from sales taxes. There are two basic types of sales taxes: 1) a *general sales tax* that applies to all retail sales transactions, and; 2) *special sales taxes* that apply only to sales of certain goods and services, such as gasoline, cigarettes, alcohol, and gambling. Some states tax construction, personal trainers, catering, and other professional services, while many do not. Many special sales taxes are administered as excise taxes. Like with the income tax, sales tax revenues are derived from a tax rate applied to a taxable base. A state's

	Property Tax	Sales Tax	Income Tax	Charges and Fees
Vertical Equity				
Elasticity				
Stability				
Administrative Costs				
Horizontal Equity				
Efficiency				

Strength
Weakness
Mixed

sales tax base is all the retail sales of personal property that happen within its borders. The challenge is that it's not always clear what is included in that taxable base. For instance, a business will remit state sales tax only if it has a substantial portion of its business, known as a *sales tax nexus*, in that state. When a company does business in multiple states, or in multiple countries, it must use complicated calculations, known as tax apportionment formulas, to determine the sales tax it owes in each state. Online retailers like Amazon.com have argued they should not pay state sales tax because they do not have a nexus in any one state. Some states require consumers to pay a *use tax* if they purchase a good without paying sales tax. In many states, the goods and services purchased by businesses, for the purposes or producing are good or delivering a service, are exempt from sales taxes. For these and other reasons sales tax administration is quite complex.

- Approximately 18% of total state revenues are from individual and corporate income taxes. For states that have them – 10 states do not have an income tax – income taxes are always the largest or the second largest revenue source. State income taxes are administered much like the federal income tax. In fact, most states apply the federal government's definition of taxable income to determine state taxable income. Interestingly, overall spending has grown much slower in states that do not have an individual income tax.

- All state governments depend to some extent on intergovernmental revenues (IGR). For the states, most intergovernmental revenue is transfers from the federal government for its share of certain mandated programs. Medicaid (see below) is the largest and most important for most states. The federal government also sends states money for transportation infrastructure, the child health insurance program (or S-CHIP), federal student loan assistance, and many other programs. Federal IGR falls into roughly two categories: *categorical grants* that are restricted to specific purposes, and *block grants* that are less restricted but must produce measurable outcomes or deliverables. Federal funds for highways and university research are good examples of categorical grants. The Community Development Block Grant program is a good example of a block grant.

- Most state revenues are from the sales tax, income tax, and IGR. That said, states do depend on a variety of other smaller revenues. Some states levy a limited property tax (see below) on transactions of certain personal property, like vehicles. States also generate revenue through fees attached to everything from hunting to running a tavern to practicing medicine. Some states also tax private electricity and water utility operators.

As mentioned, most state spending is around health, education, and corrections.

- About one-third of total state spending is related to health. Most of that one-third is state *Medicaid* programs. Medicaid is the federal government's healthcare program for the poor. It's delivered through a partnership with the states. Each state designs its own Medicaid program, and the federal government covers 50-70% of the spending related to that program. That's why it's actually part of "Assistance/Cash Transfers" in the figure above. Medicaid is non-discretionary spending. In most states, an individual qualifies for it if their income falls below a certain level. It's also the default health insurer for many vulnerable populations, including foster children, the permanently disabled, and the mentally ill. Older individuals who are poor or disabled often qualify for both Medicare and Medicaid. They are known as *dual-eligibles*. Medicaid is to the states what Medicare is to the federal government: a massive health insurance program that is expected to cover more people and become vastly more expensive over time. In fact, in most states the primary source of growth in Medicaid spending is spending on nursing homes and other long-term care for the elderly. Health and hospitals spending also includes public hospitals and free health clinics run by state governments, and state public health services like vaccinations, diabetes prevention, and outreach programs to prevent sexually-transmitted diseases.

Medicaid Expansion (and Contraction?)

As part of Affordable Care Act (i.e. "Obamacare"), the federal government offered states a once-in-a-generation opportunity. If states expanded their Medicaid programs to cover more uninsured people, the federal government would cover up to 90% of the costs for that expansion. By 2014 a total of 31 states had expanded or were seriously exploring expansion options. In early 2017, President Trump and Congressional Republicans called for the federal government to reduce or even eliminate its contribution to that Medicaid expansion, a move that would remove tens of millions of Americans from Medicaid-sponsored health insurance. If and how to do "Medicaid Contraction" is one of the central issues in health care policy today.

- Around 20% of state spending is related to *public education*. In most states, public education is delivered by local school districts but paid for in large part by the state government. Virtually every state constitution has language that calls out funding primary (Kindergarten through 8th grade) and secondary (9th through 12th grade) public education as the state's principal responsibility. In most states, the state funding for public education is distributed to local school districts through a formula based on the number of students in the district, the district's local demographic circumstances, and the district's financial condition. Public education also includes community colleges and state universities, both of which are paid for through a combination of state funding and student tuition payments.

- *Corrections* and *judicial services* are around 5% of total state spending. This includes prisons, parole officers, state court systems, and state crime prevention programs.

- Highways are 5-12% of state spending, with lots of variation across the states. Rural states like Kansas and Texas have large and elaborate networks of state highways. They spend 10-12% of their annual budgets maintaining and building state highways. By contrast, in New England, the state highway systems are far smaller, so state highway spending is not nearly as large a share of overall state spending. State governments finance most of their highway and other infrastructure projects by borrowing money, usually through *bonds* that they repay over time.

- The other category includes state parks, state environmental conservation programs, law enforcement officials such as the state patrol, and interest on state government debt. Pensions and other post-employment benefits (OPEB) for retired state government workers are one of the most important and fastest growing components of this "other" category (see below).

The Problem with Pensions

The chronic underfunding of public sector retirement systems is arguably one of the most significant fiscal challenges facing states and local governments to date. The *unfunded actuarial accrued liability* or *UAAL* is a plan's net position (or market value of plan investments minus actuarial accrued liabilities (AAL)). The AAL represents the projected cost of benefits for retirees and active employees that will eventually retire and draw benefits. If assets exceed liabilities, a retirement plan is fully funded, otherwise, it's underfunded or simply, unfunded.

A vast majority of retirement plans are unfunded! The nation's state-run retirement systems reported a $934 billion gap in FY2014 (Pew, 2016). When combined with the more than 3,000 local pension systems, the UAAL is in excess of $1.5 trillion. *Funded ratios* (ratio of market value of assets divided by plan liabilities) plunged 14 percentage points from 89 cents for every $1.00 in liabilities in 2002 to 75 cents for every $1.00 in 2011. Aggregate funded ratios of state-sponsored retirement plans in Connecticut, Illinois, Kentucky, and New Jersey are less than 50 cents for every $1.00 in liabilities. Distressed local governments, including those that recently filed for Chapter 9 Bankruptcy protection (e.g., City of Detroit MI, City of Central Falls RI) reported equally low funded ratios.

Why would pension underfunding present a fiscal challenge to governments? First, pension obligations are akin to general obligation (GO) debt in that general tax dollars will be used to make payments on retiree benefits. However, unlike general government long-term debt obligations, liabilities associated with retirement benefits are less visible to the public, face no constitutional or statutory limitations, and do not require voter approval. What's more, once granted, governments can do little to modify benefits to existing employees, retirees, or their beneficiaries. They therefore represent a substantial reallocation of future cash flows on what are in essence unpaid historical costs.

While the Great Recession exacerbated the public sector retirement crisis, it did not create it. Before the downturn, many states opted to increase employee pension benefits in lieu of annual wage adjustments. At the same time, they either failed to make the necessary contributions or fell short of their *annual required contribution* (ARC). Instead, they relied on robust returns on investments and above average discount rates to value their long-term obligation. The result of which was inflated assets and understated liabilities.

For states (and local governments) to adequately fund their retirement systems, they will need to make structural changes to retirement systems that would ensure fiscal sustainability. While reforms have faced legal setbacks, a number of states have been able to scale back on their plan benefits including limiting benefits to current employees, demanding higher contributions, limiting or ending eligibility for new employees, and creating defined contribution plans or hybrid retirement plans. While policy changes represent improvements on the margin, they do not resolve plan insolvency. Governments will need to contribute at or above ARC to ensure retirement systems are sustainable. A sluggish economic recovery has made this even more difficult as politicians must choose between funding retirement benefits, a historical cost, or paying for schools, roads, and public safety.

The discretionary vs. non-discretionary spending distinction is also critically important to the states. Medicaid and primary/secondary education are effectively non-discretionary programs. State legislators can change their state Medicaid laws and policies, and many have. But without a policy change, Medicaid spending is formula-driven and locked in. Primary/secondary education spending is also driven by formulas that requires the state to send a given amount of money to local school districts each year, barring some substantial policy change. States must also pay the interest on their debts, and make good on their pension and OPEB promises. A quick glance at the figure above shows that non-discretionary spending is around 70% of total spending in most states. That's why when revenues fall short of expectations, and states need to balance their budgets, they have little choice but to scale back on the 30% that remains in discretionary areas like higher education and public health. We've been reminded of this fact since the Great Recession. From 2008-2015, state governments cut spending on higher education by an average of 35%, and public health by an average of 50%.

MUNICIPALITIES

There are just over 19,000 "municipal" governments in the US. They include cities, villages, towns, and a few incorporated townships. In 2015 these governments spent around $1.8 trillion, most of it in three core service areas: public safety, infrastructure, and community development.[2] When we think of local governments we think of police officers, firefighters, municipal parks, and local streets.

But beyond those core services, no two municipal governments are alike. Some operate their own electric utilities and water companies. Some operate golf courses, swimming pools, and other recreational facilities. Some have programs to fight homelessness and promote affordable housing, both areas that until recently were managed by the state and federal governments. Others have programs to fight climate change, promote tourism, and acclimate new immigrants to their communities. Of all the levels of government, municipalities offer the most variety in their size and scope of services.

The figure below shows revenues and spending for the 50 largest (by population) US cities from 1977 through 2012. This figure is similar to the previous figure for the states. All the shaded areas above 0 are revenues, and all the area below 0 is spending. All figures are expressed in 2015 per capita dollars.

At a glance, this chart shows the enormous variety in the size of municipal governments. Many of them collected and spent less than $1,000 per capita each year since 1977. They have not grown or shrunk in any appreciable way. By contrast, cities like Baltimore, Boston, Nashville, New York, Philadelphia, and San Francisco have grown substantially. Financially speaking, these municipalities are more like states than cities. They fund and manage public schools, utilities, large cash-transfer assistance programs, and major infrastructure networks. As a result, their total spending and the

2. This $1.8 trillion figure does not include the nearly $400 billion spent by local school districts.

growth in total spending is orders of magnitude larger than many other cities. Cities like Austin, Jacksonville, and Seattle have financial structures dominated by large public utilities. To these jurisdictions, their utilities are both a major revenue source and a major spending item.

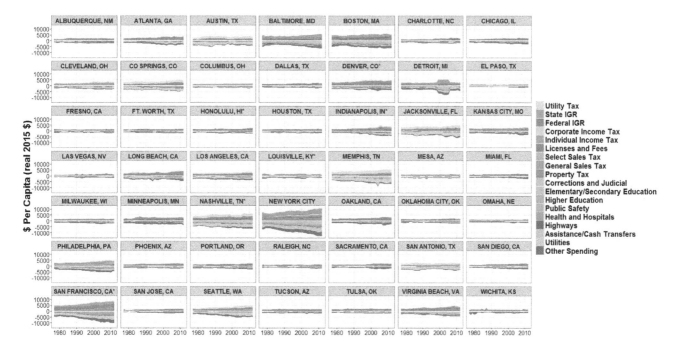

Revenues and Spending of the 50 Largest US Cities, 1977-2012; Source: Authors' calculations based on US Census of Governments data

Municipalities depend on the same revenue sources as states, but in much different configurations.

- *Property taxes* are the local revenue workhorse. They are the oldest local revenue source and the only tax found in all 50 states. For the past two decades, they have accounted for at least 30% of all local government revenues. There are good reasons for this. Property taxes are simple and transparent. They follow the same basic taxable base times tax rate concept you've already seen with both the income tax and the sales tax (see below for more detail on property tax administration). And yet, property taxes are wildly unpopular. Taxpayers get angry when their tax bill increases, but their income does not. They also struggle to understand how the government determines their property value. That's why the property tax is often called the "necessary evil" of local revenue systems.

A Primer on Property Taxes

The amount of property taxes a jurisdiction collects is called the *tax levy*. The tax levy is determined by three factors: the tax base, the tax rate, and any tax preferences. The *property tax base* is the value of all private land and buildings, and all business-related land and buildings within a jurisdiction. The local *tax assessor* determines that value. The assessor's job is to determine the price someone would pay for a particular property and/or building in the current real estate market. This is broadly known as a property's *market value*. It's difficult to determine market value because real estate is not bought or sold that often. Assessors solve this problem by using statistical models to infer the market price of a property from the prices of similar properties that were recently sold.

Policymakers decide what percentage of the market value is subject to taxation. This is known as the *assessed value*. They must also decide the amount of the tax as a percent of the assessed value. This is the *tax rate*.

Tax rates are important, but some of the most consequential decisions about property taxes are about exceptions to the base-rate relationship. For example, non-profit organizations are not required to pay property taxes. Many senior citizens pay reduced property taxes as a way to keep home ownership affordable to people on a fixed income. Many municipalities and counties offer property tax abatements, or temporary property tax reductions or exemptions, to encourage businesses to locate, stay, or grow within their borders.

If a property's assessed value increases, but the tax rate stays constant, the tax levy will still increase. In fact, if a property is subject to special assessments, or property taxes that apply only to certain properties, its levy can increase even if its assessed value decreases.

- In 33 states, the state government has authorized local governments to levy a *local sales tax*. In all, around 6,500 municipalities have a local sales tax, and since World War II sales taxes have grown from less than 5% of total local revenues to nearly 15%. Applicable rates and taxable bases vary. Some municipalities have a general sales tax to fund general local services. Rates on these general local sales taxes are usually between 2-3%. Other local sales taxes are much smaller rates but for more specific purposes like public safety, public health, or tourism. For example, in 2000, voters in Brown County, WI authorized a 0.5% sales tax to fund improvements to Lambeau Field, home of the Green Bay Packers of the National Football League (NFL).

- *Local income taxes* are common in areas with lots of commuters. In fact, they're often called *commuter taxes* or *head taxes*. Central cities often lament commuters work in the central city and use central city services, but do not pay for those services because they own property outside the central city. Local income taxes impose a tax on wages, income, and other earnings in the jurisdiction where that income is earned. This is the logic behind local income taxes in several large cities like Birmingham, Denver, Kansas City, New York City, Philadelphia, St. Louis, and Washington, DC. Several municipalities in greater Portland, OR impose a local income tax to help fund Tri-Met, the regional light rail system. This is an interesting twist on the commuter tax model. Ohio authorizes all of its municipal governments to levy a local income tax. The central criticism of local income taxes is that they drive away business. That is, if a local business can avoid paying the local income tax simply by moving to another jurisdiction, it will have a strong incentive to do so.

- Municipalities depend on a variety of *intergovernmental revenues*. Many state governments offer municipalities grants to fund a variety of needs, especially infrastructure. Many states have grants and *revolving loan* programs to help municipalities pay for roads, bridges, drinking water systems, stormwater management systems, and other basic infrastructure. Federal intergovernmental revenues also assist municipalities with transportation infrastructure, affordable housing and community development, community policing, and many other initiatives. In a few states, municipalities receive up to 30-40% of their revenues through state *revenue sharing* programs. This is most common in states where local governments are not authorized to levy a local sales tax or are subject to strict property tax limits.

- Municipalities also employ dozens of "other" revenue sources. Some tax utilities, both publicly-owned and privately-owned, within their borders. Municipalities also impose fees on licenses for everything from owning a pet to operating a tavern to practicing massage therapy. Municipal courts also impose a variety of fines on everything from illegal parking to vagrancy. Like the sales tax, fees and other miscellaneous charges have become a much larger part of municipal revenue portfolios throughout the past two decades.

The figure above also illustrates that it's difficult to broadly characterize municipal spending. That said –

- *Public education* accounts for around 30% of total municipal spending. However, that figure is driven by a few large school districts and a few states where municipal governments are obligated to provide or pay for public education. Most municipal governments are not directly responsible for public education.

- Most US municipalities spend 30-50% of their money on *public safety*. This includes police, fire, and emergency medical services. Public safety is also one of the fastest growing spending areas. On average, municipal spending on public safety has grown at more than three times the rate of inflation in the broader economy.

- The rest of municipal spending is split roughly between infrastructure and community development. Municipal infrastructure includes streets, sidewalks, bridges, drinking water treatment, wastewater treatment, stormwater management, electricity, cable television, and telecommunications. Many of our most basic human needs are met by municipal infrastructure. Community development includes programs to encourage small business growth, promote arts and culture, make neighborhoods safer and more walkable, among others.

- As mentioned above, the scope of municipal governments around the country has expanded dramatically in the past two decades. Today, many municipalities have programs and services designed to mitigate climate change, stop the emerging nationwide heroin epidemic, protect the civil rights of the LGBTQ community, prepare recent parolees for careers in emerging industries, promote international trade, and assist newly arriving refugees. In the past, these issues were considered state, national, or even international issues. What difference can a city make, the argument went, around a problem so vast as climate change? But in the midst of chronic political gridlock in state capitals and in Washington, DC, and in a new environment where "symbolic politics" are more potent than ever, many municipal officials feel compelled to go it alone.

When is a Business Not a Business?

The "sharing economy" is exciting unless you're a tax collector. In April 2016 the San Francisco (CA) Office of the Treasurer and Tax Collector imposed a new requirement that all drivers for ride-sharing services like Uber and Lyft register as business owners. As a result of the requirement, drivers are now required to pay a business license fee of up to $15,000 depending on how much revenue they generate. Uber's management bitterly opposed this measure, arguing that its drivers are not business owners but rather entrepreneurs who deliver a contracted service arranged through its app. This same basic challenge of defining and taxing a "business" applies to other sharing platforms like AirBnB, HomeAway, TaskRabbit, InstaCart, and many others.

COUNTY GOVERNMENTS

Counties are often called the "bottom of the fiscal food chain." They deliver expensive and human capital-intensive services like public health, elections, tax administration, and regional transit systems, but they receive most or all of their money from property taxes with limited growth potential, from highly constrained sales taxes, and from categorical grants from the state that arrive with many "strings attached." That's why many counties have structural deficits that cannot be addressed without substantial policy changes. In some sense, counties are the opposite of municipalities. Where the scope of municipal government has expanded, the scope of county government has narrowed by about the same margin.

There are 3,144 counties in the US. The figure below shows revenues and spending for the 50 largest (by population) from 1977 through 2012. It's similar to the figures above for states and municipalities. All the shaded areas above 0 are revenues, and all the area below 0 is spending. All figures are expressed in 2015 per capita dollars.

This figure shows that county governments are generally smaller and more narrow in scope than municipalities. According to the US Census of Governments, counties' average per capita spending in 2012 was just over $1,200, where municipalities' average spending was nearly $3,000 per capita. However, this figure also highlights some important exceptions. In the southeastern US county governments are often the major local service provider. They are responsible for schools, roads, public safety (i.e. the county sheriff), stormwater management, and most other major services. Municipal governments in the southeast have comparatively limited powers and responsibilities. That's why Fairfax (VA), Mecklenberg (NC), Montgomery (MD), Prince Georges (MD), Shelby (TN), and Wake (NC) are orders of magnitude larger than most others. We see a similar dynamic in California. For most of California's rural communities, the county government is the main service provider.

In general, counties derive one-third of the revenues from property taxes, one-third from intergovernmental sources, and one-third from other sources including sales taxes, charges and fees, utility taxes, and others. All counties in Maryland and Indiana levy a local income tax.

On the spending side, counties have the same basic spending patterns as municipalities. Public safety and infrastructure are typically the largest spending items. At the same time, counties also manage services where a broader geographic reach, relative to municipalities, is more practical and economical. Elections, for example, are usually a county function. Instead of dozens of municipalities

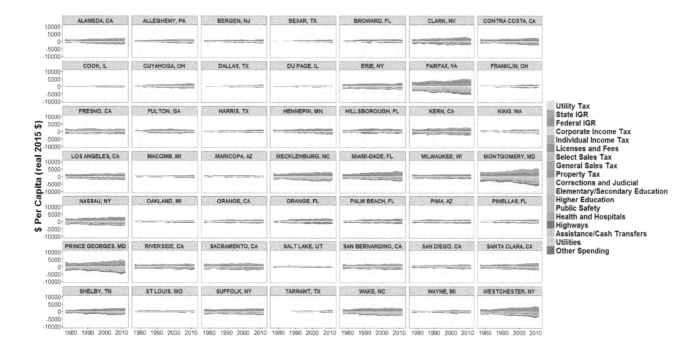

Revenues and Spending of the 50 Largest US Counties, 1977-2012; Source: Authors' Calculations Based on US Census Data

conducting their own elections, county governments manage county-wide elections that cover all the municipal and county officials elected within the county. Tax administration is another example. Property assessors are usually positioned within a county government but execute property assessments for all the municipalities and other taxing jurisdictions within their county. For this same reason counties are usually responsible for a majority of human service programs including public health and mental health services.

SPECIAL DISTRICTS

Special districts are local units of government that are independent from counties and municipalities. They are called many different things, including *public authorities, special-purpose districts, autonomous governments, special taxing districts,* and *public corporations,* among others. By definition, they're narrow in scope. Most special districts are authorized by their respective state governments to deliver one particular service. School districts are authorized to collect property taxes and operate public schools. Utility districts are authorized to deliver electricity to customers and collect fees in exchange. Hospital districts are authorized to operate public hospitals and collect fees, grants, and other revenues to that effect. And so forth.

The term "special district" means radically different things in different settings. Consider the following examples:

- The Milwaukee (WI) Metropolitan Sewerage District (MMSD) is a regional agency that provides wastewater and stormwater management services for about 1.1 million people. Its service area covers 411 square miles that includes six watersheds. It is one of the largest urban sewerage districts in the country. In 1996 it contracted out most of its basic operations to the private firm

United Water, making it the largest urban sewer system in the US under private management. It collects revenues from charges to businesses and homes who use its sewer system, a .5% property tax on all land within the District, state and federal grants, and sales of "Milorganite," an organic compost product it developed and patented, among other revenue sources. In 2015 it spent $252 million and employed 1,200 people.

- The Port of Seattle (WA) manages one of the fastest growing airports in the world (Seattle-Tacoma International Airport), the third largest cargo container port on the west coast, a real estate portfolio worth more than $15 billion, and a variety of technical education programs that train young people to work in the maritime and aviation industries. It employs 1,800 people and in 2015 it spent $336 million. It collects revenues from rental fees paid by airlines and shipping companies, fees on cargo and airline passengers, and real estate rentals and sales. It also has authority to levy a property tax.

- The Barberton-Norton (OH) Mosquito Abatement District manages populations of "biting arthropods" across 60 square miles of northeast Ohio. In its own words, the District is successful if "you can prepare a picnic, play cards by moonlight, even sit on your front porch without the hassle of mosquitoes." It employs 3 full-time staff and in 2015 it spent $784,000. It's sole revenue source is a .05% property tax.

- The Holley-Navarre (FL) Fire District began as a volunteer fire squad with no equipment or funding. It operated from 1965 through 1980 using borrowed equipment and was funded solely by donations. In 1980 the District was created by a special act of the Florida legislature. Today it covers approximately 50 square miles in the Florida "panhandle," with 30 full time firefighters across four fire stations. In 2015 it spent $2.5 million. All its revenue is from property taxes and *impact fees* (i.e. excise taxes levied on new construction).

- The New Jersey Sports and Exposition Authority (NJSEA) is the planning and land use agency for a 30 square mile area just across the Hudson River from New York City. It was created in 1971 to develop sports and entertainment facilities near the "Meadowlands," a marshy and heavily polluted former industrial area (see the opening credits of "The Sopranos"). Today it manages Met Life Stadium (home of the New York Giants and New York Jets of the NFL), IZOD Arena (former home of the New Jersey Devils of the National Hockey League), and several other racetracks, convention facilities, aquariums, and amusement parks. In 2015 the New Jersey Meadowlands Commission, the authority originally tasked with land use planning and restoration of the Meadowlands, was folded into the NJSEA. As a result of that merger the NJSEA now delivers services that include planning, zoning, floodplain management, solar energy, methane recovery, a marina, and pontoon boat cruises. In 2014 it employed 85 full-time staff and spent $90 million. It derives most of its revenue from rental fees and leases, and a local tourism tax paid on hotel rooms and rental cars.

- The Utah Housing Corporation is a statewide authority created by the Utah legislature in 1975. It's mission is to raise funds to make housing affordable for lower-income Utah households. It does this mostly by offering home loans – or *mortgages* – to first time home buyers and to developers building or renovating affordable apartment projects. The Authority is self-supporting and raises hundreds of millions of dollars each year through prartnerships with banks, real estate developers, realtors, and others. In 2015 it employed 80 people and spent $75 million. It collects interest payments on its mortgages, it buys and sells mortgages for a profit, and it receives corporate donations.

Special districts deliver a wide variety of local government services, and the variation in their scope and scale is staggering.

They are the most dynamic area of public finance today. According to the US Census Bureau, in 1977 there were just under 26,000 special districts in the US. Today there are just under 40,000. The figure below shows the growth in special district revenues and spending from 1977-2012. Each line represents the total revenues (solid lines) and total spending (dashed lines) for eight different types of special districts. Most districts increased their total revenues and spending by 30-75% during this period. Spending and revenues in the "other" category – which includes soil and water conservation, libraries, cemeteries, parks and recreation, and many other types of districts – increased more than 200% during this time. Also note that like state and local governments, special districts' aggregate spending is less than their aggregate revenues. This is because special districts, like states, municipalities, and counties, must balance their budgets.

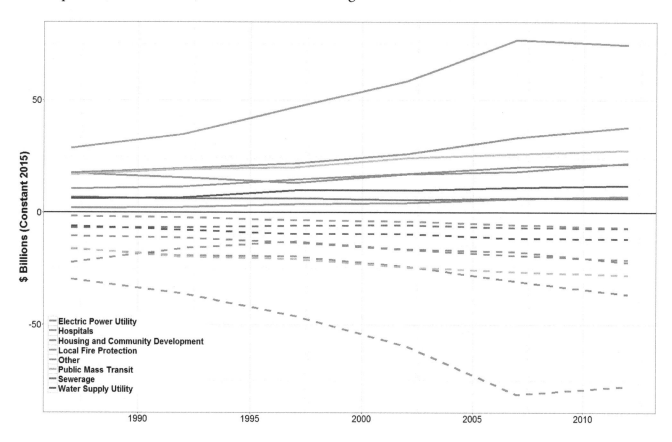

Total Special District Revenues and Spending by Type of District, 1987-2012; Source: Authors' Calculations from US Census of Governments Data; Note: School Districts excluded.

The next figure shows the composition of special districts' revenues. This figure is based on data from 2012 only. It shows each revenue source as a percentage of total revenues for each type of special district. For example, in 2012 public hospitals derived 77% of their revenues from charges and fees. In other words, a typical hospital earns revenue by collecting fees from patients (and patients' health insurers including Medicare and Medicaid). Public hospitals levy property taxes (12%) and receive federal (4%) and state (7%) intergovernmental revenues.

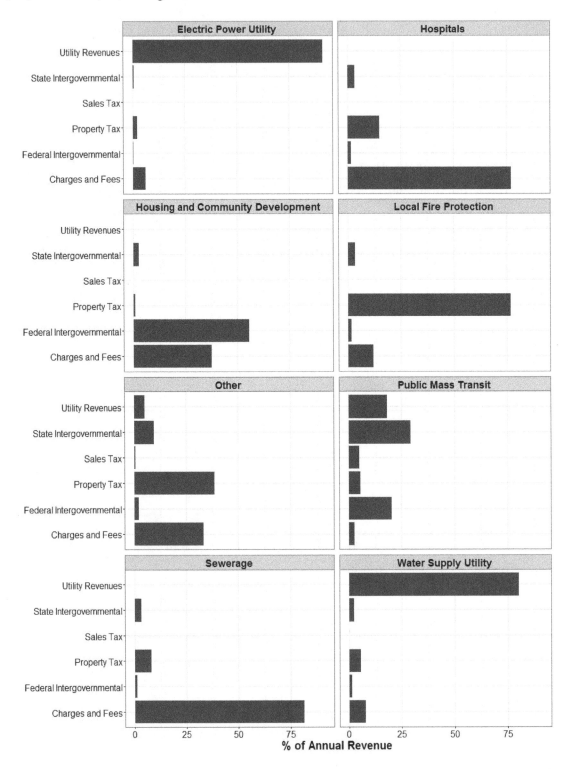

Revenue Composition of US Special Districts by Type of District, Year 2012; Source: Authors' Calculations Based on US Census of Governments Data; Note: Figures may not add to 100% due to rounding and excluding of smaller categories

The key takeaway from this chart is that most special districts depend on one or two main revenue sources. This is not a coincidence. State and local legislatures typically grant special districts limited taxing authority. That said, many districts are deeply engaged in business-type activities where they deliver a specific service to a particular customer in exchange for a fee. This is quite different from state and local governments where taxpayers pay general revenue sources like property and sales taxes, and receive general services like public safety and public health.

What accounts for the explosive growth of special districts? Two, sometimes contradictory factors. First, special districts allow for more direct taxpayer control. If citizens receive a service through their municipal or county government, and they wish to change how they pay for that service or how that service is delivered, they can only affect that change through their city council member or other local representative who must also attend to dozens of other service delivery concerns. With special districts, citizens elect a separate governing body that attends only to that specific service, and they pay taxes or fees dedicated to that service. The relationship between governance, funding, and service delivery is, in concept, much clearer.

Fire protection is a good example. Citizens in unincorporated areas (i.e. areas that fall outside the boundaries of any municipality) often receive fire protection from a county government or nearby municipality. In rural communities that are growing often want better fire protection. In the event of a fire, they'd rather not wait for the county or nearby municipal fire service to arrive. They'd much rather have local firefighters who understand the local terrain and can offer specialized services that a municipal or county fire service is less likely to deliver, like wilderness rescue and wildfire prevention and outreach. So they'll create a local fire protection district, pay a specialized property tax to that district, and elect a specialized fire protection district board. We see a similar dynamic in service areas like flood control, agricultural irrigation, and parks. It's also quite common in the western US, where local political culture tends to favor populist, local control of government. For instance, Tennessee and Washington State have roughly the same population. Tennessee has 347 municipal governments and 475 special districts. Washington State has 281 municipal governments and 1,670 special districts.

Special districts have also proliferated because they can help citizens circumvent tax and expenditure limitations. Sometimes those limitations are political. For instance, taxpayers across the country have voted often to move traditional municipal services like libraries and parks from their municipal government to a special district. When these services are delivered through a special district they have a dedicated revenue source. They need not compete with public safety, roads, water/sewer, and other municipal services for limited tax dollars. And sometimes those limitations are legal. For example, school districts in many states must get voter approval for new school buildings. Before a district can borrow money to build, voters must approve the additional property taxes needed to pay back that borrowed money. Voters in many districts are reticent to approve those additional property taxes. So as an alternative, a district can authorize the creation of a school building authority. That authority will borrow money, build the new school building, lease the building to the district, and then repay the borrowed money with the district's lease payments. At one point in the early 2000s, nearly half the public school buildings in Texas were financed through this "leaseback" model.

This proliferation presents a variety of trade-offs for governance and accountability. Special districts do offer more local control, but the evidence suggests they often do the opposite. Voter turnout for special district elections is usually among the lowest for all elected offices. Academic research shows citizens rarely know that special districts even exist, and almost never know who they voted for in the last special district election. So there's little evidence that special districts offer better democratic accountability. Another practical concern is that the proliferation of special districts has drastically increased the total amount of local government debt outstanding. This raises a variety of concerns about whether local governments are able to repay those debts.

NON-PROFITS

Non-profits are big business! According to the National Center for Charitable Statistics, in 2013 there are approximately 1.4 million nonprofit organizations registered with the Internal Revenue Service (IRS). They collected $1.73 trillion of revenue and spent $1.62 trillion. Collectively, they contribute an estimated $900 billion to the US economy each year and employ almost 10% of the entire US workforce.

To understand where non-profits get their money and where their money goes you must first understand the many different types of organizations that comprise the "non-profit sector."

The table below illustrates some of these differences. It shows the ten largest non-profits by expenses in 2014. The "All" category covers all non-profits, and the other four categories are specific types: environment, human services, international, and civil rights. Abbreviations in parentheses are the state where that non-profit is incorporated. Most of the organizations listed here are incorporated in one state but have a national presence.

All		Environment		Human Services		International		Civil Rights	
Kaiser Foundation Health Plan Inc (OR)	$ 41,982,288,055	National Geographic Society (DC)	$504,309,459	American National Red Cross (DC)	$3,356,880,480	Gavi Alliance (DC)	$1,031,021,275	American Civil Liberties Union Foundation Inc (NY)	$89,345,364
Kaiser Foundation Hospitals (OR)	17,878,889,604	Foothills Land Conservancy (TN)	237,063,788	Feeding America (IL)	1,886,998,720	Food for the Poor Inc (FL)	1,028,028,428	Core Physicians LLC (NH)	83,052,527
Partners Healthcare System Inc (MA)	10,292,631,012	Zoological Society of San Diego (CA)	229,979,506	Park Nicollet Group Return (MN)	1,220,002,816	World Vision (WA)	970,739,732	American Bar Association Fund for Justice and Education (IL)	66,791,540
Upmc Group (PA)	8,743,867,259	World Wildlife Fund Inc (DC)	220,790,782	National Collegiate Athletic Association (in)	842,072,422	Nature Conservancy (VA)	752,216,964	Anti-Defamation League (NY)	58,137,559
Dignity Health (CA)	8,317,741,661	Wildlife Conservation Society (NY)	218,361,953	Partnership for Supply Chain Management Inc (VA)	752,337,203	Compassion International, Inc. (CO)	710,449,180	Arctic Slope Native Association Ltd (AK)	57,384,445
Cleveland Clinic Foundation (OH)	6,825,082,036	American Society for the Prevention of Cruelty To Animals (NY)	173,064,741	Navigate Affordable Housing Partners Inc (AL)	504,940,631	Americares Foundation Inc (CT)	660,160,492	American Jewish Committee (NY)	43,559,818
Ochsner Clinic Foundation (LA)	5,497,859,163	Ducks Unlimited Inc (TN)	153,845,715	California Affordable Housing Initiatives Inc (CA)	391,038,126	Family Health International (NC)	653,826,994	Patient Advocate Foundation Inc (VA)	43,412,007
John Hopkins University (MD)	5,028,927,000	Eckerd Youth Alternatives Inc (FL)	151,673,476	Community Care Inc (WI)	346,411,119	Save the Children Federation, Inc (CT)	653,826,460	National Association for the Advancement of Colored People (MD)	42,597,074
Battelle Memorial Institute (OH)	4,813,672,278	Conservation International Foundation (VA)	143,663,423	Legal Services Corporation (DC)	343,144,208	Plan International Inc (RI)	628,676,279	National Council on the Aging Inc (DC)	41,568,450
Providence Health & Services Washington	4,753,674,523	The Conservation Fund (VA)	141,551,350	Pac-12 Conference (CA)	332,555,484	Population Services International (DC)	579,319,073	Christian Advocates Serving Evangelism Inc (GA)	38,850,143

Ten Largest Non-Profits by Total Expenses in 2014, by Type of Organization; Source: National Center for Charitable Statistics

A few key trends stand out. Eight of the ten largest US non-profits are health care organizations. Some are health systems that employ physicians, nurses, and other networks of health care providers. Others are health insurance companies. Some are research institutions that focus on health care. It's also noteworthy that many of these large health care organizations defy the conventional wisdom that "non-profit" means "not profitable." For instance, Dignity Health, the fifth largest overall non-profit, reported profits in excess of $550 million in 2015. The other health care organizations are similarly profitable.

How can an organization be so profitable yet remain "non-profit"? <u>Because "non-profit" is a tax distinction, not a business model</u>. Non-profit organizations do not pay state and local taxes, and they receive a considerable subsidy through a tax preference (see below). We grant them these benefits because they deliver goods and services that benefit the public. Most non-profit hospitals accomplish this by delivering free or low-cost health care to people who can't afford it. As long as they provide that service, there's little if any restriction on how much profit they can earn.

Note also the staggering variety of services provided and populations served. Many of those services are not unlike governments. Non-profits conserve land for future generations, manage affordable housing programs, and provide pro bono legal services for the poor. Like governments, most of their money is spent on employee wages and benefits. And like governments, the non-profit sector is comprised of thousands of small organizations but dominated by a handful of larger organizations. In fact, by some estimates, more than half of all non-profits have total annual revenues less than one million dollars.

But non-profits are also quite different from governments. Many non-profits are deeply engaged in political advocacy. They fight for everything from endangered species to vulnerable populations around the world. And unlike governments, who are funded mostly through general taxes, almost half of non-profit revenue is "fee-for-service" or "exchange like" transactions. This includes everything from tuition payments to revenues from sales of specialty goods, club memberships, patient revenues etc.

That said, keep in mind that non-profits and governments interact in two crucial ways. Revenues from government sources, including government contracts and Medicare/Medicaid, account for just under one-quarter of non-profit revenues. Government grants represent another eight percent. Put differently, more than one-third of non-profit revenue is directly connected with government. Also note that government revenues are not distributed evenly across non-profits. In fact, a large portion of non-profits, perhaps as much as 20-30%, depend on governments for more than half of their revenues. This suggests that many non-profits are not necessarily independent entities with their own mission and organizational capacity, but rather low-priced government contracts. In later chapters we explore some of the advantages, disadvantages, and criticisms of this part of the nonprofit-government nexus.

Governments also support the non-profit sector through a powerful tax preference. The federal government and most state governments offer a tax deduction for charitable giving. Donors give to non-profits for many reasons. Perhaps they like a non-profit's mission or strategy. Maybe they or someone they know received that organization's services. Or, maybe the decision to give had a lot to do with tax planning. When a donor gives to a non-profit, that donor's taxable income is reduced by the amount of that gift. So for many individuals and corporations, in addition to supporting their favorite non-profit, charitable giving can also reduce their income tax liability, by sometimes up to

50%. According to the US Congress' Joint Committee on Taxation, the charitable deduction costs the federal government about $50 billion annually, in foregone revenue.

There is considerable controversy around the deduction. Some believe it only benefits the wealthy and does little to encourage giving. Others believe that highly profitable non-profit organizations, including many of the health care entities listed above, do not need or deserve an implicit government subsidy.

Practice Problems

1. What are the three biggest financial challenges that public organizations will face in the next decade? What opportunities do those challenges present to sophisticated public financial managers?

2. You are the City Manager of the City of Whoville and are considering options to raise new revenues. Describe the advantages, disadvantages, and implications for fairness of the following:

   ◦ Increase property taxes

   ◦ Increase user charges and fees

   ◦ Implement a local sales tax

3. In 2013 the City of Pittsburgh, PA sued the University of Pittsburgh Medical Center (UPMC). The goal of the lawsuit was to strip UPMC of its tax-exempt status. According to the City's compliant, UPMC does not deliver adequate charity care to justify its tax-exempt status, does not contribute any payments in lieu of taxes (PILOTs), and pays its executives lavish compensation packages. Had the City won in court, it planned to impose a .55% income tax on wages earned by UPMC employees. UPMC counter-sued, claiming it had been unfairly singled-out among Pittsburgh's dozens of large tax-exempt organizations. The City dropped its suit in July 2014, and both sides have since been negotiating a solution. What are the advantages and disadvantages of the City's proposed income tax? How would you suggest Pittsburgh and UPMC resolve this conflict?

4. You are the chief finance officer (CFO) of the City of Pulaski and are about to borrow $10 million for repairs to your city sewer system. A week before you're scheduled to close on the borrowing with your lender, the Federal Reserve announces its intention to increase the Federal Funds Rate by 0.25%. How will this affect your sewer system project?

5. Throughout the 2016 Presidential election virtually every candidate has proposed "comprehensive federal income tax reform" that would require "closing the loopholes and lowering the rate." What are these "loopholes," and how would closing them allow for a lower federal income tax rate? What other financial or economic implications might follow from closing those loopholes? Is a lower tax rate good fiscal policy?

6. In 2014 voters in the City of Seattle, WA voted to create a Metropolitan Parks District. This new District has the power to levy its own property tax, and its borders are contiguous with the City of Seattle. Through an interlocal agreement, the City agreed to receive all of its parks services from the new District for the next 20 years. What are the advantages and disadvantages of this approach to funding parks?

CHAPTER 2.

THE BASIC FINANCIAL STATEMENTS

FINANCIAL STATEMENTS: THE "FINANCIAL STORY"

Financial statements help managers answer a variety of questions:

- Where does this organization's money come from? Where does it go?

- Is this organization's mission aligned with its money? Do its revenues and spending reflect is core mission, priorities, and strategy?

- How much of this organization's spending does it control? How much of its spending is directed by outside stakeholders like donors, clients, or investors?

- How much, if any, does this organization report in "reserves" or "rainy day fund"? Given its operations, what would be the optimal level of reserves?

- Does this organization have enough financial resources to cover its obligations as they come due?

In November 2013 the Contra Costa County (California) Board of Supervisors voted to end nearly $2 million in contracts with the non-profit Mental Health Consumer Concerns (MHCC). The reason: MHCC's savings account had grown too large.

Since the late 1970s MHCC had offered patient rights advocacy, life skills coaching, anger management classes and several other mental health-related services to some of the poorest residents of the Bay Area. Much of its work was funded by and delivered through contracts with local governments.

In 2007 its Board of Trustees began to divert 10-15% of all money received on government contracts to a reserve account (or rainy day fund). MHCC's management concluded this policy was necessary after several local governments began to consistently deliver late payments on existing contracts. This new policy was designed to guarantee MHCC would never again be exposed to these types of unpredictable cash flows. MHCC's Board and management considered this a prudent use of public dollars, and a necessary step to protect the organization's financial future. From 2007-2011 nearly $400,000 flowed into the new rainy day fund.

Contra Costa County disagreed. They interpreted the contracts to mean that reimbursements were only for actual service delivery expenses. They also pointed out that those contracts prohibited carrying over funds from year to year. A reserve fund containing County funds was therefore a violation of those contracts, and the contracts were terminated. MHCC pointed out that they disclosed the reserve fund strategy in their annual financial reports, and that the reserve allowed them to deliver better, uninterrupted services even during the worst financial moments of the Great Recession. Contra Costa County Supervisor Karen Mitchoff responded by saying MHCC's financial statements were not the appropriate channel to communicate such a contentious policy choice. She added, "I am not sympathetic to the establishment of the reserve, and the nonprofit board knows they had a fiduciary responsibility to be on top of this."

The contracts were canceled, and MHCC dissolved in early 2011.

This episode illustrates two of the key take-aways from this chapter. First, an organization's financial statements are a vital communication tool. They tell us about its mission, priorities, and service delivery strategy. In this particular case, MHCC made a policy decision to deliver less service in the near-term in exchange for the ability to deliver more consistent and predictable services in the future. That choice was reflected several places in MHCC's financial statements. It's unrestricted net assets were higher. It's direct expenses were lower. They also disclosed the rainy day fund policy in the notes to its financial statements. Second, and more important, financial statements are only useful if the audience knows how to read them. In this case, Contra Costa County failed to understand how the rainy day fund policy was communicated in the financial statements, and how that policy affected MHCC's finances and its ability to accomplish its mission. But without the ability or desire to interpret the financial statements, the County considered MHCC's actions a breach of contract. Whether a rainy day fund is a direct service expense is an interesting policy question. So is the question of if and how a government should use financial statements for oversight of its non-profit contractors. But to engage these and many other questions, one must first understand how a public organization's financial statements tell its "financial story."

Learning Objectives

After reading this chapter you should be able to:

- Identify the fundamental equation of accounting.
- Identify the basic financial statements – balance sheet, income statement, and cash flow statement – for public organizations.
- Know what information each statement is designed to convey about an organization.
- Contrast the basic financial statements for non-profits to those same statements for governments and for-profit organizations.
- Recognize the key elements of the financial statements – assets, liabilities, revenues, and expenses.

BUDGETING VS. ACCOUNTING

If you want to know how an organization connects its money to its mission, read its budget. If the budget calls for more spending in one program and less in another, that tells us a lot about that organization's priorities. If one of its programs operates at a loss, but another program's profits subsidize that loss — that's also a clear statement about how that organization carries out its mission. We can think of many other ways an organization's money does or does not connect to its mission. A public organization's budget lays out the many, unique ways it makes those connections.

But sometimes we want an "apples-to-apples" comparison. Sometimes we want to know if an organization's mission-money nexus is the same, or different, from similar organizations. Sometimes we want to know how efficiently an organization accomplishes its mission compared to its peers. Sometimes we want to know if an organization is in comparatively good or bad financial health. To answer these types of question you need information found only in financial statements. In this chapter, we walk through the basic financial statements that most public organizations prepare, and the essential concepts from accounting you'll need to understand the numbers that appear in those statements.

Moreover, we may need to compare an organization's finances to the finances of other organizations. If our organization's expenses exceeded its revenues we might consider that to be a failure. Unless, of course, we see that all organizations like it also struggled. If it failed to invest in its capital equipment, we might think it was neglecting its own service delivery capacity, unless we saw other organizations make that same trade-off. These types of comparisons demand financial information that's based on standardized financial information from a broadly-shared set of assumptions. Budgets are rarely standardized that way.

Fortunately, we can get that information from an organization's financial statements. Financial statements are the main "output" or "deliverable" from the organization's accounting function. Accounting is the process of recording, classifying, and summarizing economic events in a process that leads to the preparation of financial statements. Unlike budgets, the numbers reported in financial statements are based on *generally accepted accounting principles (GAAP)*, that prescribe when and how an organization should acknowledge different types of financial activity.

Who Makes Accounting Standards?

The *Financial Accounting Standards Board (FASB)* produces GAAP for publicly-traded companies and for non-profits. The *Governmental Accounting Standards Board (GASB)* produces GAAP for state and local governments. Both the FASB and the GASB are governed by the *Financial Accounting Federation (FAF),* a non-profit organization headquartered in Norwalk, CT, just outside of New York City. Both Boards are comprised of experts from their respective groups of stakeholders: accounting, auditing, "preparer" (entities that prepare financial statements, like companies and governments), and academia. The *Securities and Exchange Commission (SEC),* the federal government agency that regulates public companies, designates the FASB as the official source of GAAP for public companies. The GASB has not been designated as such, but it is the de facto source of GAAP for governments because key stakeholders like bond investors and the *credit ratings agencies* have endorsed its standards. GAAP for federal government entities is produced by the *Federal Accounting Standards Advisory Board (FASAB)*. The FASAB is comprised of accountants and auditors from federal government agencies. Federal government GAAP is still an emerging set of concepts and practices.

GAAP tells us when an organization can say it "owns" an asset, or when it has "earned" revenue for delivering a service, among many other types of financial activity. These are known as principles of accounting *recognition*. The key point here is that GAAP is a shared set of "rules of the game" for summarizing and reporting an organization's financial activities. If an organization offers up GAAP-compliant financial information, we can compare its finances to itself over time, and to other organizations.

Standardized rules aren't the only difference between budgeting and accounting. Broadly speaking, if budgeting is the story, then accounting is the scorecard. An organization's budget tells us the activities it wants to do and how it plans to pay for those activities. Politicians and board members love to talk about budgets because budgets are full of aspirations. They're how leaders translate their dreams for the organization into a compelling story about what might happen.

Financial statements tell us what actually happened. Did the organization the organization's revenues exceed its expenses? Did it pay for items with cash, or *on credit*? Did its investments gain value or lose value? How much revenue would it need to collect in the future to pay for capital improvements and equipment? Accountants often see themselves as the enforcers of accountability. That's why budget-makers and accountants often don't see eye-to-eye.

These two world views are different in many other important ways. As mentioned, budgeting is prospective (i.e., about the future) where accounting is retrospective (i.e., focused on the past). Budgets are designed primarily for an internal audience – elected officials and board members, department heads and program managers, etc. – where accounting produces financial reports mostly for an external audience of taxpayers, investors, regulators, and funders. Budgeting focuses on the resources that will flow in and out of an organization, also known as the *financial resources focus*. Accounting focuses on the long-term resources the organization controls and its long-term spending commitments, also known as the *economic resources focus*. Budgeting is about balance between revenues and spending, where accounting is about balance between an organizations assets and the claims against those assets. These main differences between the two perspectives are summarized in the table below.

THE FUNDAMENTAL EQUATION OF ACCOUNTING

Everything we do in accounting is organized around the *Fundamental Accounting Equation*. That equation is:

$$\textbf{Assets = Liabilities + Net Assets}$$

How are Budgeting and Accounting Different?

Characteristic	Budgeting	Accounting
Metaphor	"The Story"	"The Scorecard"
Time Frame	Prospective	Retrospective
Format	Idiosyncratic/Customized	Standardized
Main Audience	Internal	External
Focus of Analysis	Inputs/Investments	Solvency/Financial Health
Organizing Equation	Planned Revenues = Planned Spending	Assets = Liabilities + Net Assets
Measurement Focus	Financial Resources	Economic Resources
Cost Measurement	Market Price	Historical Cost

An **asset** is anything of value that the organization owns. There are two types of assets: 1) short-term assets, known more generally as *current assets*; and 2) *long-term assets or non-current assets*. A current asset is any asset that the organization will likely sell, use, or convert to cash within a year. Most organizations have supplies or inventory they expect to use to carry out normal operations. Those are the most common current assets.

When someone outside the organization owes the organization money, and the organization expects to collect that money within the year, that's also a current asset known as a *receivable*. An organization recognizes an *account receivable* or *A/R* when it delivers a service to a client and that client or customer agrees to pay within the current fiscal year. Many non-profits also report *donations receivable* or *pledges receivable*. Donations and pledges receivable represent a donor's commitment to give at a future date. The same logic applies to *grants receivable* from foundations or governments.

Most public organizations own buildings, vehicles, equipment, and other assets they use to deliver their services. These are *long-term assets*. They have long *useful lives* and it's unlikely the organization would sell these assets, as that would diminish their capacity to deliver services. State and local governments maintain roads, bridges, sewer systems, and other *infrastructure assets*. These are among the most expensive and important long-term assets in the public sector.

By contrast, a *liability* is anything the organization owes to others. Or to put it in more positive terms, liabilities are how an organization acquires its assets. Here the short vs. long-term distinction also applies. *Short-term liabilities* are liabilities that the organization expects to pay within the next fiscal year. The most common are *accounts payable* for goods or services the organization has received but not yet paid for, and *wages payable* for employees who have delivered services but not yet been paid.

Long-term liabilities are money the organization will pay at some point beyond the current fiscal year. When an organization borrows money and agrees to pay it back over several years, it recognizes a *loan payable* or *bonds payable*. Many public sector employees earn a *pension* while they work for the government, and they expect to collect that pension once they retire. If the government has not yet set aside enough money to cover those future pension payments, it must report a *pension liability*.

What's left is called *net assets*. Technically speaking, net assets are simply the difference between assets and liabilities. For private sector entities, this difference is known as *owner's equity*.

Owners = Equity Holders

In for-profit organizations the fundamental equation is Assets = Liabilities + Owners' Equity. Conceptually, a for-profit company's owners have a claim to all its assets that do not have an offsetting liability. Or put differently, the company's owners have a claim to all of its assets not otherwise promised to creditors or suppliers. When you buy stock (or "shares") of a for-profit company you are, in effect, buying a portion of that company's owner's equity. That's why stocks are also known as *equities*. If a company's assets grow faster than its liabilities, its equity will become more valuable, the price of its stock will increase, and investors who hold that stock will make money. For instance, some extraordinarily fortunate investors purchased Facebook's original stock at around $5/share. Today Facebook stock sells for around $120/share. As the Facebook's user base and annual revenues have grown, its assets have grown much faster than its liabilities, and its stock price has steadily increased.

Public organizations don't have "owners." Instead, they have *stakeholders*, or anyone who has an interest, financial or otherwise, in how well the organization achieves its mission. For governments, taxpayers are a rough analog to owners. But unlike investors in a for-profit company, taxpayers don't have a legal claim to the government's assets. Taxpayers' main interest is that the government delivers the services they expect it to deliver. Donors and funders who give money to a non-profit organization care about its financial health, but they also don't expect to get their money back if the organization fails. Mostly, they care that the organization will continue to serve its clients and the community at large. For these reasons, net assets are an important part of a government and non-profit finances, but they don't have quite the same meaning as owners' equity for a for-profit entity.

That said, we can think of net assets as an indicator of the organization's financial strength or financial health. If its net assets are growing, that suggests its assets are growing faster than its liabilities, and in turn, so is its capacity to deliver services. If its net assets are shrinking, its service-delivery capacity is also shrinking.

We also have to think about the restrictions on net assets. Net assets are reported as either *unrestricted net assets, temporarily restricted net assets* or *permanently restricted net assets. Unrestricted* net assets have no donor-imposed stipulations but may include internal or board-designated restrictions. *Temporarily* restricted net assets represent assets with time and/or purpose restrictions stipulated by a donor. *Permanently* restricted net asset represent assets with donor restrictions that do not expire.[1] We are therefore interested in whether the growth in an organization's capacity is limited to donor-funded programs (i.e., temporarily or permanently net assets) or whether the growth is in its unrestricted position.

THE BASIC FINANCIAL STATEMENTS

All organizations that follow GAAP, both public and private, produce three *basic financial statements*:

---

1. Note that these net asset restriction categories are for non-profit organizations. Governments use a separate classification scheme for net asset restrictions. We describe that scheme later.

1. **Balance Sheet**. Presents the organization's assets, liabilities, and net assets at a particular point in time.
2. **Income Statement**. Presents the organization's revenues, expenses, and changes in net assets throughout a particular time period.
3. **Cash Flow Statement**. Shows how the organization receives and uses cash to carry out its mission.

In the discussion that follows you'll see more detail about each statement and how the information it contains can inform key management and policy decisions.

When considering an organization's financial statements keep one central point in mind: <u>Net assets are the focal point.</u> Changes in assets, liabilities, revenues, expenses, and cash flows will affect net assets differently. Each of the three financial statements illuminates different dimensions of those changes. Regardless of the organization's structure or mission, its financial statements are organized around changes in net assets.

Also, each statement's presentation style and terminology can vary depending on the type of organization that prepared it. This table summarizes those differences.

Many of the differences in labeling are intended to contrast the mission orientation of non-profits and governments with the profit orientation of for-profits. We see this most clearly in the income statement. For-profit organizations often call the income statement the "profit/loss statement," given its purpose is to distinguish its profitable products and services from its non-profitable products and services. For governments and non-profits, the focus is on "activities." The question here is not whether the organization's activities are profitable, but rather how to do those activities advance its mission. In the aggregate, they must take in more revenue than they spend, or they will cease operating. <u>But "profitability" is not their main goal.</u>

Statement	What For-Profits Call It	What Non-Profits Call it	What Governments Call It		
			Government-Wide Statements	Governmental Fund Financial Statements	Proprietary Fund Financial Statements
Balance Sheet	Balance Sheet; Statement of Financial Position	Statement of Financial Position	Statement of Net Position	Balance Sheet	Balance Sheet
Income Statement	Income Statement; Profit & Loss Statement; "P&L"; Operating Statement	Statement of Activities	Statement of Activities	Statement of Revenues, Expenditures, and Changes in Fund Balances	Operating Statement
Cash Flow Statement	Cash Flow Statement; Statement of Cash Flows	Statement of Cash Flows	N/A	N/A	Cash Flow Statement

You'll also note several differences in what governments call these statements. We've talked already about how financial statements illuminate *operational accountability,* or how efficiently and effectively an organization used its financial resources to advance its mission. Taxpayers want to know their government delivered services efficiently and effectively. To that end, state and local governments prepare a set of "government-wide" financial statements. These statements present the government's overall financial position, and they offer some insight into its ability to continue to deliver services in the future. These government-wide statements are, with a few modifications, conceptually similar to the basic financial statements for a non-profit or for-profit.

The government-wide balance sheet is called the *Statement of Net Position,* and the government-wide income statement is called the *Statement of Activities.* By calling the income statement, the Statement of Activities, the governmental accounting standards-setters have sent a clear message: governments exist not to generate income, but to produce activities. This also explains why there's no government-wide cash flow statement. Information about how a government generates and uses cash does not necessarily help us understand if it is achieving its mission.

But with governments, operational accountability is only part of the story. Taxpayers also want to know their government did what they told it to do. They want to know if it delivered the services they wanted with the revenues they gave it. That's *fiscal accountability.*

When we think of fiscal accountability in government we usually think of the budget. A government's budget is not just a plan; It's the law. Most governments' constitutions or charters require them to lay out their planned revenues and spending in a special law called an *appropriations ordinance.* They must literally pass a law that makes their budget intentions clear. If they spend more than their budget allows or spend money in ways not specified in their budget ordinance, they are breaking the law.

Budgets are enshrined in law because they are one of our most effective tools to ensure inter-period equity. *Inter-period equity* is the idea that if a government follows its budget, it is living within its means and it is less likely to pass costs onto future generations.

Fiscal accountability and inter-period equity are so important that they're built not just into a government's budget, but also into its financial statements. For instance, imagine that a school district levies a special sales tax to pay for school buildings. Taxpayers want to see how much revenue that tax generated, how much money the school district borrowed to build those buildings, how much of that revenue has been used to repay that borrowed money, and so on. They'll want fiscal accountability on that special tax.

For taxpayers to assess this they'll need to see those revenues, expenditures, assets, and liabilities presented separately from all other operations. To do that, the school district will present those finances in a stand-alone *special revenue fund.*

A *fund* is a stand-alone, self-balancing set of accounts with a specific purpose. A government's *general fund* is where it accounts for its general services that are paid for through general revenue sources. It's where local governments account for police, fire, public health, and other services paid for through property taxes and general sales taxes. It's also where state governments account for their Medicaid programs, state parks, state patrol, and other general services paid for through state income taxes and statewide general sales taxes. For most governments the general fund is the largest and most carefully-watched. According to GAAP, a government's general fund, special revenue funds, and *capital projects funds* are collectively called its *governmental funds.* You can think of the governmental funds as a government's core services and operations.

Like the budget, governmental funds are focused on near-term revenues and spending. For that reason the information you see in funds is prepared using a different set of accounting principles. Those principles are known as *modified accrual accounting* (or "fund accounting") and are described later in this chapter.

Since funds are self-balancing, we rewrite the fundamental equation for the modified accrual context as:

Assets = Liabilities + Fund Balance

Funds are so important to governments that they are required to present a separate set of fund financial statements, prepared on the modified accrual basis of accounting. The balance sheet in the governmental funds is simply called the balance sheet, and the income statement is called the *Statement of Revenues, Expenditures, and Changes in Fund Balance*. Like with the government-wide statements, there is no cash flow statement for the governmental funds.

Governments also deliver goods and services whose operations are quite similar to what we'd find in the private sector. Examples include water utilities, golf courses, swimming pools, waste disposal facilities, and many others. These are known as *business-type activities* or *proprietary activities.* In concept, business-type activities should cover their expenses with the revenue they generate through fees and charges for their services. In fact, many governments operate business-type activities because those activities are profitable and can subsidize other services that cannot pay for themselves. Since business-type activities are expected to pay for themselves, we account for them on the *accrual basis* and prepare a separate set of *proprietary fund financial statements.* Accrual basis accounting, assumes an organization records a transaction when that transaction has an economic impact, regardless of whether it spends or receives cash. Those statements follow the traditional titles of balance sheet, income statement, and cash flow statement.

What is the Audit Report?

At the beginning of every set of financial statements, you'll find an *audit report*. This report is formatted as a letter, prepared by an external financial auditor, presented to the organization's board and management and incorporated in the audited financial statements. That auditor reviews the organization's statements, tests its procedures and systems to prevent fraud and abuse (also known as *internal controls*), interviews its staff, examines a selected group of specific transactions, and performs other work designed answer a simple question: Are the organization's financial statements a fair presentation of its actual financial position? Usually, the audit report expresses an *unqualified opinion*, meaning the auditor believes the financial statements are a fair presentation of the organization's financial position. An unqualified audit report will contain language to the effect of "...these financial statements present, fairly, and in all material respects, this organization's financial position." If the auditor has reason to believe the financial statements do not present that position fairly they will issue a *qualified opinion*, or, in rare cases, an *adverse opinion*.

THE BALANCE SHEET

The balance sheet is designed to answer a simple question: What is this organization's current *financial position*? Financial position has both a short-term and a long-term component. If current assets exceed current liabilities, then the organization is in a good short-term financial position. If long-term (i.e. non-current) assets exceed long-term liabilities, the organization is in a good long-term financial position.

For that reason, a point of emphasis for the balance sheet is the relationship between the organization's assets and liabilities. If assets grow faster than liabilities, net assets will increase. And vice versa. Later we'll cover some more precise measures, also known as *financial statement ratios*, you can use to answer these questions.

The balance sheet offers a lot this sort of detail on why net assets do or do not increase. To that point, when looking at an organization's balance sheet you should ask a few questions:

1. Do its total assets exceed its total liabilities? If they do, that's a good indicator of a good long-term financial position.
2. Do its current assets exceed its current liabilities? If they do, that's a good indicator of a strong short-term financial position.
3. What portion of its current assets are reported under cash? Does it appear to have a lot of cash relative to its other assets and liabilities? Cash is critical. At the same time, it's possible for an organization to have too much cash. If it has more cash than it needs to cover its day-to-day operations, then it could invest some of that idle cash in marketable securities or other safe investments, and earn a small investment return.
4. What portion of its assets are reported as receivables? What proportion of receivables are due in 12 months or less? What proportion of receivables due are from a single donor or grantor? This can be a source of financial uncertainty or even weakness, depending on the donors or payees in question.
5. What is the relationship between its current and non-current assets? How much does the organization report in buildings and equipment? The organization will likely need to use cash, and other short-term assets, to pay for and maintain its long-term assets.
6. What portion of net assets are unrestricted? Are temporarily restricted? Are permanently restricted? Unrestricted and temporarily restricted net assets can be use to cover short-term spending needs, if they are used within the confines of the donor restrictions.
7. Does the organization have non-current liabilities? How might these affect the organization's current assets in the future? Long-term liabilities like loans, bonds, legal settlements, and pensions increase demand for current assets like cash.

It's important to keep in mind that the balance sheet is a snapshot in time. When an organization's accounting staff prepare a balance sheet they simply report the balances in each of organization's main financial accounts on a particular day. Usually, that day is the last day of the fiscal year. Keep in mind that if an organization has a dynamic balance sheet – i.e., it has a lot of receivables or payables, or it has a lot of investments whose value fluctuate – then its total assets and total liabilities can look quite different from one week to the next or from one month to the next.

Let's look at an example. Here you'll see Fiscal Year 2015 Balance Sheet – i.e. the Statement of Financial Position – for a non-profit organization called Treehouse. Treehouse supports children in foster care with tutoring and other educational support (e.g., counseling, food, clothing). It was founded in 1988, and serves nearly 8,000 children in greater Seattle, WA.

TREEHOUSE

STATEMENT OF FINANCIAL POSITION
September 30, 2015
(With Comparative Totals for 2014)

ASSETS	2015	2014
Current Assets		
Cash and cash equivalents	$ 2,713,337	$ 3,053,277
Investments	1,324,922	980,248
Current pledges receivable, net	2,056,445	1,349,314
Contribution receivable for rent	193,357	45,369
Contracts receivable	252,784	99,030
Inventories	239,615	296,017
Unemployment trust deposits	86,007	46,725
Prepaid expenses	131,529	32,589
Total current assets	6,997,996	5,902,569
Long-Term Assets		
Long-term portion of receivables, less current portion		
Pledges receivable, net	1,061,300	1,410,876
Contribution receivable for rent, net	240,946	
Furniture and equipment, net	468,397	53,867
Endowment investments	3,444,637	3,683,988
Other investments	401,134	423,764
Total long-term assets	5,616,414	5,572,495
Total assets	$ 12,614,410	$ 11,475,064
LIABILITIES AND NET ASSETS		
Current Liabilities		
Accounts payable	$ 48,975	$ 37,053
Accrued salaries and related costs	418,486	348,719
Total current liabilities	467,461	385,772
Net Assets		
Unrestricted	5,255,411	4,549,404
Temporarily restricted	3,446,901	2,855,900
Permanently restricted	3,444,637	3,683,988
Total net assets	12,146,949	11,089,292
Total liabilities and net assets	$ 12,614,410	$ 11,475,064

See Notes to Financial Statements

The balance sheet is organized in order of *liquidity*. The most liquid assets appear first, and the least liquid assets appear near the bottom. Liquidity refers to how quickly an asset can be converted to cash with minimal loss in value. We can convert an asset to cash by selling it, or, in the case of receivables, by collecting on it. Cash is, of course, the most liquid asset. That's why it's listed first. Cash equivalents (e.g., *commercial paper*, and *marketable securities* like *money market mutual funds* and *overnight re-purchase agreements* or "Repos") are extremely safe investments that can be converted to cash immediately at low or no cost.

Book Value vs. Market Value

Accountants usually report assets at *historical cost*, or the cost the organization paid to acquire them. Historical cost is also called *"book value"* because it's the value at which the accountant recorded that asset in the organization's "books." For instance, if an organization purchased a building for $500,000 ten years ago it will report a book value of $500,000 on its balance sheet. Meanwhile, an *appraiser* might estimate that a buyer would be willing to pay $1,000,000 for that building today. This is an estimate of the building's *market value*. Accountants prefer historical cost. In fact, that preference is so strong it's called the *historical cost rule* of accounting. Until that building is actually bought or sold for $1,000,000, that figure is just a guess that's too unreliable as a basis for financial reporting.

Treehouse reports the most typical current assets:

- *Investments (current assets)*. Investments includes holdings of stocks, bonds, and other typical financial instruments. By definition, investments reported as current assets are bought and sold less frequently and less liquid than marketable securities.

- *Receivables*. When someone pays money they owe to the organization that money, that receivable is converted to cash. Treehouse reports receivables for pledges, rent (it owns property that it rents to others), and contracts. Also note that it reports net receivables. This means it has subtracted from that receivables figure, the portion of those receivables it has determined it cannot collect. Those removals are known as **bad debt expense**, and are described later in this chapter.

- *Inventory*. This includes goods that the organization intends to sell or give away as part of delivering its services. Much of Treehouse's inventory is held in its "Wearhouse," a thrift store where children can pick up clothing and personal items for free. Many organizations (Treehouse not included) report a separate category for *supplies*. These are goods and materials, usually *commodities*, that the organization intends to use while delivering its services. Unlike marketable securities and investments, there may not be a robust market for supplies and inventory, so they are among the least liquid current assets.

- *Pre-paid Expenses*. When an organization pays in advance for services it will use later – such as insurance, memberships, subscriptions, etc. – that's known as a pre-paid expense. If the organization can cancel, renegotiate, or otherwise change a pre-paid and get cash back in return, then the pre-paid can be converted to cash. This is rare.

Treehouse also reports the most common long-term assets. These are also listed in order of liquidity:

- *Long-term Receivables*. Some receivables are received over multiple fiscal periods. This is especially true for long-term grants and contracts, and for donors who choose to give at regular intervals over several years. These long-term receivables are also reported net of bad debt.

- *Furniture and Equipment*. Reported at *historical cost* (see below) and net of *depreciation* (see later in this chapter). These are also known as capital assets or property, plant, and equipment (PPE). They are illiquid as there may or may not be an interested buyer. If Treehouse owned a building the value of that building would also be reported here.

- *Endowment Investments* represent donated funds with a explicit restriction that funds not be expended, but rather, invested for the purpose of producing income. This is the precise reason why these investments are reported as long-term assets. Its not because the owner cannot sell — or that they cannot be sold, but rather if they are sold, they must be replaced by an equivalent financial instrument. Earnings from endowment investments can be used to advance the organization mission as long as the organization exists. Treehouse maintains a sizeable pool of endowment investments. For some organizations, endowment investments may not be explicitly reported in the balance sheet, but these are often disclosed in the notes to the financial statements.

- *Other Investments*. Many investments are not liquid because their owner is not allowed to sell them. This is usually true of holdings in hedge funds, private equity, and other investment vehicles where investors give up liquidity, but expect a more profitable investment in return. Some investments are less liquid because there are simply fewer potential buyers. Commercial real estate, for instance, can take some time to sell because there are simply fewer potential investors interested in those types of properties compared to, say, residential real estate. All these investments are reported as "other" long term assets.

Fair Value vs. Historical Cost

Investments are an important exception to the historical cost rule. Most investments trade on an exchange like the New York Stock Exchange or the NASDAQ. The prices quoted on those exchanges are a good estimate of the price at which that organization could sell that asset. In this case, an accountant would replace historical cost with a *fair value estimate* based on the price from an exchange. So for instance, say a non-profit bought 1,000 shares of stock for $50,000 three years ago at historical cost is $50/share. If on the last day of the current fiscal year, that stock was trading for $75/share, the accountant would record that stock on the balance sheet at a *mark-to-market* fair value estimate of $75,000. Accountants are comfortable relaxing the historical cost rule for investments because for most investments, we can quickly and easily observe an accurate market price.

Liabilities are also listed in reducing order of liquidity. Liquidity of a liability refers to how quickly the organization will need to pay it. Treehouse's balance sheet includes the two most common current liabilities – accounts payable and accrued salaries and related costs (i.e. wages payable). These are liabilities that will come due within the fiscal year. Like many non-profits, Treehouse does not report any long-term liabilities. If it had a mortgage, loan payable, or other liabilities that will come due over multiple years it would report them as long-term liabilities.

At a glance, three key features of Treehouse's balance sheet stand out. First, its current assets far exceed its current liabilities. This indicates a strong near-term financial position. Treehouse has more than enough liquid resources on hand to cover liabilities that will come due soon. However, roughly one-third of those current assets are pledges receivable. This introduces some uncertainty into Treehouse's overall asset liquidity. What's more, a substantial proportion of Treehouse's net assets are reported as either temporarily restricted or permanently restricted. This indicates that a good amount of Treehouse's overall spending is for donor-directed programs. Taken together, the findings suggest Treehouse is in a strong financial position, has good balance across its current and long-term assets, and does not have long-term liabilities. At the same time, it does not have full autonomy over its financial resources.

FOR GOVERNMENTS – THE STATEMENT OF NET POSITION

Governments prepare government-wide financial statements that are similar to the basic financial statements for a non-profit or for-profit entity. These government-wide statements answer some of the key questions taxpayers ask about their government:

- Has its overall financial position improved or deteriorated?

- How much has it invested in its infrastructure and other capital assets?

- Were its current year revenues sufficient to pay cover full cost of current year services?

- How much does it depend on user fees and other exchange-like revenues compared to general tax revenues?

- How does its financial position compare to other, similar governments?

To illustrate, let's look at the financial statements for the City of Overland Park, KS. Overland Park (OP) is a large suburban community just west of Kansas City, MO. In 2015 its population was just under 175,000.

Let's start with OP's government-wide balance sheet, known formally as the Statement of Net Position. It shows OP's balances for its assets, liabilities, and other accounts on the final day of its fiscal year, December 31. This statement includes separate presentations for *governmental activities* and *business-type activities*. Governmental activities are supported by taxes and other *non-exchange revenues*. Business-type activities, or proprietary activities, are supported by *exchange-like revenues*, or fees the government charges for goods and services it delivers. For local governments, government-owned utilities, recreational facilities, golf courses, and other enterprises are almost always considered business-type activities. For state governments, business-type activities usually include programs like workers compensation/unemployment funds, state lotteries, university tuition assistance programs, private corrections facilities, and many other activities.

On the asset side, we see many of the same assets we saw at Treehouse. OP has cash, investments, and accounts receivable. Like a non-profit, current assets are assets it expects to collect within the fiscal year. The same applies to the liabilities side. OP has accounts payable, unearned revenue, accrued expenses, and other items we'd see at a non-profit or for-profit entity.

But there are several important differences. First, note the two new categories of *deferrals*. A government records a deferred inflow of resources when it receives resources as part of a non-exchange transaction in advance. Pre-paid property taxes are a good example. Imagine a property owner in OP paid their property taxes for 2016 in July of 2015. OP might be tempted to call this *deferred revenue* because it received payment in advance for services it will deliver next year. However, that would be incorrect because property taxes are a *non-exchange revenue*. Taxpayers in OP don't pay property taxes for specific services at specific times; they pay for a variety of services delivered at

City of Overland Park
Statement of Net Position
December 31, 2015

	Primary Government		
	Governmental Activities	Business-Type Activities	Total
Assets			
Current assets:			
Cash and cash equivalents and investments	$ 91,154,714	$ 2,278,786	$ 93,433,500
Taxes receivables	18,505,422	-	18,505,422
Accounts receivables	2,019,538	601,601	2,621,139
Due from other governments	3,103,137	-	3,103,137
Current property taxes receivable	39,011,577	-	39,011,577
Special assessments	407,664	-	407,664
Other current assets	777,877	634,277	1,412,154
Total current assets	154,979,929	3,514,664	158,494,593
Noncurrent assets:			
Special assessments	1,075,046	-	1,075,046
Cash and investments restricted for:			
Unspent bond proceeds	11,006,155	-	11,006,155
Debt service	-	16,689,167	16,689,167
Workers' comp and medical claims	1,957,850	-	1,957,850
Capital Assets:			
Land, improvements and construction in progress	50,520,788	1,535,263	52,056,051
Capital assets, net of depreciation	1,001,900,796	48,225,827	1,050,126,623
Total capital assets	1,052,421,584	49,761,090	1,102,182,674
Total noncurrent assets	1,066,460,635	66,450,257	1,132,910,892
Total assets	1,221,440,564	69,964,921	1,291,405,485
Deferred Outflows of Resources			
Deferred outflow from pensions	14,680,265	-	14,680,265
Deferred charge on refunding	1,597,240	5,837,346	7,434,586
Total deferred outflows	16,277,505	5,837,346	22,114,851
Liabilities			
Accounts and claims payable	7,889,468	3,320,971	11,210,439
Accrued expenses	3,820,519	4,331,901	8,152,420
Contract payable	6,754,823	-	6,754,823
Unearned revenue	2,341,053	25,754	2,366,807
Long-term liabilities:			
Due in one year	21,571,154	2,316,002	23,887,156
Due in more than one year	178,650,123	106,316,974	284,967,097
Total liabilities	221,027,140	116,311,602	337,338,742
Deferred Inflows of Resources			
Deferred inflows from pensions	2,452,360	-	2,452,360
Unavailable revenue - property taxes	39,097,004	-	39,097,004
Total deferred inflows	41,549,364	-	41,549,364
Net Position			
Net invested in capital assets	921,477,236	(49,536,373)	871,940,863
Restricted for:			
Debt Service	-	12,812,874	12,812,874
Restricted for capital and other projects	-	3,876,293	3,876,293
Workers' compensation and medical claims	1,191,377	-	1,191,377
Street improvements	4,896,795	-	4,896,795
Unrestricted	47,576,157	(7,662,129)	39,914,028
Total net position	$ 975,141,565	$ (40,509,335)	$ 934,632,230

The accompanying notes are an integral part of the basic financial statements.

various times throughout the year. There's no real exchange. So in this case, OP would recognize the taxpayer's cash as an asset, but simultaneously recognize a *deferred inflow of resources*. Next year, when OP delivers the police, fire, and other services funded by those property taxes, it will reduce cash and reduce that deferred inflow.

The inverse is true for deferred outflows. Say, for example, that most of OP's employees belong to the Kansas Public Employees' Retirement System. That System sends OP a bill for $14.86 million to cover pensions and other costs related to the OP employees now in the System. That bill is due on January 20, 2016. In December 2015 OP closes its books and prepares its financial statements, but its City Council signs papers acknowledging their commitment to make that $14.86 million shortly after the start of the coming fiscal year. Those resources are effectively unavailable for the coming year.

OP might be tempted to call this accounts payable because it has owes money for a service it's already received. But that's not entirely true. A state retirement system is not a service, and even if it was, it wouldn't deliver that service until the next fiscal year. So instead, OP will book this as a deferred outflow of resources, and book a corresponding increase in liabilities. By not booking a liability, and not actually spending the cash, OP's FY15 balance sheet looks much stronger. At the same time, it has committed resources to the future, and that will impact its operations in the coming year. By recognizing a deferred outflow of resources, OP has offered us a clearer picture of how well the resources it collects each year cover its annual spending needs.

That's How We Roll

Most governments have dozens, if not hundreds, of individual funds. It's not feasible to report on all of them. So to simplify the reporting process governments draw a distinction between *major funds* and *non-major funds*. Different governments define "major" differently, but most use a benchmark of 5-10%. That is, a fund is major if it comprises at least 5-10% of the total revenues of all government activities or all business-type activities. GAAP requires a set of financial statements for each major fund. The remaining non-major funds are "rolled up" into a single set of financial statements.

Critics of government financial reporting often say that governments have too many funds. When a government's finances are spread across so many different reporting units it's difficult, if not impossible, to develop a clear picture of its financial position. Supporters of the status quo say that funds, while cumbersome, are our best available means to ensure fiscal accountability.

With the addition of deferrals, we re-write the fundamental equation for the government-wide financial statements as:

Assets + Deferred Outflows = Liabilities + Deferred Inflows + Net Position

In the traditional fundamental equation, we use "net assets" to identify assets minus liabilities. When we add deferrals, the "net assets" label no longer captures everything on the right side of the equation, but "net position" does.

Going back to OP's assets, we see items that we'd only see on a government's financial statements.

- *Taxes Receivable.* Taxes, usually property taxes, that OP is owed for 2015 and expects to receive early in 2015.

- *Special Assessments.* Recall special assessments are taxes, usually property taxes, levied on specific parcels of property or groups of properties. Special assessments are reported separately from general property taxes because they are used to fund specific assets like sidewalks and street lighting, and specific services like economic development.

- *Due from Other Governments.* Local governments routinely partner with other local governments. These *inter-local agreements* or *cross-jurisdictional sharing* arrangements are common in areas like emergency management, police and fire response, and public health, among many other service areas. If those agreements require one government to pay another government, those payments appear as "due to other governments."

Like with most governments, the majority of OP's liabilities are long-term liabilities. State and local governments finance most of their infrastructure improvements with long-term bonds (either general obligation bonds or revenue bonds), usually paid off over a 20 up to 30 year period. When a government issues bonds it recognizes a long-term liability, and the borrowed cash as an asset. Cities, counties, and school districts rarely go bankrupt or cease operations, so investors are willing to invest in them for such long periods of time. This is quite different from non-profits or for-profits, where the *going concern* question is not always so clear.

Net position and its components are also a uniquely governmental reporting feature. Here OP is similar to other states and local governments.

- *Net Investment in Capital Assets* is the value of OP's infrastructure assets (net of depreciation) minus the money it owes on the bonds that financed those assets. All capital assets are reported in this component of net assets, even if there are legal or other restriction on how the government is to use them for service delivery.

- Governments restrict portions of their net position for many purposes. *Restricted net position* is virtually the same as restricted net assets for a non-profit. According to governmental GAAP, a portion of net position is restricted if: 1) an external body, like bondholders or the state legislature, can enforce that restriction, or 2) the governing body passes a law or other action that imposes that restriction. For most state and local governments, the largest and most important portion of restricted net position is *restricted for debt service*. In 2001 OP created a non-profit organization called the Overland Park Development Corporation (OPDC). OP includes OPDC in its financial statements as a *component unit* (see below). Shortly after its creation OPDC financed, constructed, and now owns a Sheraton Hotel that's designed to bolster local convention business. OP agreed to levy a small tax on hotel rooms and car rentals within the city – a "transient guest tax" – to pay the debt service on the bonds OPDC used to finance that hotel. Almost all of OP's restricted net position is related to that debt service and to capital spending required to maintain the hotel.

- A government's *unrestricted net position* is akin to a non-profit's unrestricted net assets. These are net assets available for spending in the coming fiscal year.

What's a Street "Worth"?

When we look at Net Investment in Capital Assets we're forced to ask, what's the "book value" of a capital asset. Recall that most organizations, public and private, record their tangible capital assets at historical cost. That means they record a new asset at whatever it cost to construct or purchase it, and then depreciate it over it's useful life. Most of the assets non-profits carry on their books – buildings, vehicles, office furniture, etc. – have useful lives of 10-30 years. But how does a government determine the book value of a street? Or a school building? Or a sewer system? Many of these assets were built long before governments started preparing modern financial statements, and many of them have useful lives of more than 100 years.

States and localities dealt with precisely this issue when they implemented Governmental Accounting Standards Board (GASB) Statement 34. This statement – euphemistically known as "*GASB 34*" – required governments, for the first time, report the book value of their capital assets. Prior to GASB 34, they reported what they spent each year on capital assets as an expense, but they did not include their full book value. In other words, they did not *capitalize* their infrastructure assets.

Fortunately, many governments were able to reconstruct historical cost figures by reviewing old invoices, purchase orders, construction plans, and other historical documents. Public works staff at states and local governments around the country spent thousands of hours researching old records to determine what they spent to build their original streets, bridges, sewer systems, university buildings, and other key pieces of infrastructure. Those assets were then grouped into fixed asset networks, assigned a useful life and a depreciation schedule, and depreciated to the present day. That depreciated figure became the original capitalized infrastructure asset value.

So for most governments the figure Net Investment in Capital Assets is the original capitalized value depreciated to a present day, plus any investments since implementing GASB 34. A few governments take a different approach allowed under GASB 34 known as the *modified method*. Here a government capitalizes its infrastructure assets, but instead of depreciation, it estimates how much it will need to spend each year to maintain those assets in good working condition. If it can demonstrate that it's making those investments, it need not depreciate, and the book value does not change.

Why take the time and effort to do this? Because investors and taxpayers want to know if their government is taking care of its vital infrastructure. If the Net Investment in Capital Assets is stable or increasing, it suggests a government is making precisely those investments.

THE INCOME STATEMENT

The Income Statement is designed to tell us if an organization's programs and services cover their costs? In other words, is this organization *profitable*?

It's organized by *revenues* and *expenses*. In GAAP, revenue is defined as what an organization earns for delivering services or selling goods. Expenses are the are the cost of doing business. Whenever possible, think of expenses in terms of the revenues they help to generate. For non-profit organizations this relationship is sometimes clear, and sometimes not. For example, imagine that a non-profit conservation organization operates guided backpacking trips. Participants pay a small fee to participate in those trips. To run those trips the organization will incur expenses like wages paid to the trip guides, supplies, state permitting fees, and so forth. These are expenses incurred in the course of producing backpacking tour revenue. Here that relationship between revenues and expenses is clear.

This same organization might sell coffee mugs, water bottles, and other merchandise, and then use those revenues to support it's conservation mission. The expenses to produce those mugs are known as *cost of goods sold*. Here again, the revenue-expense relationship is clear. When that link is clear, we can determine if a program/service/product is *profitable*. That is, does the revenue it generates exceed the expenses it uses up? In for-profit organizations, profitability and accountability are virtually synonymous.

But for public organizations profitability has little to do with accountability. For instance, our conservation non-profit might accept donations from individuals in support of its conservation work. Which expenses were necessary to "produce" those revenues? The development director's salary? The administrator's travel expenses to go visit a key donor? The expenses from a recent marketing campaign? Here the revenue-expense link is less clear. Same for in-kind contributions (i.e. donated goods and services) the organization receives in support of its mission. This link is even murkier for governments, where taxpayers pay income, property, and sales taxes, but those taxes have no direct link to the expenses the government incurs to deliver police, fire, parks, public health, and other services.

To put this in the language of accounting, public organizations have a mix of *exchange-like transactions*, such as the backpacking trips and coffee mugs, and many more *non-exchange-like* activities like conservation programs and public safety functions that are just as, if not more central, to their mission as their exchange-like activities. That's why profitability is one of many criteria we need to apply when thinking about the finances of a public organization.

Notes to the Financial Statements

GAAP imposes uniformity on how public organizations recognize and report their financial activity. But at the same time, all public organizations are a bit different. They have different missions, financial policies, tolerance for financial risk, and so forth. Also keep in mind that large parts of GAAP afford organizations a lot discretion on how and when to recognize certain types of transactions. For these reasons, numbers in the basic financial statements don't always tell a complete financial story about the organization in question. That's why it's essential to read the Notes to the Financial Statements. The Notes are narrative explanations at the end of the financial statements. They outline the organization's key accounting assumptions, share its key financial policies, and explain any unique transactions or other financial activity.

That said, the main point of emphasis on the income statement is the relationship between revenues and expenses. As mentioned, net assets are a good indication of that relationship. If revenues increase faster than expenses, then net assets increase. If expenses increase faster than revenues, net assets will decrease. The income statement can help illuminate several follow-up questions to understand an organization's revenues-expenses relationship at some detail:

1. How much did net assets increase since last year? How much of that increase was in unrestricted net assets? How much was in restricted net assets? Growth in unrestricted net assets generally indicates that the organization's core programs and services are profitable. Growth in restricted net assets can mean many other things.
2. What portion of revenue is from *earned income* vs. revenue from contributions? Earned revenue, or revenue generated when the organization sells goods or services, is attractive because managers have direct control of expenses needed to generate income. Contributions are less predictable and less directly manageable, but do not have an immediate offsetting expense.
3. What percentage of earned revenue is from the organization's core programs and services? What percentage is from other activities and other lines of business? It's common for non-core programs and services to subsidize core programs and services, but is that the right policy for this organization to pursue its mission?
4. To what extent does this organization rely on in-kind contributions? Investment income? In-kind contributions – such as legal services provided to the organization for free by a donor – and investment income make up a smaller portion of overall revenues but often allow the organization report a positive change in net assets.

To illustrate, let's examine Treehouse's FY2015 Income Statement (i.e. Statement of Activities). Treehouse's FY2015 Income Statement reports the four most common types of revenues: contributions and grants, in-kind contributions (i.e. donated goods and services), contract revenue, and "other" revenues. The Income Statement reports revenues by restrictions – i.e., unrestricted, temporarily restricted, and permanently restricted. It also reports revenues, expenses, and change for FY 2014.

For FY 2015, Treehouse reported $10,625,911 in revenues. Of that, $7,484,460 was from contributions and grants, $1,879,833 from in-kind contributions, $1,261,618 from contracted revenue and $1,396,194 released from restrictions. Net assets released from restrictions identifies restricted net assets that became unrestricted once the conditions defining the restriction has been met. For example, if a non-profit receives a grant that is temporarily restricted to the provision of specific services to a specific group of beneficiaries, and it delivers those services, it will then convert those temporarily restricted net assets to unrestricted net assets. On the Statement of Activities that conversion will appear as a reduction of temporarily restricted net assets and an increase in unrestricted net assets. These releases do not indicate new revenues, but rather a re-classification across the different types of net asset restrictions.

In reviewing financial statements, we want to take note of important trends. In the case of Treehouse, there was substantial growth in Contributions and Grants — up from $6,337,712 in FY2014, a more than 18% increase.

Turning to the expense part of the Statement, we see that expenses for program services (i.e. services for foster children, consistent with Treehouse's mission) were $7,447,627 in FY2015, nearly 80% of total expenses. Total expenses grew by 14.5% from FY2014 to FY2015, a growth rate that is lower than the rate of revenue growth.

TREEHOUSE

STATEMENT OF ACTIVITIES
For the Year Ended September 30, 2015
(With Comparative Totals for 2014)

		2015			
	Unrestricted	Temporarily Restricted	Permanently Restricted	Total	2014
Revenue					
Contributions and grants	$ 5,616,195	$ 1,868,265	$ -	$ 7,484,460	$ 6,337,712
In-kind contributions	1,879,833			1,879,833	1,315,232
Contract revenue	1,261,618			1,261,618	1,368,092
Other					7,767
Net assets released from restrictions	1,396,194	(1,246,597)	(149,597)		
Total revenue	10,153,840	621,668	(149,597)	10,625,911	9,028,803
Expenses					
Program services	7,447,627			7,447,627	6,560,098
Management and general	495,941			495,941	391,208
Fundraising	1,438,030			1,438,030	1,239,095
Total expenses	9,381,598			9,381,598	8,190,401
Changes in net assets before investment income and loss on pledge receivable	772,242	621,668	(149,597)	1,244,313	838,402
Investment income (loss)	(66,235)	(19,767)	(89,754)	(175,756)	477,175
Loss on pledge receivable		(10,900)		(10,900)	(225,065)
Change in net assets	**706,007**	**591,001**	**(239,351)**	**1,057,657**	**1,090,512**
Net assets, beginning of year	4,549,404	2,855,900	3,683,988	11,089,292	9,998,780
Net assets, end of year	$ 5,255,411	$ 3,446,901	$ 3,444,637	$ 12,146,949	$ 11,089,292

See Notes to Financial Statements

The expenses part also highlights how investment income affected the change in net assets. In FY2015 Treehouse's investments lost value, and reduced net assets by $175,756. This is a substantial change from FY2014, where those same investments added $477,175 to net assets.

Change in net assets is, as mentioned before, the focal point for the Statement of Activities. To see the change in net assets we compare across the "Change in Net Assets" row. We see Treehouse's total net assets grew from by $1,057,657, an increase of almost nine percent. Much of that increase is attributable to growth in both contributions and grants and in-kind contributions.

FOR GOVERNMENTS – THE STATEMENT OF ACTIVITIES

A government's Statement of Activities presents much of the same information we see on the income statement for a for-profit or non-profit. It lists a government's revenues and expenses or expenditures, and the difference between them. It reports the change in net assets and offers some explanation for why that change happened. Like an income statement, it tells us where the government's money came from, where it went, and whether its core activities pay for themselves.

That said, the Statement of Activities is also quite different from a traditional income statement. *Expenses* in the upper left, are presented by major function or program, with the *governmental activities* presented separately from the *business-type activities*. Governmental activities and business-type activities together comprise the *primary government*. Next to expenses you'll occasionally see (although not with OP) indirect expenses the government has allocated to each activity (more on this in Chapter 4).

City of Overland Park
Statement of Activities
For the Year Ended December 31, 2015

| | | Program Revenues | | | Net (Expense) Revenue and Changes in Net Position | | |
| | | | | | Primary Government | | |
Functions/Programs	Expenses	Charges for Services	Operating Grants and Contributions	Capital Grants and Contributions	Governmental Activities	Business-type Activities	Total
Primary government:							
Governmental activities:							
General government	$ 33,678,644	$ 10,874,123	$ 888,625	$ -	$ (21,915,895)	$ -	$ (21,915,895)
Public safety	56,811,306	7,458,653	3,149,365	86,442	(46,116,847)	-	(46,116,847)
Public works	84,779,317	3,086,611	8,285,925	34,666,441	(38,740,340)	-	(38,740,340)
Parks and recreation	16,427,499	5,516,395	1,385,731	-	(9,525,373)	-	(9,525,373)
Planning and development services	7,818,756	4,246,668	405,401	-	(3,166,687)	-	(3,166,687)
Interest on long-term debt	6,381,217	-	-	-	(6,381,217)	-	(6,381,217)
Total governmental activities	205,896,739	31,182,450	14,115,047	34,752,883	(125,846,359)	-	(125,846,359)
Business-type activities:							
Golf course	4,444,788	5,004,110	-	-	-	559,322	559,322
Soccer complex	1,155,103	1,303,552	-	-	-	148,449	148,449
OP Development Corporation	27,134,815	23,503,118	-	-	-	(3,631,697)	(3,631,697)
Total business-type activities	32,734,706	29,810,780	-	-	-	(2,923,926)	(2,923,926)
Total primary government	$ 238,631,445	$ 60,993,230	$ 14,115,047	$ 34,752,883	(125,846,359)	(2,923,926)	(128,770,285)
			General Revenues:				
			Property taxes		36,981,306	-	36,981,306
			Sales taxes		51,903,813	-	51,903,813
			Franchise taxes		10,832,504	-	10,832,504
			Transient guest tax		10,057,212	-	10,057,212
			Grants and contributions not restricted to specific programs		28,230,807	-	28,230,807
			Unrestricted investment earnings		238,184	28,864	267,048
			Miscellaneous		5,185,716	270,560	5,456,276
			Transfers		(2,966,247)	2,966,247	-
			Total general revenue and transfers		140,463,295	3,265,671	143,728,966
			Change in net position		14,616,936	341,745	14,958,681
			Net position - beginning, as restated		960,524,629	(40,851,080)	919,673,549
			Net position - ending		$ 975,141,565	$ (40,509,335)	$ 934,632,230

The accompanying notes are an integral part of the basic financial statements.

Program revenue includes two types of revenues. One is fees directly linked to these functions and programs for "exchange-like" transactions. OP reported $4.25 million in charges for services for Planning and Development Services. Most of that was building permit fees. As another example, it reported $7.5 million in charges for Services for Public Safety, and that was mostly parking ticket and speeding ticket revenue. And so forth.

The other type of program revenue is grants and contributions, which are broken out by operating grants and contributions, and capital grants and contributions. These are usually revenues from other governments. For instance, in 2015 OP received $3.1 million in Public Safety operating grants. Most of that was payments for fire protection services OP delivers to neighboring jurisdictions that lack a full-service fire department. It also received a $34.7 million capital grant from the State of Kansas' clean water revolving fund for upgrades to its stormwater infrastructure. That money was recorded as a capital grant to Public Works. These are just a few examples of program revenues that governments are likely to report.

Beneath the total expenses and program revenues for business-type activities, we see totals for the *primary government*. The primary government is the governmental activities and business-type activities combined. It does not include the government's component units (see below). The primary government plus any *component units* comprise the government's *reporting entity* or the total scope of financial operations covered by its financial statements. OP does not report any component units.

Are We Components?

A *component unit* is a legally separate entity for which the government is financially accountable. The primary government is financially accountable if it can appoint a voting majority the unit's governing body, if the component unit can impose financial burdens on the primary government, or if the unit is fiscally dependent on the primary government. Special districts like local development authorities, transportation improvement districts, and library districts are typical local government component units. Common state component units include housing authorities, tollway authorities, public insurance corporations, state lotteries, and state universities.

Most component units are small relative to the primary government. But some are quite large. The Cherokee Nation of Oklahoma, for example, counts among its component units three casinos, a housing development company, a home health services company, a public health insurance company, a waste management company, a large community foundation, a historic preservation society, and an economic development corporation, among others. In 2015 the total expenses in its primary government were just over $500 million, but the total expenses in its component units were $750 million.

Shifting to the right, we see a group of columns with the heading "Net (Expense) Revenue and Changes in Net Position." The totals listed here are total program revenues minus total expenses. OP lists a deficit in public safety of $46,116,847. This number is its charges for services plus operating grants and contributions plus capital grants and contributions minus expenses, or (($74,58,653 + $3,149,365 + $86,442) − $56,811,306) = -$46,116,847. This reporting structure is called the *net cost format*. It nets program revenues from program costs (i.e. program expenses).

This deficit tells us that, not surprisingly, OP's public safety services do not pay for themselves. Put differently, in 2015 OP had to finance $46 million for public safety using general revenues. We see similar deficits across all of OP's governmental activities. None of these services are profitable, and the total "deficit" across all governmental activities was $125,846,359.

Should OP's leaders be concerned that their core services are hemorrhaging money? Not really. We don't want basic local government services like public safety, planning, and zoning to pay for themselves because there's not a clear link between the users and the beneficiaries of these services. OP exacts fines on people who break the law when they park illegally or speed on city streets, but those fees are designed to deter those behaviors. Perpetrators who pay these fines really don't receive a service, and as we saw in Ferguson, MO and elsewhere, bad things happen to local governments that try to turn fines into a viable revenue source.

But that leaves open an important question. Citizens who follow the law and want public safety to keep their community safe are the real beneficiaries of public safety services. How do they help to fund public safety?

To answer that question skip down to the lower right corner of the statement. Here we see a list of General Revenues like property taxes, sales taxes, and others. General revenues are not directly connected to a specific activity. When we add up these general revenues and take away any transfers of general revenues to other parts of OP's government, the "Total general revenue and transfers" is $140,463,295. Compare that figure to the $125,846,359 "deficit" for the governmental activities, and we're left with an increase in net assets for the governmental activities of $14,616,936. In other words, OP's general revenues cover the governmental activities expenses not covered by program revenues, plus almost $15 million more. To put this a bit differently, OP's core services generate about one-third of the revenues they need to cover their costs. The remaining two-thirds comes from general revenues. This relationship between expenses, program revenues, and general revenues is one of the most important things to observe on a government's activity statement.

For the business-type activities, this expenses-program revenues link is much clearer. Recall business-type activities are designed to pay for themselves through charges and services. For OP, we see that the Golf Course had net positive revenue of $559,332 and the Soccer Complex had net positive revenue of $148,449. As expected, these activities were profitable. They generated more revenue than expenses. But that was not true for OPDC. It ran a net deficit of more than $3.6 million. Like with the governmental activities, this deficit was covered by general revenues.

Business-type activities present many different challenging strategic and policy questions. How profitable is too profitable? Should business-type activities be profitable enough to subsidize the governmental activities? If a business-type activity like a golf course is not profitable, does it offer enough indirect benefits in areas like economic development and tourism to justify that lack of profitability? With a careful look at the Statement of Activities, you can begin to put numbers to these and other questions.

THE CASH FLOW STATEMENT

The Cash Flow Statement is just as the title suggests. It tells us how an organization receives and uses cash.

It might seem strange to devote an entire financial statement to a specific asset. But cash is not just any asset. **Cash is king.** For small organizations, especially small non-profits, it's possible to run out of cash. If that happens, nothing about that organization's mission, clients, or impact on society will matter. Its employees, vendors, and creditors won't take compelling mission statement as a form of payment. If you're out of cash, you're out of business. To that end, the Cash Flow Statement is quite useful if we want to answer a few key questions about how a public organization receives and uses cash:

1. Do this organization's core operations generate more cash than they use? If not, why not?
2. Does this organization depend on cash flow from investing activities and financing activities to support the cash flow needs of its basic operations? How predictable are are cash flows from investing and financing activities?
3. How much of this organization's cash is tied up in transactions it cannot directly control, such as receivables and payables?
4. How much of this organizations' cash flow is related to sales of goods and inventory? How predictable are those sales?

From the cash flow statement we can learn a lot about the specific ways an organization generates and uses cash. The statement breaks cash flows into three categories: operations, investing activities, and financing activities. Euphemistically, we call this "OIF" (pronounced "oy-f"):

1. *Cash Flow from Operations.* This is how the organization receives cash and uses cash for its core activities. Negative cash flow from operations indicates the organization's basic operations use more cash than they produce. Without positive cash flow from other sources, this is not sustainable.

2. *Cash Flow from Investing Activities.* In this case investing includes investments in financial instruments like stocks and bonds, and investments in capital assets like buildings. For most non-profits this section is focused on cash earned from investments. If those investments produced more cash than what was spent acquire them, then they produce *positive cash flow.* Purchases of buildings and equipment are a *cash outflow,* and if the organization sells any buildings or equipment the receipts from those sales also appear here as a cash inflow. In general, we expect positive cash flow from investing activities. It's important, however, to know the origins of that positive cash flow. If the organization sold a building, that might produce positive cash flow, but at the expense of its ability to deliver services in the future. It might see negative cash flow from investing activities if, for instance, it moves idle cash into short-term investments.

3. *Cash Flow from Financing Activities.* Financing activities are cash the organization borrows to finance its operations. Most of the activity in this section has to do with borrowed money. For-profit entities use this section of the cash flow statement to show how selling stock produces a cash inflow. For non-profits and governments, the cash inflow from issuing bonds or from taking out a loan will appear here. For non-profits with an *endowment* or other *permanently restricted net assets* that produce unrestricted investment income that cash flow will also appear here.

Like with the balance sheet and the income statement, net assets are a key part of most public organizations' cash flow statement, especially Cash Flows From Operations. It might seem strange that net assets are the point of departure for a statement about cash, but it makes sense if we're willing to make a few assumptions. Recall that the most common way for net assets to increase is for revenues to exceed expenses. To understand the cash flow statement take this idea a step further. Assume that a public organization's total cash will increase during a fiscal period if the cash inflows from its main operating revenues exceeds the cash it pays out to cover its main operating expenses. The "Cash Flow from Operations" part of the cash flow statement is based on precisely this idea. It starts with the assumption that an organization's change in net assets is a good indicator of its cash flows from operations.

Most sizable public organizations follow this concept and report their cash flows from operations using the *indirect method.* This method starts with the change in net assets, assuming that change is the result of cash flows from operations. But of course, not all changes in net assets are the result of positive or negative cash flow. As you'll see later in this chapter, many different transactions and accounting procedures can affect revenues or expenses without affecting cash flow. A typical example is depreciation. Depreciation is when an organization "uses up" some portion of an asset in the process of delivering services. The portion of that asset's value that is used up is recorded as a depreciation expense. Like all expenses, depreciation reduces net assets. But at the same time, there is no cash flow associated with depreciation. You won't find any checks written to an entity called "Depreciation." The same is true for changes in the value of an organization's investments. Its stocks, bonds, and other investments can increase in value, but unless it sells those investments that increase in value won't produce any positive cash flow. Depreciation and changes in the value of investments are both examples of *reconciliations*. These are transactions that affect net assets but do not involve a cash flow.

In FY15 Treehouse produced its Statement of Cash Flows according to the indirect method. In the second column of the statement you can see that its net assets increased by $1,057,657 from the start of FY2015 (October 1, 2014) to the end of FY2015 (September 30, 2015). Skip down to the row "Net cash flows from operating activities" and you'll see that in FY2015 Treehouse's operating activities resulted in a net cash outflow of $199,299. In other words, the cash its operating activities used was almost $200,000 more than the cash those activities generated. This begs a natural question: How could Treehouse have more than a million dollars of new net assets even though its basic operations lost $200,000 of cash? This seems inconsistent with the idea that growth in net assets will correlate with growth in cash holdings.

To answer this question look at the reconciliations in the third/fourth row (i.e. "Adjustments to reconcile change in net assets to net cash flows from operating activities"). Recall that the figures in this part of the statement are reconciliations, so we interpret them inversely. Activity that would otherwise decrease net assets is shown here as an increase because we're "adding back" those decreases to arrive at net cash flows from operations. Activity that would otherwise increase net assets is shown as a reduction (in parentheses) because we're "backing out" those increases to arrive at net cash flows from operations.

Treehouse reported several reconciliations in FY2015, but a few of the larger ones deserve special attention. We see that Treehouse's net assets increased because it received $163,767 of donated investments and $600,265 of donated computer equipment. These two transactions alone increased net assets by $764,032, but did not produce any positive cash flow. Computer equipment is equipment, not cash. Investments increase the asset called investments, but do not immediately result in a cash flow. So we can see how net assets can increase substantially without any change in cash flow. The opposite is true for depreciation and an *unrealized loss* on investments (i.e. when the market value of an investment is less than the book value, also known as a *"paper loss"*; the opposite is also true for *unrealized gains* or *"paper gains"* on investments). These reconciliations decreased net assets by $198,775 and $271,087 respectively, so here they are added back to total net assets.

Below the reconciliations you'll see "Change in Operating Assets and Liabilities." The figures listed here are also reconciliations, this time to reconcile changes in assets and liabilities that do involve cash to changes in net assets.

The key here is we're focused on assets and liabilities driven by cash flows. So to make sense of the Change in Operating Assets and Liabilities section, first think about how typical assets and liabilities interact with cash. Most assets will increase if cash decreases. If we purchase inventory with cash, for instance, inventory will increase and cash will decrease. It follows that decreasing an asset will almost always bring about an increase in cash. For example, if we sell marketable securities or collect on accounts receivable, those assets will decrease, but cash will increase. When liabilities like loans or

TREEHOUSE

STATEMENT OF CASH FLOWS

For the Year Ended September 30, 2015
(With Comparative Totals for 2014)

	2015	2014
Cash Flows from Operating Activities		
Change in net assets	$ 1,057,657	$ 1,090,512
Adjustments to reconcile change in net assets to net cash flows from operating activities		
Depreciation	198,775	62,914
Donated investments	(163,767)	(245,822)
Net realized and unrealized losses (gains) on investments	271,087	(384,639)
Interest and dividends restricted for long-term investments	(62,412)	(53,610)
Changes in allowance and discounts on receivables	(14,055)	(10,513)
Donated computer equipment	(600,265)	
Change in operating assets and liabilities		
Pledges receivable	(343,500)	(90,231)
Contribution receivable for rent	(388,934)	179,874
Contracts receivable	(153,754)	(42,387)
Cy pres award receivable		750,000
Inventories	56,402	(99,043)
Unemployment trust deposits	(39,282)	(23,695)
Prepaid expenses	(98,940)	98,129
Accounts payable	11,922	(26,463)
Accrued salaries and related costs	69,767	82,838
Deferred revenue		(45,000)
Net cash flows from operating activities	(199,299)	1,242,864
Cash Flows from Investing Activities		
Purchase of investments (including reinvested income)	(1,488,331)	(1,892,570)
Proceeds from sale of investments	1,298,318	1,707,962
Purchase of furniture and equipment	(13,040)	(49,857)
Net cash flows from investing activities	(203,053)	(234,465)
Cash Flows from Financing Activity		
Interest and dividends restricted for reinvestment	62,412	53,610
Net change in cash and cash equivalents	**(339,940)**	**1,062,009**
Cash and cash equivalents, beginning of year	3,053,277	1,991,268
Cash and cash equivalents, end of year	$ 2,713,337	$ 3,053,277

See Notes to Financial Statements

a mortgage increase, so does cash (otherwise, most increases in liabilities don't correspond to a cash flow). When we pay down an account payable or a loan payable, cash decreases.

Now, recall that with the indirect method, the goal is to arrive at cash flows from operations by adjusting changes in net assets. To that end, we need to undo the effects of these asset/liability changes on net assets, this time focusing on how cash flows affect those specific types of assets and liabilities. The table below lays out how these reconciliations work.

Change in Asset/Liability	Reconciliation
Asset account increases	Reduce Net Assets
Asset account decreases	Increase Net Assets
Liability account increases	Increase Net Assets
Liability account decreases	Decrease Net Assets

To illustrate these mechanics let's return to Treehouse's cash flow statement for FY15. First look at the "Change in Operating Assets and Liabilities" section and focus on the reconciliation for inventory. We know that an increase in inventory will correspond to decrease of cash, and vice versa. Look at the table above to see how that translates into a reconciliation. If inventory increased, we would reconcile by reducing net assets. That's because that inventory increase would produce a cash outflow. We want our reconciled net assets figure to reflect that cash outflow, so we reduce it. The opposite is also true. If inventory decreased, we'd see a cash inflow, so we'd want to reconcile by increasing net assets. We'd want the reconciled net assets figure to show that reducing inventory produced new cash flow from operations. That makes sense, given that reductions of inventory usually associate with sales of goods, and those sales will increase cash.

For Treehouse, we see a reconciliation for inventory of $56,402. Since the reconciliation is asking us to increase net assets, we can assume this means inventory decreased. That's evident in the Statement of Net Position. Again, if inventory decreased, then cash increased, so we want our reconciled net assets to be larger as a result. That's why Treehouse "added back" this inventory reconciliation. Recall that a big part of Treehouse's mission is operating a thrift store for children in foster care. This inventory reconciliation is likely because it sold a particular product to a customer in its store.

Consider another example: pledges receivable. Here we see a reconciliation that reduces net assets by $343,500. Returning to the table, we see that a reduction in net assets means that asset increased. Practically speaking, this means Treehouse increased its pledges receivable. That's generally a good thing, but it did not produce a cash inflow. In fact, you can think of increases of receivables as transactions that "tie up" operating cash. Treehouse won't have access to that cash until its donors make good on their pledges. So in terms of day-to-day operations, receivables don't really "produce" cash from operations. So Treehouse took that $343,500 out of net assets. Note that all of Treehouse's receivables increased throughout FY15. Treehouse has brought in lots of new receivables, but until its collects those receivables we can't consider them cash flow from operations.

Turning to the liability side, we see a reconciliation for accounts payable of $11,922. In the table above we see that an increase of a liability requires a reconciliation that increases net assets. If Treehouse increased its accounts payable, that means it purchased something it would otherwise have purchased with cash. By acquiring goods it needs to operate, but acquiring those goods without a cash outflow, Treehouse has "saved" cash for other parts of its operations. Although it seems counter-intuitive, on the cash flow statement we consider this a cash inflow from operations. Why? Because by committing to a future cash outflow, Treehouse has "freed up" cash it can use today. That's why increasing a liability leads to a reconciliation that adds back to net assets.

Of course, this can't go on forever. At some point Treehouse will need to pay off those payables. When they do that liability will decrease, but so will cash. That's why when liabilities decrease, we see a reconciliation that also decreases net assets.

As mentioned, most organizations prepare their cash flow statement according to the indirect method. It's convenient, and it can be prepared using information that most organizations have readily available. Even if they don't carefully track their cash flow, they do carefully track changes in assets, liabilities, and net assets. As you've seen, those changes are the basis for the cash flow statement prepared with the indirect method. However, as you've also seen, the indirect method does not produce a clear illustration of exactly how cash moves through the organization.

Less complex organizations are able to address this problem by reporting their cash flow from operations using the *direct method*. Here the organization "directly" reports the actual cash flows. Instead of deriving those cash flows from changes in net assets, it reports the difference between its total cash inflows and outflows from different parts of its operations. Those parts are usually reported in discrete, useful categories like "Cash Received from Donors," "Cash Received from Clients," "Cash Paid to Employees," or "Cash Paid for Supplies."

The direct method is simple and intuitive. So why don't more organization's use it? Simply put, most large organizations have thousands or even millions of transactions throughout their fiscal year. They use cash in so many different ways it's not feasible add up all of their cash inflows and all of their cash outflows. So as counter-intuitive as the indirect method might seem, it's the only feasible method.

Cash Flows from Investing Activities and Cash Flows from Financing Activities sections are more intuitive, and are the same for both the direct and indirect method. Here we interpret the figures directly. No reconciliations or conversions. An increase means cash increased, and a decrease means cash decreased.

Returning to Treehouse, we see that in FY2015 it purchased $1,488,331 of investments with cash. We also see that it sold some investments, and those sales increased cash by $1,298,318. In Cash Flows from Financing Activities we see a cash inflow of $62,412. Recall that for non-profits, the proceeds from endowments and other permanently restricted net assets are reported as financing activities.

We can draw two immediate and important conclusions from Treehouse's cash flow statement overall. First, we see that in FY2015 its operations used more cash than they produced. We also see that overall cash also decreased by $339,940. This is noteworthy because it's a big change from FY14, when cash flow from operations and overall cash flow were both positive by more than one million dollars. Normally we'd think such a big change in cash flow might have to do with big increases in capital items or investments, but that's not the case here. Cash flows related to investments and capital items had essentially the same effect on cash flows in both FY14 and FY15. In fact, the main difference is the "Cy pres award receivable" in FY14. We see a reconciliation that added back $750,000 to net assets. Practically speaking, this means Treehouse collected on a large receivable in FY14 that did not appear in FY15. This raises a natural question: Was FY14 an outlier year with respect to receivables and cash flow? If it was, then an important second conclusion is that Treehouse's basic operations don't produce as much positive cash flow as the "Net cash flows from operating activities" line on the cash flow statement suggests. In turn, Treehouse depends to some degree on positive cash flow from investing and financing activities. That's not a weakness, per se, but it does change how we think about Treehouse's operational and financial strategy.

STATEMENT OF FUNCTIONAL EXPENSES

One of the central questions in non-profit financial management is: How well does this organization accomplish its mission? From a financial standpoint, one way to answer this question is to determine how much of the organization's expenses are related to its core, mission-related services. In the language of accounting, this distinction is *program services* vs. *support services* (i.e. *administrative services*). According to paragraph 28 of FASB Statement 117, program services are "activities that result in goods and services being distributed to beneficiaries, customers, or members that fulfill the purposes or mission for which the organization exists." Support services are everything else: fundraising, communications, management, administrative support, and other activities necessary to deliver program services.

Donors want to support a non-profit's main goals. They want to know their contribution improved a child's education, fed hungry people, advanced scientific research, or advanced whatever objectives are outlined in that organization's mission. They are less interested in funding rent, insurance, professional memberships, administrator's salaries (gasp!), or other support services. To be clear, support services are essential. They're just not sexy. That's why one of the most closely-watched numbers in non-profit financial management is the program expense ratio, computed as total program service expenses/total expenses. Many donors look for organizations with comparatively high program expense ratios, and many non-profit leaders work hard to minimize their support service expenses for that same reason.

In fact, the program services vs. support services distinction is so important that GAAP for non-profits calls for a fourth basic statement to illustrate it. This statement is called the *Statement of Functional Expenses*. It shows three basic categories of expenses:

1. **Program.** Many non-profits report their program expenses separately for each of their major mission or program areas.
2. **Management and General.** This is principally salaries and benefits for administrators, technical support services like accounting, and reconciliation expenses in areas like depreciation.
3. **Fundraising.** Includes expenses related to fund raising and special events, identifying and contacting donors, and other expenses associated with soliciting and generating contributions.

Let's return to Treehouse and examine its Statement of Functional Expenses. Treehouse reports expenses for each of its main programs in the first three columns from the left. Education programs are by far the largest spending area. In FY 2015 they comprised 46% of the organization's total expenses. The previously-mentioned "Wearhouse" program was 20% of total spending, and all "other" programs were 14%. Total expenses in all program services in 2015 were $7,447,627, or 80% of total spending. In other words, the program service ratio is 80%. To put it one more way, 80 cents of every dollar Treehouse spends is for services provided directly to foster children. As you'll see in the next chapter, 80% is a commonly-observed program service ratio.

One appealing feature of the Statement of Functional Expenses is that the expense categories are intuitive. Items like payroll, occupancy (i.e. expenses related to maintaining buildings), licenses and fees, transportation, etc. are self-explanatory.

Like many other human services-focused non-profits, most of Treehouse's spending on support services is for fundraising, and most of its spending on support services overall is for payroll. The same applies to spending on the education programs. All these functions are labor-intensive. Also, note that total spending increased by more than 14.5% from FY2014 to FY2015. Much of that increase was in payroll and payroll taxes. This would suggest Treehouse expanded its service delivery capacity. However, some of that increase was also due to a big increase in depreciation expense. That increase may or may not reflect a qualitative change in how Treehouse delivers its services.

TREEHOUSE

STATEMENT OF FUNCTIONAL EXPENSES
For the Year Ended September 30, 2015
(With Comparative Totals for 2014)

| | Program Services | | | | Support Services | | Totals | |
| | Education Programs | Enrichment Programs | | Total Program Services | Management and General | Fundraising | 2015 | 2014 |
		Wearhouse	Other					
Payroll	$ 2,961,283	$ 254,559	$ 297,039	$ 3,512,881	$ 207,608	$ 803,007	$ 4,523,496	$ 3,808,143
Wearhouse distributions		1,105,563		1,105,563			1,105,563	1,039,882
Payroll taxes and benefits	661,899	67,702	72,198	801,799	42,373	170,827	1,014,999	891,310
Occupancy	108,936	199,366	16,936	325,238	61,628	32,374	419,240	406,863
Assistance to specific individuals			412,720	412,720			412,720	378,059
Holiday Magic purchases			343,792	343,792			343,792	333,673
Other in-kind expenses	7,327	162,330	92,633	262,290	1,617	20,416	284,323	238,829
Professional services	132,687	5,825	20,409	158,921	44,960	34,593	238,474	197,606
Licenses and fees	48,231	4,003	7,246	59,480	14,251	28,286	102,017	81,124
Postage and shipping	2,221	180	41,095	43,496	825	55,947	100,268	80,075
Transportation	83,262	1,968	1,423	86,653	849	5,337	92,839	78,855
Printing and publications	4,759	497	12,048	17,304	2,429	70,910	90,643	88,495
Special events						87,260	87,260	172,958
Supplies	46,258	6,392	5,184	57,834	8,181	7,325	73,340	53,170
Staff training	54,806	2,163	962	57,931	7,591	6,339	71,861	62,062
Telephone	37,136	1,367	426	38,929	7,180	6,222	52,331	51,611
Meetings	17,402	920	1,356	19,678	6,104	21,951	47,733	36,424
Credit card fees			744	744		38,710	39,454	42,588
Equipment leases	8,306	1,250	991	10,547	6,925	2,670	20,142	15,297
Insurance	7,281	783	869	8,933	6,070	2,341	17,344	24,304
Depreciation	83,444	8,973	9,959	102,376	69,571	26,828	198,775	62,914
Other	15,972	1,943	2,603	20,518	7,779	16,687	44,984	46,159
Total expenses - 2015	$ 4,281,210	$ 1,825,784	$ 1,340,633	$ 7,447,627	$ 495,941	$ 1,438,030	$ 9,381,598	
Percent of total - 2015	46%	20%	14%	80%	5%	15%	100%	
Total expenses - 2014	$ 3,605,605	$ 1,701,631	$ 1,252,862	$ 6,560,098	$ 391,208	$ 1,239,095		$ 8,190,401
Percent of total - 2014	44%	21%	15%	80%	5%	15%		100%

See Notes to Financial Statements

FOR GOVERNMENTS - THE FUND STATEMENTS

Recall that in governmental accounting, a fund is a stand-alone, self-balancing set of accounts. Funds are one of our main tool's to assess a government's *fiscal accountability*. That is, did it follow taxpayers' directives on how to collect and spend its money? This is a rather different focus from the economic resources focus or a focus on operational accountability that runs throughout the government-wide statements.

Funds are so important that governments prepare an entirely separate set of fund-based financial statements. Moreover, those statements are prepared on a different basis of accounting, known as *modified accrual* accounting, that's designed to reflect this unique focus on short-term, fiscal accountability. Here we start with a quick tour of those fund financial statements, and then talk about how we recognize different types of financial activity in the modified accrual framework.

At the outset we must first recognize yet another small adaptation to the fundamental equation. In the fund financial statements, we care most about the difference between assets and liabilities within the fund. To that end, for those fund financial statements we express the fundamental equation as:

Assets + Deferred Outflows = Liabilities + Deferred Inflows + Fund Balance

Fund balance is perhaps the most closely-watched number in all of governmental accounting. Taxpayers seem to understand the core idea that if a government is living within its means, then its assets will slightly exceed its fund balance, and it will record a small positive fund balance. Policymakers seem to understand that ending the fiscal year with a fund balance, especially in the general fund, means there's a bit of money to spend in the next fiscal year. That's why many fiscal policy and financial strategy discussions often come back to a simple "Goldilocks" question: Is our general fund balance too large, too small, or just right?

Governments prepare three different types of fund financial statements: 1) governmental funds; 2) proprietary funds; and 3) fiduciary funds. Each type is covered herein.

The Governmental Funds Statements

GAAP requires governments to prepare a balance sheet that shows the assets, liabilities, and fund balance in every major governmental fund, and also shows the combined assets, liabilities, and fund balance in non-major funds. OP's balance sheet is presented here. It shows five discretely-presented governmental funds. They include the General Fund, which accounts for all of OP's general revenues; three special revenue funds (One-Eighth Cent Sales Tax Street Improvement, Stormwater Utility, and Street Improvement), the debt service fund, and the combined non-major funds (presented as "Other Governmental Funds"). Recall that the proprietary (i.e. business-type activity) funds are presented elsewhere.

OP's General Fund has $114.7 million in total assets, more than two-thirds of its total governmental funds assets. The basic distribution of cash and receivables in the general fund is quite similar to the distribution we saw earlier in the government-wide Statement of Net Position. OP also has few General Fund liabilities relative to its General Fund assets. As you'll see a bit later, most general fund spending is on salaries and other expense/expenditure items that do not generate a liability. And like the Statement of Net Position, OP also reports deferred inflows related to pre-paid property taxes, special assessments, and other revenues.

According to GAAP there are five types of fund balance, each corresponding to the strength of restrictions on how fund balance resources can be spent:

- *Non-spendable* fund balance is, as the name suggests, not available for spending in the next fiscal period. Governments usually record non-spendable fund balance for items like legal settlements,

City of Overland Park
Balance Sheet
Governmental Funds
December 31, 2015

	General	One-eighth Cent Sales Tax - Street Improvement	Stormwater Utility	Street Improvement	Debt Service	Other Governmental Funds	Total Governmental Funds
Assets							
Cash, cash equivalents and investments	$ 60,313,574	$ 4,816,249	$ 761,894	$ 5,778,177	$ 313,725	$ 15,839,605	$ 87,823,224
Cash restricted for unspent bond proceeds	-	-	-	6,356,688	-	4,649,467	11,006,155
Taxes receivable	13,607,181	1,052,455	-	-	-	3,845,786	18,505,422
Accounts receivables	1,548,333	-	-	-	-	454,653	2,002,986
Due from other funds	3,117,825	-	-	552,960	-	-	3,670,785
Due from other governments	15,198	-	-	2,102,854	-	985,085	3,103,137
Current property taxes receivable	36,093,601	-	2,917,976	-	-	-	39,011,577
Other current assets	-	-	-	-	-	777,877	777,877
Special assessments							
Current	-	-	-	-	407,664	-	407,664
Noncurrent	-	-	-	-	1,075,046	-	1,075,046
Total assets	$ 114,695,712	$ 5,868,704	$ 3,679,870	$ 14,790,679	$ 1,796,435	$ 26,552,473	$ 167,383,873
Liabilities:							
Accounts payable	$ 4,615,518	$ 262,310	$ 14,831	$ -	$ 58,725	$ 1,081,840	$ 6,033,224
Accrued expenditures	2,404,377	-	27,051	-	-	-	2,431,428
Contracts payable	-	-	-	3,139,498	-	3,615,325	6,754,823
Due to other funds	-	-	-	-	-	3,670,785	3,670,785
Unearned revenue	44,375	-	-	-	-	2,296,678	2,341,053
Total liabilities	7,064,270	262,310	41,882	3,139,498	58,725	10,664,628	21,231,313
Deferred Inflows of Resources							
Unavailable revenue - property taxes	36,179,028	-	2,917,976	-	-	-	39,097,004
Unavailable revenue - special assessment	-	-	-	-	1,482,710	-	1,482,710
Unavailable revenue - other	-	-	-	142,963	-	-	142,963
Total deferred inflows of resources	36,179,028	-	2,917,976	142,963	1,482,710	-	40,722,677
Fund Balances:							
Restricted	-	5,606,394	657,602	6,356,688	250,000	17,202,901	30,073,585
Assigned	30,249,453	-	62,410	5,151,530	5,000	2,996,659	38,465,052
Unassigned	41,202,961	-	-	-	-	(4,311,715)	36,891,246
Total fund balances	71,452,414	5,606,394	720,012	11,508,218	255,000	15,887,845	105,429,883
Total liabilities, deferred inflows of resources and fund balance	$ 114,695,712	$ 5,868,704	$ 3,679,870	$ 14,790,679	$ 1,796,435	$ 26,552,473	$ 167,383,873

The accompanying notes are an integral part of the basic financial statements.

small trust funds or endowment funds, or other long-term investments where the corpus of the investment must remain intact. OP did not report any non-spendable fund balance.

- *Restricted* fund balance is similar to restricted net assets. It can only be spent for the specific purposes prescribed in the government's constitution, enabling legislation, or some action from an external funder. OP is similar to other cities in that it reports restricted fund balance in both its special revenue funds and its debt service fund. It's common for bond holders to require minimum *coverage* levels or *contingency* funds. These are financial reserves designed to ensure the government will be able to make regular payments on its bonds especially if revenues fall short of expectations.

- *Committed* fund balance includes amounts that can be used for purposes determined by a formal action of the governing body. State and local legislators will occasionally commit fund balance for particular capital projects, for legal settlements or other one-time spending needs, or for *rainy day funds* or other *stabilization funds* designed to prevent spending cuts in the General Fund during an economic downturn. OP did not report any committed fund balance.

- *Assigned* fund balance is restricted by some action other than a governing body commitment or other enforceable restriction. Usually this means restrictions that management places on fund balances without the approval of the governing body. OP assigned $30.2 million of general fund balance for a variety of purposes including back wages it expected to pay as part of a new labor contract with its firefighters, and an "informal" rainy day fund that management maintains internally.

- *Unassigned* fund balance is the portion of fund balance without any other restrictions. In 2015 OP reported unassigned fund balance of $41.2 million. General fund unassigned fund balance is one of the most closely-watched indicators of a government's overall financial position.

Some readers review the governmental funds balance sheet and ask an intuitive question: Do the fund balances in the governmental funds equal the net assets in the governmental activities that we see on the government-wide Statement of Net Position? Fund balance and net assets are both the residual that left when we subtract liabilities from assets, so shouldn't fund balance equal net position. The answer is no. Why? Because, these two statements are prepared according to different bases of accounting. Recall that the Statement of Net Position is prepared on the accrual basis, where the Balance Sheet for the Governmental Funds is prepared on the modified accrual basis. As you'll see below, the modified accrual basis calls for slightly different recognition of some key types of financial transactions. Those differences can cause fund balance to diverge substantially from net assets.

The Statement of Revenues, Expenditures, and Changes in Fund Balance is like an income or activity statement for the governmental funds. It lists the revenues, expenditures, and changes in fund balances for the governmental funds. In this case, changes in fund balance are akin to changes in net assets.

From OP's Statement of Revenues, Expenditures, and Changes in Fund Balances we see that its two largest overall tax revenue sources are property taxes (just under $37 million total) and sales taxes ($51.9 million). It also relies on intergovernmental revenues (almost $29 million total), mainly in its street improvement fund, and $27.8 million of other general grants and contributions.

An expenditure is roughly equivalent to an expense, albeit on the modified accrual basis of accounting (more on this below). More than half of OP's general fund expenditures are for public safety. This is typical for mid to large suburban cities. Almost half of OP's total governmental funds expenditures are in the general fund. The other half is mostly for debt service and capital spending in the special revenue and debt service funds. This illustrates one of the key take-aways from this statement: In general, non-capital expenditures in the general fund are a good proxy for a government's "operating costs." Most of its salaries, benefits, and other operational spending will appear as general fund expenditures. By contrast, most of the revenues and expenditures in the special revenue and debt service funds will be related to capital spending and debt repayments, neither of which are considered day-to-day operations costs.

At the bottom of this statement, we also see "other financing sources." These are inflows and outflows of resources that affect fund balance but do not result in a revenue or expenditure. Refunding bond issue, for instance, refers to a restructuring of some of OP's existing debt. In 2015 OP borrowed new money at relatively low-interest rates to pay off some of its outstanding bonds that were issued with higher interest rates in the past. As a result of this refinancing, OP will now pay back $20,685,000 less than it was scheduled to pay back over time. This new "savings" appears as an increase to "other financing sources (uses)" in the debt service fund.

The last two lines of other financing sources are an important and sometimes controversial part of governmental accounting: *inter-fund transfers*. Transfers in are movements of resources into a fund from some other fund. Transfers out are movements of resources out of a fund into some other fund.

City of Overland Park
Statement of Revenues, Expenditures and Changes in Fund Balances
Governmental Funds
For the Year Ended December 31, 2015

	General	One-eighth Cent Sales Tax Street Improvement	Stormwater Utility	Street Improvement	Debt Service	Other Governmental Funds	Total Governmental Funds
Revenues							
Property taxes	$ 33,914,093	$ -	$ 2,750,891	$ -	$ -	$ 316,322	$ 36,981,306
Sales taxes	45,809,887	5,767,085	-	-	-	326,841	51,903,813
Franchise taxes	10,832,504	-	-	-	-	-	10,832,504
Transient guest tax	-	-	-	-	-	10,057,212	10,057,212
Charges for services	5,512,750	-	-	-	-	9,601,575	15,114,325
Licenses and permits	7,229,833	-	-	-	-	105,941	7,335,774
Fines and penalties	7,458,653	-	-	-	-	-	7,458,653
Use of money	130,358	-	-	-	-	602,361	732,719
Intergovernmental	2,562,014	-	-	18,839,986	-	7,573,889	28,975,889
Contributions	1,806,186	-	-	-	649,769	1,286,027	3,741,982
Capital / operating grants	-	6,629	3,823,176	-	-	7,967,163	11,796,968
Grants / contributions not restricted to specific programs	27,368,513	-	-	-	-	486,890	27,855,403
Total revenues	142,624,791	5,773,714	6,574,067	18,839,986	649,769	38,324,221	212,786,548
Expenditures							
Current:							
General government	18,956,273	-	-	-	-	16,062,682	35,018,955
Public safety	52,642,089	-	-	-	-	463,257	53,105,346
Public works	13,100,014	-	3,207,368	-	-	1,239,155	17,546,537
Parks and recreation	9,667,549	-	-	-	-	2,113,194	11,780,743
Planning and development services	7,339,195	-	-	-	-	245,646	7,584,841
Capital improvements	47,511	-	-	36,661,302	-	23,061,024	59,769,837
Principal / Interest on long-term debt	-	-	-	-	22,597,369	-	22,597,369
Bond Issuance Costs	-	-	-	49,068	341,931	103,826	494,825
Total expenditures	101,752,631	-	3,207,368	36,710,370	22,939,300	43,288,784	207,898,453
Excess of revenues over (under) expenditures	40,872,160	5,773,714	3,366,699	(17,870,384)	(22,289,531)	(4,964,563)	4,888,095
Other financing sources (uses)							
General obligation bonds issued	-	-	-	8,532,282	-	7,592,718	16,125,000
Refunding bond issue	-	-	-	-	20,685,000	-	20,685,000
Issuance: Premium	-	-	-	468,482	1,541,036	413,571	2,423,089
Payment to refunded bond escrow agent	-	-	-	-	(19,624,998)	-	(19,624,998)
Capital lease issuance	47,511	-	-	-	-	-	47,511
Transfers in	15,493,691	451,420	-	28,383,958	19,693,493	17,508,884	81,531,446
Transfers out	(42,356,015)	(3,075,120)	(2,798,000)	(13,575,187)	-	(22,793,371)	(84,597,693)
Total other financing sources (uses)	(26,814,813)	(2,623,700)	(2,798,000)	23,809,535	22,294,531	2,721,802	16,589,355
Net change in fund balances	14,057,347	3,150,014	568,699	5,939,151	5,000	(2,242,761)	21,477,450
Fund balances (deficits) at beginning of year	57,395,067	2,456,380	151,313	5,569,067	250,000	18,130,606	83,952,433
Fund balances (deficits) at end of year	$ 71,452,414	$ 5,606,394	$ 720,012	$ 11,508,218	$ 255,000	$ 15,887,845	$ 105,429,883

The accompanying notes are an integral part of the basic financial statements.

In 2015 OP transferred $15.5 million into its General Fund, and transferred $42.4 million out of its General Fund. Transfers like these are a necessary because, as you saw above, the General Fund finances operations across the entire government. For that to happen, OP's financial staff transferred a good amount of money out of the general fund. Critics say governments use inter-fund transfers to perpetuate a financial "shell-game." By transferring money in and out of funds at just the right moment, they argue, finance officials can obscure a government's actual financial position. How and when transfers can and should happen are important parts of financial strategy and policy.

When Transfers are Fraud?

In September 2016 the former mayor and finance director of the City of Miami, FL were convicted in federal court of defrauding investors. Their crime, according to prosecutors from the federal Securities and Exchange Commission (SEC), was that they improperly transferred into the City's General Fund money that had been committed to debt service in other funds. City officials argued those transfers were common and were necessary to bolster the City's financial position just before the bond rating agencies updated its credit rating. SEC officials and the jury disagreed. In their view, those transfers misled investors into thinking the City was financially stronger than it really was. Shortly after the verdict, City officials began negotiating a financial settlement with the SEC.

The Proprietary Fund Statements

Governments account for their business-type activities – or *proprietary funds* – on the accrual basis of accounting. As such, GAAP requires governments to supply a separate presentation of the financial activity in those proprietary funds. What follows is a quick tour of those proprietary fund statements. At the outset, keep in mind that these statements are quite similar to non-profit or for-profit financial statements given their basis of accounting and their overall scope of activity.

Governments show their proprietary fund assets, liabilities, and net position in a *Combining Statement of Net Position*. Like the Statement of Net Position, here OP has drawn a distinction between major and non-major proprietary funds. It's only major fund, shown in the second column is the Overland Park Development Corporation (OPDC). OPDC ended 2015 with $64.6 million in total assets and $115.8 million in total liabilities. Most of the assets are related to OPDC's ownership of the leasing rights to the Sheraton Hotel project, identified here as "other capital assets, net of depreciation." Most of the liabilities – more than $100 million – are connected to the bonds issued to finance that project.

This statement implies that OPDC is highly leveraged. That is, it owes others far more than the value of its assets today. That's not a problem, so long as the hotel project generates its expected revenues. The other non-major proprietary funds ended 2015 with total assets of $5.4 million, and total liabilities $477,056.

This statement is called the "combining" statement because it combines the government's proprietary funds with its internal service funds. *Internal service funds* are activities within the government that serve other parts of the government. OP has four internal service funds. Two are related to employee "self-insurance." For instance, OP's city manager, engineers, attorneys, and other professionals need to hold professional liability insurance to protect them in the event they are sued for malpractice. By pooling their risk across the entire city, they are able to purchase insurance at much lower rates than if they purchased individual policies. OP also uses this same model to offer workers compensation and catastrophic health insurance to its employees. Internal service funds can also include everything from motor pool to information technology repair to internal consulting services.

Internal service funds are designed to be self-balancing, so they are also accounted for on the accrual basis and presented on the Combining Statement of Net Position. In 2015 OP's governmental activities internal service funds reported total assets of $5.3 million, and total liabilities of $1.9 million.

Also note that governments can restrict portions of net position in the proprietary funds. OP has net position restricted for a typical array of needs such as debt service, capital spending, and compensation claims.

Federal Government Financial Reporting

The federal government does, in fact, prepare a set of audited financial statements known as the *Financial Report of the United States Government*. A division of the US Treasury known as the Bureau of the Fiscal Service prepares this

	OPDC	Total Nonmajor Enterprise Funds	Total Enterprise Funds	Governmental Activities Combined Internal Service Funds
Assets				
Current assets:				
Cash, cash equivalents and investments	$ 240,182	$ 2,038,604	$ 2,278,786	$ 3,331,490
Receivables, net	584,318	17,283	601,601	16,552
Inventory	336,141	152,348	488,489	-
Other current assets	145,788	-	145,788	-
Total current assets	1,306,429	2,208,235	3,514,664	3,348,042
Noncurrent assets:				
Capital assets:				
Land and construction in process	110,063	1,425,200	1,535,263	-
Other capital assets, net of depreciation	46,505,713	1,720,114	48,225,827	-
Total capital assets	46,615,776	3,145,314	49,761,090	-
Cash and cash equivalents restricted for				
workers' compensation	-	-	-	1,957,850
Reserved for debt service	16,689,167	-	16,689,167	-
Total noncurrent assets	63,304,943	3,145,314	66,450,257	1,957,850
Total assets	64,611,372	5,353,549	69,964,921	5,305,892
Deferred outflows or resources,				
Deferred charge on refundings	5,837,346	-	5,837,346	-
Liabilities				
Current liabilities:				
Accounts payable	3,092,987	227,984	3,320,971	166,939
Accrued payroll	1,581,130	90,277	1,671,407	-
Accrued interest payable	2,660,494	-	2,660,494	-
Unearned revenue	-	25,754	25,754	-
Unpaid claims	-	-	-	1,689,305
Bonds payable	2,285,000	-	2,285,000	-
Capital lease obligation	-	31,002	31,002	-
Total current liabilities	9,619,611	375,017	9,994,628	1,856,244
Long-term liabilities				
Accrued compensated absences	-	36,205	36,205	-
Bonds payable, net	102,752,973	-	102,752,973	-
Capital lease obligation	-	65,834	65,834	-
Ground lease obligation	1,059,008	-	1,059,008	-
Subordinated asset and				
property mgmt fee payable	2,402,954	-	2,402,954	-
Total long term liabilities	106,214,935	102,039	106,316,974	-
Total liabilities	115,834,546	477,056	116,311,602	1,856,244
Net Position				
Net investment in capital assets	(52,584,851)	3,048,478	(49,536,373)	-
Restricted for workers' compensation claims	-	-	-	987,076
Restricted for employee medical claim allocations	-	-	-	204,301
Restricted for debt service	12,812,874	-	12,812,874	-
Restricted for capital and other purposes	3,876,293	-	3,876,293	-
Unrestricted	(9,490,144)	1,828,015	(7,662,129)	2,258,271
Total Net Position	$ (45,385,828)	$ 4,876,493	$ (40,509,335)	$ 3,449,648

The accompanying notes are an integral part of the basic financial statements.

report according to a set of accounting principles developed by the Federal Accounting Standards Advisory Board (FASAB). Those principles are similar to modified accrual accounting in that they focus on financial resources and fiscal accountability. They also incorporate some recognition concepts that speak to the unique nature of federal appropriations and budget authority. The Government Accountability Office (GAO) then audits those statements according to those standards.

To date, the federal government has never received an audit opinion on these financial statements. GAO has refused to issue an opinion due to several material weaknesses on internal controls, especially at the Department of Defense (DOD). That said, the federal government has substantially improved its financial reporting processes. Today almost all of the 24 major cabinet agencies have received an unqualified audit opinion, and the DOD has convened a high-level task force to address its internal control shortcomings.

Governments also produce a Combining Statement of Revenues, Expenses, and Changes in Fund Net Position for the proprietary funds. This statement is quite similar to an income statement for the proprietary funds, especially given that those funds are prepared on the accrual basis of accounting.

In 2015 the OPDC reported total operating revenue of $23.6 million, compared to $21.3 million of operating expenses. In other words, its basic operations are profitable. However, those operations do not include the $5.8 million in required debt service. This suggest that, in fact, OPDC is not generating enough revenue to cover both its operations and and its long-term liabilities. OP's leadership ought to take notice. The non-major enterprise funds reported a $911,763 operating gain, and the internal service funds reported a $1.1 million loss.

The Fiduciary Funds Statements

We've covered governmental, proprietary, and internal service funds. The final type of fund you'll see on a governments financial statements are fiduciary funds. *Fiduciary funds* are money that governments keep but do not control. The vast majority are funds related to employee pensions and retirements. Each year a government must deposit money into their employee retirement plans. Different plans are managed in quite different ways. Some are managed at the state level and include members from the state government and employees of local governments across the state. Some governments are "self-funded," meaning they manage a plan whose members come only from their own government.

Regardless of how their employees' retirement plans are managed, every government must account for the money they pay into those plans. They do not control those plans, but they are obligated to pay into them and to record their employees' portion of those plans' assets on their own financial statements. That's the motivation for fiduciary funds.

At the end of 2015 OP reported $181.3 million in assets in its employee retirement plans. Most of its employees belong to the Kansas Employee Retirement System (KPERS or "Kay-Pers"). Each year KPERS sends its member employers a listing of all the assets held by its members who are currently employed by that employer. That listing is the basis for this Statement of Fiduciary Net Position.

City of Overland Park
Combining Statement of Revenues, Expenses, and Changes in Fund Net Position
Proprietary Funds
For the Year Ended December 31, 2015

	OPDC	Total Nonmajor Enterprise Funds	Total Enterprise Funds	Governmental Activities Combined Internal Service Funds
Operating revenues:				
Charges for services	$ 23,503,118	$ 6,307,662	$ 29,810,780	$ 10,607,693
Other reimbursements	78,812	191,966	270,778	486,117
Total operating revenues	23,581,930	6,499,628	30,081,558	11,093,810
Operating expenses:				
Claims paid	-	-	-	12,460,919
Contractual services	-	-	-	(286,631)
Soccer operations	-	1,155,103	1,155,103	-
Golf course operations	-	4,191,913	4,191,913	-
OPDC Operations	18,887,779	-	18,887,779	-
Depreciation	2,449,378	252,844	2,702,222	-
Total operating expenses	21,337,157	5,599,860	26,937,017	12,174,288
Operating income (loss)	2,244,773	899,768	3,144,541	(1,080,478)
Nonoperating revenues and (expenses):				
Interest earned on investments	16,620	12,244	28,864	41,088
Loss on disposal of capital assets	-	(249)	(249)	-
Interest and amortization expense on				
long term debt	(5,797,658)	-	(5,797,658)	-
Total nonoperating revenue (expenses)	(5,781,038)	11,995	(5,769,043)	41,088
Income (loss) before transfer	(3,536,265)	911,763	(2,624,502)	(1,039,390)
Transfers in	3,415,446	117,961	3,533,407	100,000
Transfers out	-	(567,160)	(567,160)	-
Change in net position	(120,819)	462,564	341,745	(939,390)
Total net position-beginning of year	(45,265,009)	4,413,929	(40,851,080)	4,389,038
Total net position-end of year	$ (45,385,828)	$ 4,876,493	$ (40,509,335)	$ 3,449,648

The accompanying notes are an integral part of the basic financial statements.

According to this statement, $104.6 million of that $181.3 million was held in mutual funds, with the rest held allocated across equities (i.e. stocks), corporate bonds, a real estate investment trust, and other government bonds. OP does not report any liabilities because it has not incurred any. All of those liabilities reside with KPERS, who owes its members retirement benefits as those benefits come due.

OP also reports $24.3 million of both assets and liabilities in its agency funds. Agency funds refers assets held by OP in a trustee capacity for another entity. It acts in an agency capacity two ways. One is when it collects fees on behalf of the state government. Specifically, it receives payments for driver's license reinstatements and for cereal malt beverage tax licenses (a licence required for bars, grocery stores, and other entities to sell high alcohol content malt beverages). Both these taxes are collected more efficiently by cities than by the state. At the end of each year OP remits these revenues to the Kansas Department of Revenue. OP also acts as an agent on behalf of private developers. When developers take on large, multi-year projects they sometimes choose to pay their special assessments and other local fees and taxes in periodic installments. OP collects those installment payments over time and then remits them to those developers, who then use them to pay their property tax or other relevant bills.

City of Overland Park
Statement of Fiduciary Net Position
Fiduciary Funds
December 31, 2015

	Employee Retirement Plans		Private-purpose Trusts		Agency Funds
Assets					
Cash and cash equivalents	$	3,253,761	$	3,365	$ 11,793,317
Investments in equities		47,496,628		-	-
Investments in mutual funds		104,589,224		-	-
Investments in real estate investment trust		7,536,910		-	-
Investments in corporate bonds		2,014,506		-	-
Investments in U.S. Treasury and government agencie		16,381,874		-	-
Interest receivable		-		-	13,642
Sales tax receivable		-		-	958,908
Special assessment receivable		-		-	11,625,000
Total assets	$	181,272,903	$	3,365	$ 24,390,867
Liabilities					
Accounts Payable	$	-	$	-	$ 45,999
Due to other entities		-		-	24,344,868
Total liabilities	$	-	$	-	$ 24,390,867
Net Position					
Held in trust for pension benefits and other purposes	$	181,272,903	$	3,365	

The accompanying notes are an integral part of the basic financial statements.

And finally, governments also produce a *Statement of Changes in Fiduciary Net Position*. This statement is similar to an income statement for the fiduciary funds. Instead of revenues and expenditures it identifies additions and deductions to those funds. For OP most of the activity in this statement is related to its previously-mentioned KPERS contributions. In 2015 it contributed 6.4 million on behalf of its employee members, and KPERS required a $5.3 deduction to pay benefits to members who have retired and are now receiving benefits.

City of Overland Park
Statement of Changes in Fiduciary Net Position
Fiduciary Funds
For the Year Ended December 31, 2015

	Employee Retirement Plans		Private-purpose Trusts	
Additions				
Contributions:				
Employer	$	6,389,275	$	-
Plan members		84,928		-
Total contributions		6,474,203		-
Investment earnings:				
Net decrease in fair value of investments		(5,994,307)		-
Interest		93,920		23
Dividends		4,762,491		-
Total investment earnings		(1,137,896)		23
Total additions		5,336,307		23
Deductions				
Benefits		5,255,368		-
Administrative expenses		350,930		-
Total deductions		5,606,298		-
Change in net position		(269,991)		23
Net position-beginning of the year		181,542,894		3,342
Net position-end of the year	$	181,272,903	$	3,365

The accompanying notes are an integral part of the basic financial statements.

CHAPTER 3.

FINANCIAL STATEMENT ANALYSIS

Financial Statement Analysis: "How Are We Doing?"

Financial statement analysis informs a wide variety of strategic management questions, including:

- What is this organization's overall financial position? Is it liquid? Profitable? Solvent?

- How does this organization's financial position compare to its peer organizations?

- How can this organization adjust its operations and policies to strengthen its financial position?

- How much debt or other long-term liabilities can this organization afford?

On March 22, 2014 the side of a hill near the town of Oso, Washington gave out after three days of relentless rainfall. A massive landslide followed, with mud and debris covering more than a square mile. Forty-three people were killed when their homes were engulfed by the slide.

In the days that followed more than 600 personnel participated in search and recovery operations. They rescued eight people from the mud and evacuated more than 100 others to safety. Most of the rescue personnel came from the four rural Snohomish County fire districts that surround Oso.

Minutes after hearing of the slide, staff at the Washington State Office of Financial Management (OFM) – the governor's budget office – made two critical phone calls. Earlier that week they had reviewed some data on the financial health of local special districts across the state. They observed that rural fire districts in the counties north of greater Seattle were showing signs of acute fiscal stress. Those districts had seen huge growth in property tax collections during the real estate boom of the 2000's. But since the real estate crisis of 2007-2009, those revenues had fallen precipitously. Many of those districts had laid off staff, cut back on specialized training, and back-filled shifts with volunteer firefighters.

So moments after hearing of the slide, OFM staff called the fire chiefs at two of the most financially-stressed Snohomish County fire districts. Their message to those chiefs was simple: send your people. OFM agreed to reimburse the districts from state or federal emergency management funds if needed. In turn, personnel from two of those districts were among the first on the scene, and were responsible for three of the eight life-saving rescues.

A few weeks later the chiefs of both those districts acknowledged that had OFM not called, they would not have sent their personnel. Both districts were so financially stressed that they could not have afforded the overtime wages and other expenses they'd have incurred to participate in the rescue operations.

Financial condition matters. It shapes how a public organization thinks about its mission and its capabilities. In the case of the Oso mudslide, it was the focal point for some life-saving decisions. That's why all aspiring public servants need to know how to evaluate financial statements, and to measure, manage, and improve their organization's financial position.

Learning Objectives

After reading this chapter, you should be able to:

- Compute and interpret ratios that describe liquidity, profitability, and solvency.
- Contrast how those ratios mean slightly different things across the government, non-profit, and for-profit sectors.
- Compute the "Ten Point Test" for governments.
- Understand the typical strategies organizations employ to improve their liquidity, profitability, and solvency.
- Contrast short-term solvency with long-term solvency, particularly for governments.

WHAT IS FINANCIAL POSITION?

Financial position is a public organization's ability to accomplish its mission now and in the future. When stakeholders ask "how are we doing, financially?" the answer should reflect that organization's financial position.

An organization's financial position has three main components:

1. **Liquidity.** Does the organization have liquid resources – especially cash – to cover its near-term liabilities? Can it convert its less liquid assets to cash to cover those liabilities?
2. **Profitability.** Do the organization's revenues cover its operating expenses?
3. **Solvency.** Can the organization generate enough resources to cover its near-term and long-term liabilities?

Till Debt Do Us Part

Some say there are two types of non-profits: "Those that have debt, and those that don't." This is a powerful sentiment. It suggests that once a non-profit has taken on debt, none of its other stakeholders matter. If that organization encounters significant financial stress and cannot repay its creditor(s), then those creditors have a legal claim to its assets. In that circumstance, that organization's board, clients, funders, and others will have little recourse, and the mission will suffer.

In the previous chapter you learned how to extract information about an organization's financial position from its balance sheet. For example are most of its assets liquid (e.g., cash and marketable securities), or does it have assets that are more difficult to convert to cash (e.g., receivables, inventory, or prepaid expenses)?

The balance sheet also tells us a lot about solvency, namely if the organization has a lot of long-term liabilities (e.g., long-term debt or pension obligations). Long-term liabilities mean the organization will have to divert some of its resources to meet those liabilities, and that can mean fewer resources to invest in its mission. To be clear, there are times when an organization can and should take on long-term liabilities in pursuit of its mission. Sometimes it makes sense to borrow and invest in a new facility that allows the organization to effectively serve its clients. Pensions and retiree health care benefits are an important employee recruitment and retention tool, even though they result in a long-term liability.

To learn about profitability we typically look to the income statement. Recall that if an organization's revenues exceed its expenses, then its net assets will grow. The income statement makes clear the organization's major sources of revenues, which revenues are growing, and whether those revenues cover program and administrative expenses. On the income statement, we can also see depreciation, bad debt expenses, and other expenses that reduce net assets but don't necessarily impact cash. These are all profitability concerns.

While financial ratios can provide us with useful metrics, always start off with a quick review of the financial statements. Ideally, the financial statements you are working with should report on the organization's operating and financial position for at least two financial periods. Keep in mind that funding agencies and financial analysts often would need access to at least four if not five years of financial data.

What do the financial statements tell you about the organization's financial position? Operating results? Cash flows? Review the financial statements and take note of the changes in assets, liabilities, revenues and expenses. Carefully review the notes to the financial statements as they will provide you with more detailed information regarding the organization's financial position. For example, a note related to fixed assets will report fixed assets at historical cost, assets subject to depreciation, any additions or retired assets, annual depreciation expense as well as accumulated depreciation, and ending balance as reported in the balance sheet. A note for pledges receivable will report amounts due in one year (or current portion), amounts due more than one year but less than five years, and amounts due more than five years. The note will also detail bad debt expense and the discount factor used to find the present value of non-current pledges receivable. A review of the trends should inform your interpretation of the ratios.

A review of the Statement of Financial Position (or Balance Sheet) can be guided by the following questions:

- *Assets*: How have the assets changed? What proportion is current? How much is reported under cash and cash equivalents? How much is reported under property plant and equipment, net of depreciation? Were there any new investments in property plant and equipment (review notes related to fixed assets)? How much is reported under investments? What proportion of investments is restricted? Have investments changed significantly and was this the result of market gains and investment income, a capital campaign, or transfers from cash (review note on investments)? How much more or less is the organization reporting in receivables/prepaid expenses? Have changes in current assets had a negative or positive impact on cash flows (also review Cash Flow Statement)?

- *Liabilities*: How have the liabilities changed? What proportion of liabilities is the result of borrowing or financing activities? To assess long-term solvency, what proportion of liabilities are reported as long-term debt obligations? Are there any covenants or restrictions associated with these obligations? To assess short-term solvency, what proportion of liabilities are current? Of that, how much is in the form of a short-term loan or a line of credit? Are there any contingent liabilities reported in the notes to the financial statements?

- *Net Assets*: What proportion is reported as unrestricted? Of restricted net assets, what proportion is reported as permanently restricted?

Your review of the Income Statement can be guided by similar questions:

- *Revenues*: What are the major sources of revenues? Have there been significant changes in revenues? Of total revenues, what percent is unrestricted, restricted (i.e., temporarily versus permanently)? How much of the organization's revenue is driven by earned income activities? Is the organization susceptible to changes in policy or funding priorities of a governmental agency?

- *Expenses*: How much did the organization spend on programs? How much did the organization spend on administration? Fundraising? Have there been significant changes in the level of spending? Have personnel costs changed? Are there other fixed costs that limit budget flexibility? How much did the organization report in depreciation and amortization?

FINANCIAL STATEMENT RATIOS

The purpose of accounting is to help organizations make better financial decisions. *Financial statement analysis* is the process of analyzing an organization's financial statements to produce new information to inform those decisions. Public organizations make dozens of crucial decisions everyday: Should we expand a program? Should we lease or buy a new building? Should we move cash into longer-term investments? Should we take a new grant from a local government?

All of these decisions must be informed by financial statement analysis. An organization should not expand if its existing programs are not profitable. It should buy a new building only if it knows how its current rent and other operating expenses contribute or detract from its profitability. It should move cash into less liquid investments only if it knows how much liquid resources it needs to cover its operating expenses? And so on. To answer these questions with precision, we need good metrics that illustrate an organization's liquidity, profitability, and solvency.

For those metrics, we turn to *financial ratios* (sometimes called *financial statement ratios*). Financial ratios are calculations derived from the financial statements. Each ratio illustrates one dimension of an organization's overall financial health.

Analysts who evaluate public organizations' financial statements employ dozens of different financial ratios. The first table lists a set of liquidity ratios. Liquidity ratios speak to the composition of an organization's assets, and how quickly those assets can be deployed to cover the organization's day-to-day expenses. The numerator in these ratios is a measure of liquid resources — either current assets or a specific type of current asset (cash and cash equivalents, receivables etc). The denominator in these ratios is either current liabilities or a measure of average daily cash expenses. For the latter, we take total expenses and remove expenses like depreciation, amortization, and bad debt expense that do not require an outflow of liquid resources. This adjusted for spending number is divided by 365 to produce a rough measure of average daily spending.

Profitability ratios are derived from changes in net assets. Recall that net assets increase when revenues exceed expenditures. This is an intuitive measure of profitability. The *operating margin* speaks to profitability in the organization's basic (i.e., unrestricted) operations. *Net asset growth* is a more inclusive measure of profitability across the entire organization. Net asset growth will include changes in temporarily restricted and permanently restricted net assets that are not included in the operating margin.

Margin (sometimes called the profit margin) is the price at which a good or service is sold, minus the unit cost. Industries like retail clothing have extraordinarily tight margins, meaning the price exceeds unit cost by just a percent or two. Low margin businesses must be "high volume," meaning they must sell a lot of product to be profitable. Professional services like accounting, tax consulting, and equipment leasing are "high margin," meaning the price charged exceeds the unit cost by a lot, sometimes by orders of magnitude. High margin industries tend to have barriers to entry. They require highly-trained professionals, expensive equipment, and other significant up-front investments.

Profitability measures are less salient for governments because governments need not be profitable to continue operating. Unlike a non-profit or for-profit, a government can bolster its financial position by raising taxes or fees. Most governments don't have wide latitude to that effect, but they have more than other organizations. That's why profitability measures for government are focused both on growth in net assets, but also on the share of total revenue that's derived from revenue sources the government can control on its own, like general revenues and capital grants.

The solvency measures speak to where the organization gets its resources. If it depends too much on unpredictable or volatile revenues from donors, that's a potential solvency concern. The same is true of revenues from governments. Government revenues can disappear quickly if the government changes its own fiscal policies and priorities. Debt, although sometimes necessary, indicates a drain on future resources. All these factors can inhibit an organization's ability to continue to serve its mission.

Financial Statement Ratios for Liquidity

Ratio	What it Tells Us	Non-Profit	Government	For-Profit/Hybrid
Current Ratio	Will near-term assets cover near-term liabilities? Rule of Thumb: >2	(Current Assets)/(Current Liabilities)	(General Fund Current Assets)/(General Fund Current Liabilities)	(Current Assets)/(Current Liabilities)
Days of Liquid Net Assets	Will overall liquid resources cover typical operating expenses? Rule of Thumb: >180 days	((Unrestricted Net Assets-Fixed Asset,net depreciation))/(((Total Expenses-Depreciation-Bad Debt))/365)		
Quick Ratio	Will the most liquid assets cover near-term liabilities? Rule of Thumb: >1	(Cash & Cash Equivalents+Receivables)/(Current Liabilities)	(General Fund Cash +General Fund Investments)/(General Fund Liabilities-Deferred Revenue)	(Cash & Cash Equivalents+Receivables)/(Current Liabilities)
Days of Cash on Hand	Is there enough cash to cover typical operating expenses? Rule of Thumb: >90 days	(Cash & Cash Equivalents)/(((Total Expenses-Depreciation-Bad Debt))/365)		
Fund Balance OR Short-Run Financial Position	What resources are available to appropriate? Rule of Thumb: >5%		(Unassigned General Fund Bal.)/(General Fund Revenues)	
Operating Cash Flow	Do cash flows from basic operations cover current liabilities? Rule of Thumb: Positive			(Cash Flow From Operations)/(Current Liabilities)

The Internal Revenue Service (IRS) monitors the *contributions ratio* as part of its *public support test* for charitable organizations. According to this test, a non-profit must receive at least 10% of its support from contributions from the general public and/or from gross receipts from activities related to its tax-exempt purposes. Less than that suggests the public is not invested in that organization's mission. By contrast, non-profit analysts also emphasize the *tipping point* where a non-profit depends too much on individual donors. Different analysts define the tipping point threshold differently, but most agree that 80% of total revenues from individual contributions is dangerously high. At that point, a non-profit's ability to serve its mission is far too dependent on unpredictable individual donors, and not dependent enough on corporate, foundation, and government support.

For governments, the solvency ratios are focused entirely on debt and other long-term obligations. Governments can borrow money that won't be paid back for decades. If careless, a government can take on too much *leverage.* That's why these solvency ratios focus on how much money a government has borrowed in both its governmental and enterprise funds, and its ability to pay back that debt. The

Ratio	What it Tells Us	Non-Profit	Government	For-Profit/Hybrid
Operating Margin	Do typical operating revenues cover typical operating expenses? Rule of Thumb: Positive	(Change in Unrestricted Net Assets)/(Unrestricted Revenue)	(Net Revenue or Expense for Governmental Activities / Total Governmental Activities Expenses) X -1	[(Revenue – Cost of Goods Sold)/Revenue]
Net Asset Growth/Net Sales Growth	Is profitability improving? Rule of Thumb: Positive	(Change in Net Assets/Change in Unrestricted Revenue)	Change in Governmental Activities Net Position /Beginning Governmental Activities Net Position	(Current Year Operating Margin/ Prior Year Operating Margin)
Return on Assets	How well does management leverage assets to drive profitability? Rule of Thumb: Positive	(Change in Net Assets/Total Assets)		(Total Income/Net Assets)
Own Source Revenue	How much does this government depend on other governments? Rule of Thumb: < 10%		Total Primary Government Operating Grants and Contributions / Total Primary Government Revenues	
Inventory Turnover	How often is inventory sold during a year? Rule of Thumb: > 1			(Cost of Goods Sold/ Inventory)
Return on Equity	How profitable are shareholders' investments? Rule of Thumb: positive			(Net Income/Owner's Equity)

later is known as *coverage*. Bond investors, particularly for public utilities, often stipulate how much coverage a government must maintain at all times. Coverage ratios are usually expressed as operating revenues as a percentage of interest expenses.

In addition to financial health, financial statements can illuminate how efficiently a non-profit raises money and how much of its resources it devotes to its core mission. These effectiveness measures are related to, but separate from financial position. Fundraising efficiency shows the financial return a non-profit realizes for its investments in fundraising capacity.

The program expense ratio is one of the most closely-watched and controversial ratios in non-profit financial management. It tells us how much of a non-profit's total expenses are invested in its programs and services, rather than administration, fundraising, and other overhead spending. Many analysts and non-profit monitors recommend a program service ratio of at least 80%.

Non-Profit Effectiveness Ratios

Fundraising Efficiency	What is the return on $1.00 in fundraising expenses?Rule of Thumb: > 1	(Total Contributions/Fundraising Expenses)
Program Expense Ratio	What proportion of total expenses are invested in programs and services versus administration and fundraising?Rule of Thumb: > .8	(Program Expenses/Total Expenses)

Financial Statement Ratios for Solvency

Ratio	What it Tells Us	Non-Profit	Government	For-Profit/ Hybrid
Debt to Assets	What percentage of this organization's assets were financed with debt? Rule of Thumb: <1	(Total Debt/ Total Assets)		(Total Debt/ Total Assets)
Contributions Ratio	How much does this organization depend on donors? Rule of Thumb: >10% but <75%	(Contributions Revenue/Total Revenue)		
Government Revenue Ratio	How much does this organization depend on government funding? Rule of Thumb: <25%	(Government Revenue/Total Revenue)		
Near-Term Solvency	How well can this government meet its near-term obligations with annual revenues? Rule of Thumb: < 150%		[(Primary Govt Liabilities – Deferred Revenues)/Primary Government Revenues]	
Debt Burden	How much more money can this government borrow? Rule of Thumb: Depends		Primary Government Non-Current Liabilities/Population	
Coverage 1	How easily can this government repay its debt as it comes due? Rule of Thumb: < .25		(Governmental Funds Principal and Interest on Long-Term Debt/General Fund Expenditures)	
Coverage 2	How easily can this government's enterprise activities repay their debt as it comes due? Rule of Thumb: > .5		Enterprise Funds Operating Revenue/ Enterprise Funds Interest Expense	
Capital Asset Condition	Is this government investing in its capital assets? Rule of Thumb: positive		(Ending Net Value of Primary Government Capital Assets – Beginning Net Value) / Beginning Net Value	
Working Capital to Total Assets	Has this organization experienced an operating loss? Rule of Thumb: positive			(Current Assets – Current Liabilities)/ Total Assets
Total Equity	What is this organization's long-run liquidity? Rule of Thumb: > .5			(Owners' Equity/Total Assets)

Ratios and Rules of Thumb

These rules of thumb are derived from the rich academic literature and industry analysis of public organizations.

To be clear, there is no legal or GAAP-based definition of "financially healthy," or "strong financial position." Every foundation, donor, or grantor defines these metrics differently. They'll also vary across different type and size of organizations. The rules listed in this table are some of the common figures cited by across many analysts in the public and private sector.

Before going further let's consider a few key points about financial statement ratios:

- *Ratios are only part of the story.* Ratios are useful because they help us quickly and efficiently focus our attention on the most critical parts of an organization's financial position. In that sense they're are a bit like watching on ESPN the thirty-second highlight recap of a football game (or whatever sporting event, if any, you find interesting). If we want to know which team won, and who made some big plays, we'll watch the highlight reel. If we want to know the full story – the coaches' overall game plan, which players played well throughout the game, when a key mistake changed the course of the game, etc. – we need to watch a lot more than just the highlights. Ratios are the same way. They're fast, interesting, and important. If we want a quick overview and not much more, they're useful. If we don't have the time to dig deeper into an organization's operations, or if it's not appropriate for us to dig deeper, then they're the best tool we have. But they're never the whole story. Always keep this limitation in mind.

- *Always interpret ratios in context.* Ratios are useful because they help identify trends in an organization's financial behavior. Is its profitability improving? How has its overall liquidity changed over time? Are its revenues growing? And so on. But on their own, ratios don't tell us anything about trends. To reveal a trend, we must put a ratio in context. We need to compare it to that same ratio for that same organization over time. For that reason we often need multiple years of financial data. It's also essential to put ratios in an industry context. Sometimes, a broader financial trend will affect many organizations in similar ways. A decline in corporate giving will mean lower donor revenues for many non-profits. Increases in overall health care costs will impact all organizations' income statements. Reductions in certain federal and state grants will affect particular types of non-profits in similar ways. To understand these trends we need to compare an organizations' financial ratios to the ratios of organizations in similar industries. It's useful, for instance, to compare human services-focused non-profits with less than $2 million in assets to other small, human-service focused non-profits in the same region with less than $2 million in assets. We should compare fee-for-service revenue-based non-profits to other fee-for-service revenue-based non-profits to other fee-for-service revenue-based non-profits. Large non-profits with a national or international mission should be compared to each other. There are clear rules about defining comparable organizations. The only rule is that without context, an analysis doesn't tell us much.

- *Financial statement analysis raises questions.* A good financial statement analysis will almost always reveal some contradictory trends. Why does this organization's profitability look strong but the current ratio is well below the rule of thumb? Why is this organization less liquid than its peers? Why does this organization not have debt, and is far more liquid, than similar organizations? A good financial statement analysis raises many of these types granular questions about the organization's financial assumptions, program operations, and overall effectiveness. Sometimes these follow-up questions can be answered from other publicly-available information, such as the notes to the financial statements or the annual report. Sometimes they can't. If your analysis concludes with many unanswered questions, that does not mean your analysis is bad. It simply means there are limits to what we can learn from financial statements alone.

- *Ratios are retrospective.* Most organizations release their financial statements three to six months after the close of their fiscal year. Analysis based on those statements is relying on information that is at least 12 to 18 months old. A lot can happen in 18 months. Always keep this in mind when doing financial statement analysis.

What's Your Industry?

Financial analysts in the for-profit sector focus on financial trends within the industry sectors defined by the *North American Industry Classification System* or NAICS. These codes identify businesses by key aspects of their operations. For instance, according to recent estimates, there are just over 72,000 businesses in the US within NAICS code 152101 – "Single-family home remodeling, additions, and repairs." The National Center for Charitable Statistics has developed an analog classification scheme for non-profits known as the National Taxonomy of Exempt Entities (NTEE). NTEE is not as precise or specific as the NAICS, but it is a useful way to think about sub-sectors within the non-profit sector.

NON-PROFIT FINANCIAL RATIOS – AN ILLUSTRATION

To see these ratios in action let's return to Treehouse. The table below shows its computations for the key financial ratios from its FY15 financial statements. All the information for these computations is taken from Treehouse's basic financial statements included in the previous chapter.

We can summarize Treehouse's financial position as strong. Each of its ratios are at or better than their benchmarks. It's profitable, it has a robust and effective fundraising operation that produces 70% of its total revenues, it does not have debt, and it depends minimally on government revenues. [1] These are all markers of a strong financial position. Its contributions ratio suggests that going forward it should seek to diversify some of its revenues away from donations. Perhaps not surprisingly, its program service ratio is .79, almost exactly the .8 rule of thumb.

Treehouse is also quite liquid. Its current ratio suggests its current assets could cover its current liabilities almost 15 times over, and its quick ratio suggests its most liquid resources alone could cover those liabilities more than 11 times over. It also has just above the recommended days of liquid net assets and days of cash on hand. So in other words, it does not keep a startling amount of cash, but it is highly liquid. Nonprofits that depend on pledges often see precisely this dynamic. If an organization depends on pledges then it will in turn book a lot of pledges receivable that will roll in throughout the year. Those receivables are liquid resources, but they're not necessarily cash, that's available to spend. And since most of Treehouse's expenses are for salaries and other near-term spending, it carries few

---

1. These computations assume Treehouse's "contracts" are contracts with governments.

if any current liabilities. That combination of high receivables and low current liabilities can make Treehouse look more liquid than it is, especially given its modest cash holdings.

Financial Ratios for Treehouse in FY 2015

Ratio	Computation	Computation for Treehouse
Liquidity Ratios		
Current Ratio	(Current Assets)/(Current Liabilities)	($6,997,996)/($467,461) = **14.97**
Days of Liquid Net Assets	((Unrestricted Net Assets-Fixed Asset,net depreciation))/(((Total Expenses-Depreciation-Bad Debt))/365)	(($5,255,411-$0))/((($9,381,598-$198,775-$0))/365) = **208.89**
Quick Ratio	(Cash & Cash Equivalents+Receivables)/(Current Liabilities)	(($2,713,337+($2,056,445+$193,357+$252,784))/($467,461) = **11.16**
Days of Cash on Hand	(Cash & Cash Equivalents)/(((Total Expenses-Depreciation-Bad Debt))/365)	($2,713,337)/(($9,381,598-$198,775-$0)/365) = **107.85**
Profitability Ratios		
Operating Margin	(Change in Unrestricted Net Assets)/(Unrestricted Revenue)	($706,007)/($10,153,840) = **0.07**
Net Asset Growth	(Change in Net Assets)/(Change in Unrestricted Revenue)	($1,057,657)/($706,007) = **1.50**
Return on Assets	(Change in Net Assets)/(Total Assets)	($1,057,657)/($12,614,410) = **0.08**
Solvency Ratios		
Debt to Assets	(Total Debt)/(Total Assets)	($0)/($12,614,410) = **0**
Contributions Ratio	(Contributions Revenue/Total Revenue)	($7,484,460)/($10,625,911) = **0.70**
Government Revenue Ratio	(Government Revenue/Total Revenue)	($1,261,618)/($10,625,911) = **0.12**
Effectiveness Ratios		
Fundraising Efficiency	(Total Contributions/Fundraising Expenses)	($7,484,460)/($1,438,030) = **5.20**
Program Service Ratio	(Program Expenses/Total Expenses)	($7,447,627)/($9,381,598) = **0.79**

THE "TEN POINT TEST" – AN ILLUSTRATION

Throughout the past few decades, analysts have developed a popular framework to evaluate local governments' financial condition. It's known as the *"Ten Point Test."* It's comprised of ten key ratios that, when taken together, summarize a government's liquidity, profitability, and solvency. In the Ten Point Test framework a government earns "points" based on how its ratios compare to its peer governments. If its ratios are consistently better than its peers it earns a higher score. If its ratios are consistently worse than its peers, it's scores are lower and in some instance negative.

To see the Test at work let's return to Overland Park, KS. The table below shows the Ten Point Test ratios and their computations based on its FY2015 financial statements. To compute these ratios yourself refer back to OP's basic financial statements included in the previous chapter.[2]

"Ten Point Test" Ratios for Overland Park, KS in FY 2015

Ratio	Computation	Computation for Overland Park, KS
Liquidity		
Short-Run Financial Position	(Unassigned General Fund Balance)/(General Fund Revenues)	($41,202,961)/($142,624,791) = **0.29 = 29%**
Liquidity	(General Fund Cash + General Fund Investments)/(General Fund Liabilities)	($60,313,574)/($7,064,270) = **8.54 = 854%**
Profitability		
Net Asset Growth	Change in Governmental Activities Net Position /Beginning Governmental Activities Net Position	$14,616,936/$960,524,629 = **0.02 = 2%**
Operating Margin	(Net (Expense) Revenue for Governmental Activities/Total Governmental Activities Expenses) X -1	(-$125,846,359/$205,896,739)(-1) = **0.61 = 61%**
Own-Source Revenues	Primary Government Operating Grants / (Total Primary Government Revenues)	$14,115,047/($60,993,230+$14,115,057+$34,752,883+$143,728,996) = **0.06 = 6%**
Solvency		
Near-Term Solvency	(Primary Government Liabilities)/(Total Primary Government Revenues)	$21,231,313/($60,993,230+$14,115,057+$34,752,883+$143,728,996) = **0.08 = 8%**
Debt Burden	(Primary Government Non-Current Liabilities)/Population	($284,967,097)/(175,000) = **$1,628**
Coverage 1	(Governmental Funds Principal and Interest on Long-Term Debt/General Fund Expenditures)	$22,596,369/$101,752,631 = **0.22 = 22%**
Coverage 2	Enterprise Funds Operating Revenue/ Enterprise Funds Interest Expense	$30,081,558/$5,797,658 = **6.89**
Capital Asset Condition	(Ending Net Value of Primary Government Capital Assets – Beginning Net Value) / (Beginning Net Value)	($871,940,863-$863,435,252)/($863,435,252) = **.0098 = 0.98%**

OP ratios look good overall. It has plenty of liquidity. Its short-run financial position (i.e. it's "fund balance ratio") is 29%, well above the rule of thumb. It also has more than enough cash to cover its general fund current liabilities. Its net assets are growing, only six percent of its operating revenues are from sources it does not control, it has few near-term liabilities[3], and its "operating margin" (i.e. the extent to which it relies on taxes, rather than user charges to cover its operating expenses) of 0.61 is positive. For these reasons it's no surprise that Overland Park maintains the highest possible "AAA" rating from two major credit rating agencies – Moody's and Standard & Poor's.

Fortunately, the Ten Point Test framework allows us to go a step further. Instead of asking how OP

2. There are several versions of the Ten Point Test. The version presented here is based on the version recommended by Dean Mead, Research Manager at the Governmental Accounting Standards Board. A few of the ratios have been changed slightly to reflect the data available to compute national trends. For the original Mead version see Dean Mead, "A Manageable System of Economic Condition Analysis for Governments," in *Public Financial Management*, ed. Howard Frank (Boca Raton, FL: Taylor and Francis, 2006); pp.383-419.

3. Note that the near-term liabilities ratio was first presented in Karl Nollenberger (2003), *Evaluating Financial Condition: A Handbook for Local Government* (Washington, DC: ICMA Press)

compares to generic benchmarks, we have the tools to compare OP to its peer local governments. This allows us to make much more precise statements about OP's current and future financial position.

Analysts typically do these peer comparisons by computing the Ten Point Test ratios for a variety of local governments, and then assigning point values based on relative rankings. For example, to compute OP's Ten Point test score for FY 2015, refer to the table below. This table shows national trends for these same ratios. These trends are based on data from the financial statements of 3,721 city governments and 1,282 county governments from FY2005-2015.[4] The ratios are presented in quartiles. Recall that a quartile is a group of percentiles, and a percentile identifies a point in the distribution of that ratio. The table is organized by population groups. So for instance, for cities with populations between 100,000 and 250,000 (OP's peer group) the 25th percentile for short-run financial position was 8%. That means one-quarter of OP's peer cities had short-run financial position less than 8%, and three-quarters had short-run financial position equal to or greater 8%. For all the ratios shown here the first quartile starts at the lowest ratio and ends at the 25th percentile, the second quartile covers the 25th percentile through the 50th percentile, and the third quartile covers the 50th percentile through the 75th percentile. The fourth quartile includes all observations above the 75th percentile.

These quartiles are the basis for the Ten Point Test scoring. If a local government is in the second quartile for a ratio, its score for that ratio is zero. It is not qualitatively better or worse than its peers, so that ratio does not help or hurt its relative score. If a ratio is in the third quartile it earns one point. The logic here is that a ratio above the median (i.e. the 50th percentile) is a financial positive for that government. If a ratio is in the fourth quartile it earns two points. To land in the fourth quartile, a government is better than most of its peers on that particular ratio, and that indicates a source of financial strength. By contrast, a ratio in the first quartile means that government is comparatively weak on that dimension of financial health. To reflect that weakness, we subtract one point.

A local government's overall Ten Point Test score is easy to interpret. Analysts generally use the following categories:

- *A score of 10 or greater* suggests a government's financial position is "among the best." It can easily meet its immediate spending needs, it has more-than-adequate reserves to mitigate the immediate effects of recessions, natural disasters, or other unexpected events, and it has the capacity to generate adequate resources to cover its long-term spending needs. To earn that score most of its ten ratios must be as good as or better than its peer governments.

- *A score between 5 and 9* means the government is "better than most." Most of its ratios are better than its peer governments, and a few ratios are equal to its peers.

- *A score between 1 to 4* means the government is "average." Most of its ratios are equal to, or weaker than its peer governments.

- *A score between 0 and -4* means the government is "worse than most." Most of its ratios are weaker than its peer governments.

4. Merritt Research Services collects these data and makes them available through the Bloomberg Terminal.

Population < 25,000	Cities				Counties			
	First Quartile -1 point	Second Quartile 0 points	Third Quartile +1 point	Fourth Quartile +2 points	First Quartile	Second Quartile 0 points	Third Quartile +1 point	Fourth Quartile +2 points
Short Run Financial Position	< 15%	15% to 31%	32% to 54%	> 54%	< 21%	21% to 36%	37% to 55%	> 55%
Liquidity	< 77%	77% to 194%	195% to 524%	> 524%	< 62%	62% to 185%	186% to 683%	> 683%
Net Asset Growth	<-0.38%	-0.38% to 3.11%	3.12% to 7.96%	> 7.96%	< 0.26%	0.26% to 4.26%	4.27% to 10.08%	> 10.08%
Operating Margin	> 66%	51% to 66%	37% to 50%	< 37%	> 133%	87% to 144%	44% to 86%	< 44%
Own-Source Revenues	> 12%	7% to 12%	3% to 6%	< 3%	> 32%	21% to 32%	8% to 21%	< 8%
Near-Term Solvency	> 328%	198% to 328%	106% to 197%	< 106%	> 72%	43% to 72%	20% to 42%	< 20%
Debt Burden per Capita	> $2,497	$1,354 to $2,497	$615 to $1,353	< $615	> $534	$201 to $534	$59 to $200	< $59
Coverage 1	> 13.82%	6.95% to 13.82%	3.05% to 6.94%	< 3.05%	> 2.74%	1.06% to 2.74%	0.30% to 1.05%	< 0.30%
Coverage 2	< -0.66	-0.66 to 0.44	0.45 to 1.32	> 1.32	< -0.40	-0.40 to 0.84	0.85 to 2.35	> 2.35
Capital Asset Condition	< -1.87%	-1.87% to 1.27%	1.28% to 7.00%	> 7.00%	< -1.45%	-1.45% to 2.54%	2.55% to 9.43%	> 9.43%
Population 25,000 to 50,000								
Short Run Financial Position	< 9%	9% to 23%	24% to 39%	> 39%	< 16%	16% to 33%	34% to 50%	> 50%
Liquidity	< 67%	67% to 131%	132% to 287%	> 287%	< 66%	66% to 149%	150% to 498%	> 498%
Net Asset Growth	< -0.12%	-0.12% to 2.65%	2.66% to 5.95%	> 5.95%	< -0.44%	-0.44 to 3.29%	3.30% to 6.97%	> 6.97%
Operating Margin	> 55%	45% to 55%	34% to 44%	< 34%	> 154%	92% to 154%	48% to 91%	< 48%
Own-Source Revenues	> 10%	7% to 10%	3% to 6%	< 3%	> 32%	20% to 32%	6% to 19%	< 6%
Near-Term Solvency	> 254%	174% to 254%	109% to 173%	< 109%	> 79%	48% to 79%	26% to 47%	< 26%
Debt Burden per Capita	> $2,001	$1,276 to $2,001	$715 to $1,275	< $715	> $381	$204 to $381	$83 to $203	< $83
Coverage 1	> 11.05%	6.76% to 11.05%	3.09% to 11.04%	< 3.09%	> 1.45%	0.73% to 1.45%	0.15% to 1.44%	< 0.15%
Coverage 2	< -0.35	-0.35 to 0.47	0.48 to 1.25	> 1.25	< -0.13	-0.13 to 1.00	1.01 to 2.42	> 2.42
Capital Asset Condition	< -0.31%	-0.31% to 2.03%	2.04% to 6.50%	> 6.50%	< -1.94%	-1.94% to 1.59%	1.60% to 6.05%	> 6.05%
Population 50,000 to 100,000								
Short Run Financial Position	< 8%	8% to 19%	20% to 33%	> 33%	< 15%	15% to 28%	29% to 44%	> 44%
Liquidity	< 49%	49% to 108%	109% to 281%	>281%	< 58%	58% to 123%	124% to 395%	> 395%
Net Asset Growth	< 0.29%	0.29% to 2.81%	2.82% to 5.82%	> 5.82%	< -1.06%	-1.06% to 2.82%	2.83% to 7.65%	> 7.65%
Operating Margin	> 55%	48% to 55%	37% to 48%	< 37%	< 173%	105% to 73%	55% to 72%	< 55%
Own-Source Revenues	> 14%	9% to 14%	4% to 8%	< 4%	> 33%	24% to 33%	8% to 23%	< 8%
Near-Term Solvency	> 263%	178% to 263%	117% to 177%	< 117%	> 88%	57% to 88%	32% to 56%	< 32%
Debt Burden per Capita	> $2,115	$1,490 to $2,115	$843 to $1,489	< $843	> $387	$180 to $386	$82 to $179	< $82
Coverage 1	> 11.89%	7.09% to 11.89%	3.90% to 7.08%	< 3.90%	> 1.43%	0.51% to 1.43%	0.13% to 1.42%	< 0.13%
Coverage 2	< -0.31	-0.31 to 0.38	0.39 to 0.98	> 0.98	< -0.28	-0.28 to 0.80	0.81 to 2.04	> 2.04
Capital Asset Condition	< 0.39%	0.39% to 2.54%	2.55% to 5.95%	> 5.95%	< -1.28%	-1.28% to 1.82%	1.83% to 7.48%	> 7.48%
Population 100,000 to 250,000								
Short Run Financial Position	< 8%	8% to 15%	16% to 25%	> 25%	< 16%	16% to 28%	29% to 42%	> 42%
Liquidity	< 43%	43% to 117%	118% to 281%	> 281%	< 40%	40% to 95%	96% to 263%	> 263%
Net Asset Growth	< 0.27%	0.27% to 2.38%	2.39% to 5.39%	> 5.39%	< -1.40%	-1.40% to 2.95%	2.96% to 7.75%	> 7.75%
Operating Margin	> 54%	45% to 54%	37% to 45%	< 37%	> 159%	96% to 159%	59% to 95%	< 59%
Own-Source Revenues	> 11%	8% to 11%	4% to 7%	< 4%	> 33%	17% to 33%	7% to 16%	< 7%
Near-Term Solvency	> 273%	199% to 273%	140% to 272%	< 140%	> 100%	69% to 100%	43% to 99%	< 43%
Debt Burden per Capita	> $2,641	$1,613 to $2,641	$1,065 to $1,612	< $1,065	> $428	$240 to $428	$102 to $239	< $102
Coverage 1	> 10.11%	6.13% to 10.11%	3.63% to 6.12%	< 3.63%	> 2.00%	0.72% to 2.00%	0.08% to 0.71%	< 0.08%
Coverage 2	< -0.26	-0.26 to 0.38	0.39 to 0.99	> 0.99	< 0.02	0.02 to 0.73	0.74 to 1.49	> 1.49
Capital Asset Condition	< 0.32%	0.32% to 2.24%	2.25% to 4.86%	> 4.86%	< -1.44%	-1.44% to 1.56%	1.57% to 7.63%	> 7.63%
Population > 250,000								
Short Run Financial Position	< -1%	-1% to 6%	7% to 10%	> 10%	< 10%	10% to 20%	21% to 33%	> 33%
Liquidity	< 28%	28% to 62%	63% to 193%	> 193%	< 72%	72% to 155%	156% to 313%	> 313%
Net Asset Growth	< -3.80%	-3.80% to 2.28%	2.29% to 5.91%	> 5.91%	< -2.33%	-2.33% to 2.11%	2.12% to 6.17%	> 6.17%
Operating Margin	> 60%	48% to 60%	36% to 47%	< 36%	> 210%	130% to 210%	75% to 129%	< 75%
Own-Source Revenues	> 17%	14% to 16%	8% to 13%	< 8%	> 46%	33% to 46%	13% to 32%	< 13%
Near-Term Solvency	>445%	331% to 445%	230% to 330%	< 230%	> 105%	88% to 105%	63% to 87%	< 63%
Debt Burden per Capita	> $5,684	$3,368 to $5,684	$2,273 to '$3,367	< $2,273	> $563	$315 to $563	$158 to $314	< $158
Coverage 1	> 13.31%	9.52% to 13.31%	5.85% to 9.51%	< 5.85%	> 8.02%	1.33% to 8.02%	0.33% to 1.32%	< 0.33%
Coverage 2	< -0.11	-0.11 to 0.27	0.28 to 0.72	> 0.72	< -0.10	-0.10 to 0.43	0.44 to 0.85	> 0.85
Capital Asset Condition	< 1.85%	1.85% to 3.78%	3.79% to 5.65%	> 5.65%	< -0.60%	-0.60% to 2.53%	2.54% to 7.15%	> 7.15%

Quartiles of Ratios to Compute the "Ten Point Test," FY2005-2015; Source: Authors' calculations based on data from Merritt Financial Services

- *A score less than -5* means the government is "among the worst." It has major financial problems and may be insolvent. Scores this low are quite rare.

Let's return to OP, to compute its Ten Point Test Score. Recall that OP's population in FY2015 was 175,000, so we'll use the "Population 100,000 to 250,000" quartiles.

As we saw above, OP's liquidity is strong. It scores in the top quartile for both short-run financial position and liquidity. It's profitability ratios are also acceptable, but not nearly as strong as its liquidity. It was in the first quartile for net asset growth, and the third quartile for own-source revenues. These two ratios reflect the same underlying fact: OP depends mostly on general taxes like sales taxes and property taxes, and depends little on user charges and fees or on outside grants or other support. That's why its own-source revenue is comparatively high, but its operating margin is comparatively low.

OP's solvency profile is mixed. It has virtually no current liabilities in its governmental funds, and virtually no long-term debt in its proprietary funds. That's why its near-term solvency and coverage 2 ratios, respectively, are both in the top quartile. At the same time, it is quite leveraged. That fact is reflected in its comparatively high debt burden and its comparatively low coverage 1 ratio. It also appears that in 2015 OP's investment in capital assets was comparatively low, despite its comparatively high leverage.

Computing the "Ten Point Test" Score for Overland Park, KS in FY 2015

Ratio	Ratio Computed	Score
Liquidity		
Short-Run Financial Position	29%	+2
Liquidity	854%	+2
Profitability		
Net Asset Growth	2%	0
Operating Margin	61%	-1
Own-Source Revenues	6%	+1
Solvency		
Near-Term Solvency	8%	+2
Debt Burden	$1,628	0
Coverage 1	22%	-1
Coverage 2	6.89	+2
Capital Asset Condition	.98%	0
Total		**7**

Taken together, OP's ratios add up to an overall Ten Point Test score of seven. Its main financial strengths are its liquidity and its near-term solvency. At the same time, its higher than average debt load and dependence on general revenue sources, lowered that score. Recall that a score of seven suggests OP is "better than most" similarly-sized local governments.

With this overall framework you can compute and interpret a Ten Point Test score for virtually any local government.

FINANCIAL POSITION AND FINANCIAL STRATEGY

Financial statement analysis can tell us a lot about an organization's financial position. The question, then, is what to do about it? As mentioned, sometimes financial statement analysis implies some clear follow-up questions about an organization's financial operations and overall performance. Ideally, it also suggests some steps that management can take to improve that financial position and performance.

The table below identifies some of those potential steps. It is organized around liquidity, profitability, and solvency. Plus signs identify that part of the organization's financial position that is strong. Minus signs suggests a potential weakness. There is no "textbook" definition of a financial strength or weakness. However, most public sector analysts define ratios above the benchmark rule of thumb or above the median within a peer group as strong, and ratios below the benchmark rule of thumb or below the median within a peer group as weak. This is not a comprehensive list, but it does illustrate some basic management strategies that tend to follow from different patterns of financial position.

For example, the top right box lists strategies appropriate for a non-profit with good liquidity and good profitability, but concerns about solvency. An organization with these characteristics has enough resources on hand and is currently able to generate enough resources to cover its expenses. What's less clear is whether it can continue that trend into the future. Perhaps it is too dependent on donor revenues or government grants. Maybe it delivers a service that no one will want in the future. Maybe it has had to borrow a lot of money to build out its service delivery capacity. Regardless of what's driving the solvency concerns, it's clear this organization has a good, profitable business. The challenge is ensuring it has enough demand for its services to support its ongoing operations.

To that end, an organization with these characteristics could consider investing in additional capital equipment or facilities that might help it expand its client or customer base. It might also expand or extend its programs to include new lines of business that will allow it to tap into new clients/ customers. If long-term liabilities are part of the solvency concern it could consider restructuring or re-negotiating those liabilities.

"Scrubbing" Your Expenses

To "scrub" expenses is to carefully review all current major spending items for potential cost savings. Some contemporary examples include:

- Transition bills to online payments and save on transaction costs and timing delays associated with processing paper bills.
- Move employee reimbursements from checks to direct payroll deposits.

- Renegotiate premiums with your health insurance provider. Bundle different insurance policies with one carrier to improve economies of scale.

- Hire a human resources consultant to identify appropriate salary ranges for future salary negotiations and collective bargaining.

- Shift from traditional phone service to a "voice over internet" (VOI) system. VOI generally offers more lines and better reliability at a lower cost.

- Move to a "multi-platform" plan with your wireless/cellular communications provider. Save money by running phones, iPads, and other wireless devices on one plan.

- Negotiate with credit card providers for lower annual percentage rates and transaction fees.

- Consider opening a line of credit with your existing financial institution. Some institutions offer discounts for bundling banking with credit services.

- Negotiate better terms with your credit card payment processing company. Consider investing in an online processing system that does not require you to lease or purchase credit card terminals

- Move from local servers to a cloud-based, server-less computing environment.

- Explore "software as a service" for typical business applications.

Each of these tactics should happen only after careful attention to costs associated with disrupting the organization.

Contrast this with an organization that has concerns about liquidity, but is otherwise profitable and solvent. This is a good example of a "profitable but cash poor" organization. Here the challenge is to convert some of that profitability into a stronger base of liquid resources. To that end, an organization under these circumstances could consider some short-term borrowing to better manage its cash flow. This might weaken its solvency a bit, but that might be a necessary trade-off relative to weak liquidity. It might also make a specific ask to donors for a reserve fund or other financial contingency fund to bolster its liquidity.

Of course, organizations with concerns about all three aspects of financial position might consider more drastic measures like a merger with another non-profit.

In short, these strategies are some of the most typical for organizations with different financial position profiles.

Liquidity	Profitability	Solvency	Strategy
+	+	−	• Shift liquid resources to safe investments • Evaluate reserve fund policies • Broaden financing activities
+	+	−	• Invest in capital equipment, facilities • Invest in revenue-generating programs, services • Restructure/Refinance long-term liabilities
+	−	+	• Shift liquid resources to safe investments • "Scrub" current expense items • Capital investments to bolster efficiency • Renegotiate prices/reimbursements/cost recovery rates
+	−	−	• Invest in capital equipment, facilities • Scale up; increase program enrollments, client loads, etc • Explore partnerships to broaden participation, investment
−	+	+	• Short-term borrowing to smooth cash flow • Target donors for a reserve fund
−	+	−	• Target donors for an endowment • Target donors for a reserve fund • Refinance mortgages and other long-term obligations.
−	−	+	• Sell or lease capital assets • Target donors for an endowment • Downsize, partner, or outsource on key programs
−	−	−	With careful attention to minimizing impacts on key stakeholders, consider a merger, acquisition, or liquidation that will allow others to advance the organization's mission.

CASE: JONAS COMMUNITY CENTER

THE JONAS COMMUNITY CENTER, INC.

AUDITED FINANCIAL STATEMENTS

JUNE 30, 2015 AND 2014

THE JONAS COMMUNITY CENTER
BALANCE SHEET
June 30, 2015
(With comparative totals for 2014)

		2015		2014
Assets				
Current Assets				
Cash and Cash Equivalents	$	180,966	$	69,123
Accounts and Pledges Receivable, net	$	915,220	$	538,007
Prepaid Expenses	$	106,576	$	48,309
Total Current Assets	$	1,202,762	$	655,439
Property, Plant, and Equipment, net	$	2,470,444	$	2,522,449
Other				
Intangible Assets, Net	$	-	$	16,122
Deposits	$	47,289	$	48,966
Total Assets	$	3,720,495	$	3,242,966
Liabilities and Net Assets				
Current Liabilities				
Current Portion of Long-Term Debt	$	159,163	$	114,914
Notes Payable	$	165,000	$	368,000
Accounts Payable	$	538,310	$	621,747
Accrued Expenses	$	395,515	$	225,660
Deferred Revenue	$	-	$	46,400
Other Current Liabilities	$	-	$	80,792
Total Current Liabilities	$	1,257,988	$	1,457,513
Long-Term Liabilities				
Other Liabilities	$	28,352	$	33,352
Long-Term Debt	$	2,426,522	$	2,333,692
Total Long-Term Liabilities	$	2,454,874	$	2,367,044
Total Liabilities	$	3,712,862	$	3,824,557
Net Assets				
Unrestricted:	$	(4,180)	$	(604,341)
Temporarily restricted	$	11,813	$	22,750
Total Net Assets	$	7,633	$	(581,591)
TOTAL LIABILITIES AND NET ASSETS	$	3,720,495	$	3,242,966

THE JONAS COMMUNITY CENTER
STATEMENT OF ACTIVITIES
For the year ended June 30, 2015
(With comparative figures for 2014)

	Unrestricted		Temporarily Restricted		Total		Unrestricted		Temporarily Restricted		Total	
	2015		2015		2015		2014		2014		2014	
Support and Revenue:												
Grants and Donations	$	632,781	$	-	$	632,781	$	943,920	$	22,750	$	966,670
Program Service Fees	$	11,119,821			$	11,119,821	$	8,977,563			$	8,977,563
Other	$	84,924			$	84,924	$	201,401			$	201,401
Released from Restriction	$	10,937	$	(10,937)	$	-	$	-			$	-
Total support and revenue	$	11,848,463	$	(10,937)	$	11,837,526	$	10,122,884	$	22,750	$	10,145,634
Expenses:												
Program services	$	9,501,180			$	9,501,180	$	8,472,824			$	8,472,824
Management and General	$	1,707,733			$	1,707,733	$	1,507,515			$	1,507,515
Fundraising	$	39,389			$	39,389	$	-			$	-
Total expenses	$	11,248,302			$	11,248,302	$	9,980,339			$	9,980,339
					$	-					$	-
Change in net assets	$	600,161	$	(10,937)	$	589,224	$	142,545	$	22,750	$	165,295
Net Assets:												
Beginning of year	$	(604,341)	$	22,750	$	(581,591)	$	(746,886)	$	-	$	(746,886)
End of year	$	(4,180)	$	11,813	$	7,633	$	(604,341)	$	22,750	$	(581,591)

THE JONAS COMMUNITY CENTER
STATEMENT OF CASH FLOWS
For the year ended June 30, 2015
(With comparative totals for 2014)

	2015		2014	
Cash flows from operating activities:				
Increase in Net Assets	$	589,224	$	165,295
Adjustments to reconcile change in net assets to				
net cash provided by (used in) operating activities:				
Depreciation	$	159,538	$	171,835
Amortization	$	16,112	$	43,196
Gain on Sale of Real Estate	$	-	$	(116,495)
Increase in Accounts Receivable, net	$	(377,213)	$	(128,687)
(Increase) decrease in Prepaid Expenses	$	(58,267)	$	18,553
(Increase) decrease in Deposits	$	1,677	$	(16,555)
Increase (decrease) in Accounts Payable	$	(83,437)	$	40,787
Increase in Accrued Expenses	$	169,855	$	39,830
Increase in Deferred Revenue	$	(46,400)	$	(44,387)
Increase (decrease) in Other Current Liabilities	$	(80,792)	$	80,792
Increase (decrease) in Accounts Payable	$	(5,000)	$	5,000
Total	$	(303,927)	$	93,869
Net cash provided by (used in) operating activities:	$	285,297	$	259,164
Cash flows from investing activities:				
Capital Expenditures	$	(107,533)	$	(81,264)
Proceeds from the Sale of Real Estate	$	-	$	245,000
Net cash provided by (used in) investing activities	$	(107,533)	$	163,736
Cash flows from financing activities:				
Net Repayment of Notes Payable	$	(203,000)	$	(54,280)
Repayments of Long-Term Debt	$	(112,921)	$	(337,291)
Proceeds from Long-Term Debt	$	250,000		
Net Cash Used in Financing Activities	$	(65,291)	$	(391,571)
Net Increase in Cash	$	111,843	$	31,329
Cash and cash equivalents - beginning of year	$	69,123	$	37,794
Cash and cash equivalents - end of year	$	180,966	$	69,123

THE JONAS COMMUNITY CENTER, INC.

NOTES TO FINANCIAL STATEMENTS

JUNE 30, 2015 AND 2014

Note 1.   Organization

The Jonas Community Center, Inc. (the "Center") is a Washington not-for-profit corporation. The Center provides comprehensive services, including emotional and substance abuse counseling, HIV/AIDS education and prevention, residential treatment and neighborhood center services to residents of central Washington.

The Center's wholly owned subsidiary, Jonas Social Enterprises, Inc., is a taxable entity created in 2005. It is engaged in construction remodeling, repair, and maintenance, employing individuals who have been served by the Center's programs.

Note 2.   Summary of Significant Accounting Policies

The accompanying consolidated financial statements include the accounts and activities of the Center and its wholly-owned subsidiary. All intercompany balances and transactions have been eliminated in consolidation.

Net assets and revenues, gains and losses are classified based on the existence or absence of donor-imposed restrictions. Accordingly, net assets and changes therein are classified as follows:

Temporarily restricted net assets – Net assets subject to donor-imposed stipulations that may or may not be met by actions of the Center and/or the passage of time
Unrestricted net assets – Net assets not subject to donor-imposed stipulations

Grants and other contributions are reported as temporarily restricted support if they are received with donor stipulations that limit the use of the donated assets. When a donor restriction expires, that is, when a stipulated time restriction ends or purpose restriction is accomplished, temporarily restricted net assets are reclassified to unrestricted net assets and reported in the consolidated statement of activities as net assets released from restrictions. Temporarily restricted support is reported as unrestricted if the donor restrictions are met in the same reporting period. At June 30, 2015, temporarily restricted net assets are subject to time restrictions.

Management uses estimates and assumptions in preparing financial statements in accordance with accounting principles generally accepted in the United States of America. Those estimates and assumptions affect the reported amounts of assets and liabilities, the disclosure of contingent assets and liabilities, and the reported revenues and expenses. Actual results could vary from the estimates that were used.

Property, plant, and equipment are stated at cost or, if donated, at the estimated market value at the date of donation, and are depreciated on a straight-line basis over their estimated useful lives.

Intangible assets are recorded at costs and amortized on the straight-line method over periods ranging from three to seven years.

The Center is exempt from income taxes under Section 501(c)(3) of the Internal Revenue Code. Accordingly, no provision for income taxes is required. Donors may deduct contributions made to the Center within the Internal Revenue Code regulations. There are no unrecognized tax benefits and income tax returns remain subject to examination by major tax jurisdictions for the standard three-year statute of limitations.

The costs of providing the various programs and other activities have been summarized on a functional basis in the statement of activities. Accordingly, certain costs have been allocated among the programs and supporting services benefitted.

A number of unpaid volunteers have made contributions of their time to develop and operate the Center's programs. The value of this contributed time is not reflected in the financial statements since the Center does not have a clearly measurable basis for the amount to be recorded.

Certain reclassifications have been made to the 2014 financial statements in order to conform them to the 2015 presentation.

Note 3.   **Accounts Receivable**

Accounts Receivable are stated net of an allowance for doubtful accounts of $7,500 at both June 30, 2015, and 2014.

Note 4.   **Property, Plant, and Equipment**

Property, Plant, and Equipment consist of:

	2015	2014
Land, Buildings and Improvements	3,321,429	3,226,764
Furniture and Fixtures	989,209	987,201
	4,310,638	4,213,965
Less: Accumulated Depreciation	1,840,194	1,691,516
Net	**2,470,444**	**2,522,449**

Intangible Assets consist of:

	2015	2014
Computer Software	231,102	231,102
Organization Costs	75,135	75,135
Loan Origination Costs	38,750	38,750
	344,987	344,987
Less: Accumulated Amortization	344,987	328,875
Net	**–**	**16,112**

Note 6.   **Notes Payable**

	2015	2014
Notes Payable consists of:		
Note payable to a not-for-profit organization under a $350,000 line of credit agreement, due with interest payable monthly at 1.25% above the prime rate published in the *Wall Street Journal*. The note is secured by all assets of the Center	165,000	257,500
Notes payable to various individuals, due at various times through May 2014 at interest rates ranging from 0 to 12%	–	110,500
Total	**165,000**	**368,000**

Note 7.   **Long-Term Debt**

Long-Term Debt consist of:	2015	2014
Note payable to a finance company, due in monthly installments of $5,219, including interest at 9% through June 2020, secured by real estate.	250,000	–
Note payable to an employee, due in monthly installments of $250, including interest at 16%, through May 2017, unsecured.	4,665	6,568
Note payable to an employee, due in monthly installments of $1,000, including interest at 9.9%, through January 2014	–	4,496
Mortgage note payable to a bank, due in monthly installments of $22,317, including interest at 6.75%, through March 2016, at which time the monthly payment and interest rate will be adjusted based on a fifteen-year amortization schedule due March 2028, secured by a mortgage on real estate.	2,331,020	2,437,542
	2,585,685	2,448,606
Less: Current Portion	159,163	114,914
Net	2,426,522	2,333,692

Note 7.   Long-Term Debt (cont.)

Following are maturities of long-term debt for each of the next five years and in the aggregate:

Year ending June 30:	
2016	159,163
2017	181,308
2018	191,899
2019	205,715
2020	216,690
through maturity	1,630,910
Total	2,585,685

Interest expense incurred on all corporate obligations totaled $210,183 in 2015 and $204,664 in 2014. Interest paid totaled $208,822 in 2015 and $198,450 in 2014.

The mortgage note payable above includes provisions requiring the Center to maintain certain restrictive financial covenants. At June 30, 2015, all covenants were met by the Center.

Note 8.   Operating Leases

The Center leases real estate, motor vehicles, and office equipment under operating leases expiring at various intervals through 2018. The following is a summary of future minimum rental payments required under these leases as of June 30, 2015 for each of the next three years:

Year ending June 30:	
2016	217,401
2017	102,757
2018	9,599
Total	**329,757**

Rental payments made under leases with remaining terms in excess of one year totaled $158,111 in 2015 and $147,042 in 2014.

Note 9.   Concentration

The Center received a substantial amount of its support and revenue from the State of Washington. If a significant reduction in the level of this support and revenue were to occur, it may have an effect on the Center's programs and activities.

The Center also has financial instruments, consisting primarily of cash, which potentially expose the Center to concentrations of credit and market risk. Cash is held at a local bank. The Center has not experienced any losses on its cash and cash equivalents. In the ordinary course of business, the Center has, at various times, cash deposits with a bank which are in excess of federally insured limits.

Note 10.   Retirement Plans

The Center maintains a qualified contributory retirement plan under Section 403(b) of the Internal Revenue Code for all employees meeting certain age and service requirements. The Center contributes at a rate equal to fifty percent of the elective deferrals of each employee on the first $2,000 of contributions. The Center's contribution totaled $27,142 for 2015 and $22,846 for 2014.

Note 11.   Liability to the State of Washington

In 2013, the Organization recorded a liability of $28,352 to the State of Washington for non-reimbursable costs in excess of available offsetting revenue. The amount is reported in Other Liabilities in the accompanying balance sheet.

Note 12.   Related Party

Included in Notes Payable and Long-Term Debt are amounts due to members of management and the Board of Directors. Amounts due under these arrangements totaled $4,665 and $11,064 at June 30, 2015 and 2014, respectively.

The Center, as a tenant-at-will, rents a facility from a member of its Board of Directors. Rent expense incurred under this arrangement totaled $43,800 in 2015 and $42,000 in 2014.

ASSIGNMENT

1. A number of members of the Board believe Jonas Community Center (JCC) is profitable but not solvent. Others argue the nonprofit is solvent, but not profitable. Do you agree with either position? What evidence supports your argument.
2. Identify three things – two in the next six months and another in the next two years – that JCC could implement to address one or more of the issues you have identified from your review of the financial statements.

THE SAFE HOUSE

AUDITED FINANCIAL STATEMENTS

JUNE 30, 2016 AND 2015

THE SAFE HOUSE
STATEMENT OF ACTIVITIES
For the year ended June 30, 2016
(With comparative figures for 2015)

	Unrestricted	Temporarily Restricted	Total	Unrestricted	Temporarily Restricted	Total
	2016	2016	2016	2015	2015	2015
Support and Revenue:						
Contributions	$ 1,018,633 $	22,422 $	1,041,055 $	545,796 $	32,538 $	578,334
Government grants and contracts	553,214		553,214	532,052		532,052
Donated materials and services	254,537		254,537	262,213		262,213
Special event revenues,			-			-
net of direct costs (Note 11)	(29,014)		(29,014)	4,770		4,770
Rental income,			-			-
net of direct costs	20,577		20,577	32,451		32,451
Investment income	11,000		11,000	13,904		13,904
Other income	5,393		5,393	2,935		2,935
Net assets released from restrictions:			-			-
Satisfaction of purpose restrictions	49,270	(49,270)	-	247,116	(247,116)	-
Total support and revenue	$ 1,883,610 $	(26,848) $	1,856,762 $	1,641,237 $	(214,578) $	1,426,659
Expenses:						
Program services	$ 1,375,623		$ 1,375,623 $	1,375,252		$ 1,375,252
Administration	67,975		67,975	60,835		60,835
Fundraising	198,872		198,872	197,734		197,734
Total expenses	$ 1,642,470		$ 1,642,470 $	1,633,821		$ 1,633,821
Change in net assets	$ 241,140 $	(26,848) $	214,292 $	7,416 $	(214,578) $	(207,162)
Net Assets:						
Beginning of year	$ 4,038,513 $	28,348 $	4,066,861 $	4,031,097 $	242,926 $	4,274,023
End of year	$ 4,279,653 $	1,500 $	4,281,153 $	4,038,513 $	28,348 $	4,066,861

THE SAFE HOUSE
STATEMENT OF FINANCIAL POSITION
30-Jun-16
(With comparative totals for 2015)

	2016	2015
Assets		
Current Assets		
Cash and cash equivalents	$ 803,979	$ 21,652
Investments	$ -	$ 634,670
Accounts and pledges receivable, net	$ 130,323	$ 128,131
Prepaid expenses	$ 32,622	$ 29,117
Total current assets	$ 966,924	$ 813,570
Property and equipment, net	$ 3,466,636	$ 3,435,224
Total Assets	**$ 4,433,560**	**$ 4,248,794**
Liabilities and Net Assets		
Current liabilities		
Accounts payale and accrued expenses	$ 38,183	$ 68,751
Deposits	$ 7,882	$ 7,403
Deferred revenue	$ 13,500	$ -
Current portion of notes payable	$ 13,336	$ 12,935
Total current liabilities	$ 72,901	$ 89,089
Notes payable, less current portion	$ 79,506	$ 92,844
Total Liabilities	**$ 152,407**	**$ 181,933**
Net Assets		
Unrestricted:		
Undesignated	$ 868,322	$ 671,531
Board designated	$ 37,537	$ 37,537
Net property and equipment	$ 3,373,794	$ 3,329,445
Total unrestrictred	$ 4,279,653	$ 4,038,513
Temporarily restricted	$ 1,500	$ 28,348
Total Net Assets	**$ 4,281,153**	**$ 4,066,861**
TOTAL LIABILITIES AND NET ASSETS	**$ 4,433,560**	**$ 4,248,794**

THE SAFE HOUSE
STATEMENT OF FUNCTIONAL EXPENSES
For the year ended June 30, 2016

	Program Services					Administration	Fund-raising	Rental Activities	Total Expenses
	Emergency Services	Transitional Housing Services	Youth Program	Community Education and Response Advocacy	Total Program Services				
Salaries	325,176	42,190	76,222	192,455	636,043	$ 149,795	$ 89,363	$ -	$ 875,201
Payroll taxes and employee benefits	83,109	8,715	18,833	27,467	138,124	22,564	18,928	-	179,616
Professional fees	157	-	1,000	-	1,157	36,148	621	-	37,926
Consulting and contract services	2,745	150	-	-	2,895	2,000	325	16,946	22,166
Supplies	91,690	158	3,855	285	95,988	3,750	2,070	57	101,865
Telephone	8,440	798	23	53	9,314	6,648	71	-	16,033
Postage and shipping	510	64	2	4	580	1,198	1,841	-	3,619
Rent and utilities	48,190	175	-	-	48,365	-	-	8,494	56,859
Repairs and maintenance	15,892	189	-	-	16,081	2,708	-	9,288	28,077
Printing	-	-	-	507	507	7	807	-	1,321
Travel	6,721	874	926	1,807	10,328	560	1,173	-	12,061
Conferences and meetings	358	403	549	808	2,118	339	270	-	2,727
Client services and assistance	77,081	67,960	75	4,299	149,415	-	-	-	149,415
Office expense	2,908	105	575	615	4,203	9,266	4,361	-	17,830
Insurance	21,026	1,581	1,244	1,529	25,380	11,661	765	4,485	42,291
Dues, publications, subscriptions	1,496	-	-	-	1,496	60	275	-	1,831
Fundraising and media relations	-	6	-	1,118	1,124	-	45,806	-	46,930
Miscellaneous	358	-	-	-	358	583	5,703	11,465	18,109
Depreciation	96,019	185	-	402	96,606	5,617	369	16,921	119,513
Interest expense	-	-	-	-	-	-	-	2,996	2,996
Expense Allocation	29,962	12,918	47,236	45,425	135,541	(184,929)	26,124		(23,264)
Total operating expenses	811,838	136,471	150,540	276,774	1,375,623	67,975	198,872	70,652	1,713,122
Less expenses deducted directly from revenues	-	-	-	-	-	-	-	(70,652)	(70,652)
Total expenses	811,838	136,471	150,540	276,774	1,375,623 $	67,975 $	198,872 $	- $	1,642,470

THE SAFE HOUSE
STATEMENT OF FUNCTIONAL EXPENSES
For the year ended June 30, 2015

	Program Services					Administration	Fund-raising	Rental Activities	Total Expenses
	Emergency Services	Transitional Housing Services	Youth Program	Community Education and Response Advocacy	Total Program Services				
Salaries	$ 318,675	$ 38,226	$ 64,374	$ 182,824	$ 604,099	$ 177,052	$ 89,305	$ -	$ 870,456
Payroll taxes and employee benefits	77,431	8,712	16,021	37,489	139,653	31,361	15,471	-	186,485
Professional fees	53	28	-	210	291	51,806	723	248	53,068
Consulting and contract services	2,253	75	-	63	2,391	6,086	238	14,058	22,773
Supplies	77,349	146	478	455	78,428	3,844	4,052	387	86,711
Telephone	7,271	1,068	3	73	8,415	7,169	138	-	15,722
Postage and shipping	406	54	5	546	1,011	1,624	1,181	-	3,816
Rent and utilities	45,183	55	-	-	45,238	-	-	9,142	54,380
Repairs and maintenance	10,532	646	-	-	11,178	3,623	-	5,832	20,633
Printing	-	-	-	963	963	109	3,908	-	4,980
Travel	5,208	597	116	1,743	7,664	658	936	24	9,282
Conferences and meetings	1,893	500	40	54	2,487	3,799	1,268	-	7,554
Client services and assistance	55,826	56,974	52	996	113,848	-	-	-	113,848
Office expense	3,766	150	427	890	5,233	8,379	5,686	-	19,298
Insurance	19,845	-	-	1,992	21,837	20,154	-	2,584	44,575
Dues, publications, subscriptions	94	-	-	-	94	60	819	-	973
Fundraising and media relations	38	-	-	10,891	10,929	-	32,528	-	43,457
Miscellaneous	25	-	-	-	25	3,114	12,425	10,823	26,387
Depreciation	87,361	-	-	-	87,361	5,060	93	16,880	109,394
Interest expense	-	-	-	-	-	-	7	3,378	3,385
Expense Allocation	104,276	14,179	37,853	77,799	234,107	(263,070)	28,963		-
Total operating expenses	817,485	121,410	119,369	316,988	1,375,252	60,835	197,734	63,356	1,697,177
Less expenses deducted directly from revenues	-	-	-	-	-	-	-	(63,356)	(63,356)
Total expenses	$ 817,485 $	121,410 $	119,369 $	316,988 $	1,375,252 $	60,835 $	197,734 $	- $	1,633,821

THE SAFE HOUSE
STATEMENT OF CASH FLOWS
For the year ended June 30, 2016
(With comparative totals for 2015)

		2016		2015
Cash flows from operating activities:				
Change in Net Assets	$	214,292	$	(207,162)
Adjustments to reconcile change in net assets to				
net cash provided by (used in) operating activities:				
Depreciation	$	120,236	$	109,394
Less donated capitalized construction services and assets	$	(50,381)	$	(105,974)
Net realized/unrealized (gain) on investments	$	(6,282)	$	(591)
Allowance for uncollectible accounts	$	(4,000)	$	(5,600)
Gain (loss) on sale of property	$	-	$	2,131
(Increase) decrease in:				
Accounts receivable	$	1,808	$	53,511
Prepaid expenses	$	(3,505)	$	(4,526)
Increase (decrease) in:				
Accounts payable and accrued expenses	$	(30,568)	$	29,614
Deposits	$	479	$	(6,755)
Deferred revenue	$	13,500	$	-
Net cash provided by (used in) operating activities:	$	255,579	$	(135,958)
Cash flows from investing activities:				
Purchase of property and equipment	$	(101,267)	$	(324,937)
Additions to investments	$	(433,124)	$	(27,798)
Proceeds from the sale of investments	$	1,074,076	$	279,160
Net cash used in investing activities	$	539,685	$	(73,575)
Cash flows from financing activities:				
Principal payments on note payable	$	(12,937)	$	(12,555)
Net cash used in financing activities	$	(12,937)	$	(12,555)
Net increase (decrease) in cash and cash equivalents	$	782,327	$	(222,088)
Cash and cash equivalents - beginning of year	$	21,652	$	243,740
Cash and cash equivalents - end of year	$	803,979	$	21,652
Supplemental disclosures of cash flow information:				
Cash paid for interest	$	2,996	$	3,385

THE SAFE HOUSE, INC.

NOTES TO FINANCIAL STATEMENTS

JUNE 30, 2016 AND 2015

1. NATURE OF ACTIVITIES

The Safe House (the Organization) is a nonprofit human service agency that assists families in crisis by providing a foundation of hope for victims of domestic violence. Serving a diverse community made homeless by domestic violence, the Organization works to eliminate the core causes through program services and community education. Assistance includes housing, advocacy, information and referral services, community education, and other specially designed services in support of the Organization's programs. These services include emergency food, clothing and transportation, youth programs, and support groups. The Organization's programs are supported primarily through contributions and government grants. Government grants from two agencies represent 28% and 32% of total support and revenue for the years ended June 30, 2016 and 2015, respectively.

The Organization's programs are as follows:

Emergency Services: Each year approximately 300 survivors stay at the Organization's emergency shelter an average of eight weeks. It is confidentially located and can house up to 40 survivors and their children at one time. The shelter is a safe and comfortable environment where women and children can access the resources necessary to help build a violence free life.

Transitional Housing Services: The Organization operates a scattered housing transitional program. Up to 22 women are assisted through housing and ongoing advocacy for a period of up 24 months.

Youth Program: The youth program provides advocacy, safety planning and developmentally appropriate activities for emergency shelter residents under 18 years of age.

Community Education: The Safe House maintains a commitment to education and raising awareness in the community about the effects of domestic violence. Through outreach and educational programs, the Organization educates high school and middle school students on the warning signs of intimate partner violence as well as their rights within all relationships. The Organization is also committed to raising awareness about domestic violence in the workplace so businesses and employees know their rights if they or someone they know is experiencing intimate partner violence.

Response Advocacy Program: The Safe House has three advocates out-stationed at the police bureau. These advocates work specifically with survivors involved with some level of the criminal justice system. Two of these work collaboratively with other community partners through the Domestic Violence Enhanced Response Team (DVERT) working toward victim safety for high risk and high lethality domestic violence situations.

2. SUMMARY OF SIGNIFICANT ACCOUNTING POLICIES

Basis of Presentation: Net assets and all balances and transactions are presented based on the existence or absence of donor-imposed restrictions. Accordingly, the net assets of the Organization and changes therein are classified and reported as unrestricted or restricted net assets. Unrestricted net assets are those that are not subject to donor-imposed stipulations. Temporarily restricted net assets are subject to donor-imposed stipulations that will be met, either by actions of the Organization and/or the passage of time.

Cash and Cash Equivalents: For purposes of the statement of cash flows, the Organization considers all highly liquid investments available for current use with maturities of three months or less at the time of purchase to be cash equivalents.

Investments: Investments are carried at fair value. At June 30, 2015 investments consisted of various certificates of deposit held in a CDARS (Certificate of Deposit Account Registry Service) account.

Accounts Receivable: Accounts receivable are reported at the amount management expects to collect on balances outstanding at year-end. Based on management's assessment of the outstanding balances, it has concluded that realization losses on balances outstanding at year-end will be immaterial.

Property and Equipment: Acquisitions of property and equipment of $500 or greater are capitalized. Property and equipment purchased are recorded at cost. Donated assets are reflected as contributions at their estimated values on the date received.

Depreciation: Depreciation of property and equipment is calculated using the straight-line method over the estimated useful lives of the assets which range from 5 to 15 years for equipment and 40 years for buildings.

Income Tax Status: The Organization is a nonprofit corporation exempt from federal and state income tax under section 501(c)(3) of the Internal Revenue Code and applicable state law. However, income from rental activities not directly related to the Organization's tax exempt purpose is subject to taxation. No provision for income taxes is made in the accompanying financial statements, as the Organization currently has no net income subject to unrelated business income tax. The Organization is not a private foundation.

Restricted and Unrestricted Revenue and Support: Contributions, which include unconditional promises to give (pledges), are recognized as revenues in the period the Organization is notified of the commitment. Conditional promises to give are not recognized until they become unconditional, that is when the conditions on which they depend are substantially met. Management provides for probable uncollectible amounts for pledges receivable through a charge to expense and a credit to a valuation allowance based on its assessment of the current status of individual accounts. Balances that are still outstanding after management has used reasonable collection efforts are written off through a charge to the valuation allowance and a credit to accounts and pledges receivable.

Contributions received are recorded as unrestricted, temporarily restricted, or permanently restricted support, depending on the existence and/or nature of any donor restrictions. Donor-restricted support is reported as an increase in temporarily or permanently restricted net assets, depending on the nature of the restriction. When a restriction expires (that is, when a stipulated time restriction ends or purpose restriction is accomplished), temporarily restricted net assets are reclassified to unrestricted net assets and reported in the statement of activities as net assets released from restrictions.

Government grants and contracts are recognized as revenue when the services are performed.

Special event fees and sponsorships are recognized in the period the event is held. Funds received in advance are reflected as deferred revenue.

Donated Facilities, Materials, and Services: Donations of property, equipment, materials and other assets are recorded as support at their estimated fair value at the date of donation. Such donations are reported as unrestricted support unless the donor has restricted the donated asset to a specific purpose.

The Organization recognizes donated services that create or enhance nonfinancial assets or that require specialized skills and are provided by individuals possessing those skills, and would typically need to be purchased if not provided by donation. A summary of donated facilities, materials and services is as follows:

	2016	2015
Facilities	$36,960	$35,500
Materials and goods	$160,258	$121,424
Furniture and fixtures	$15,000	
Capitalized services for construction in progress	$35,381	$86,054
Legal and professional services, included in administration	$6,398	$19,235
Total donated facilities, materials, and services	**$254,537**	**$262,213**

In addition, many individuals volunteer a substantial amount of time and perform a variety of tasks that assist the Organization with specific assistance programs, campaign solicitations, and administrative duties. These volunteer services representing approximately $46,100 for 2016 and $40,600 for 2015 are not recognized as contributions in the financial statements since the recognition criteria were not met.

Expense Allocation: The costs of providing various programs and other activities have been summarized on a functional basis in the statement of activities and in the statement of functional expenses. Accordingly, certain costs have been allocated among the programs and supporting services benefited.

Use of Estimates: The preparation of financial statements in conformity with accounting principles generally accepted in the United States of America requires management to make estimates and assumptions that affect the reported amounts of assets and liabilities and disclosure of contingent assets and liabilities at the date of the financial statements and the reported amounts of revenues and expenses during the reporting period. Actual results could differ from those estimates.

Reclassifications: Certain accounts in the prior-year financial statements have been reclassified for comparative purposes to conform with the presentation in the current-year financial statements.

3. ACCOUNTS AND PLEDGES RECEIVABLE

Accounts and pledges receivable are unsecured and consist of the following at June 30, 2016 and 2015:

	2016	2015
Pledges receivable	$28,199	$35,531
Less allowance for uncollectible accounts	$(5,000)	$(9,000)
Pledges receivable, net	**$23,199**	**$26,531**
Government contracts and grants:		
City Government	$24,090	$46,286
County Government	$67,377	$43,554
Other	$15,657	$11,760
Total government contracts and grants	**$107,124**	**$101,600**
Accounts and pledges receivable, net	**$130,323**	**$128,131**

Pledges receivable at June 30, 2016 are expected to be collected within one year.

4. PROPERTY AND EQUIPMENT

Property and equipment consist of the following at June 30, 2016 and 2015:

	2016	2015
Land	$150,170	$150,170
Buildings	$4,167,783	$3,600,692
Vehicles	$5,250	$5,250
Furniture and Fixtures	$203,714	$158,486
Construction in process		$460,671
Total property and equipment	$4,526,917	$4,375,269
Less accumulated depreciation	$(1,060,281)	$(940,045)
Net property and equipment	**$3,466,636**	**$3,435,224**

Included in land and buildings is property donated to the Organization by Catholic Charities (CC) during the year ended June 30, 1999. According to CC's stipulations, at all times the property must be used in connection with the operation of a shelter and/or transitional housing for women and children who are victims of domestic violence, services for victims of domestic violence, or services consistent with the charitable purposes of the Organization. In the event that the Organization ceases to exist as a nonprofit, tax-exempt corporation, title to the property will revert to CC. As of June 30, 2016 and 2015, the Organization was in compliance with this restriction.

5. LINE OF CREDIT

The Organization has a $50,000 line of credit with Puget Sound Community Bank with interest payable monthly at an adjustable rate corresponding to the Prime Rate, but not less than 6% (6% at June 30, 2016). The line is secured by real property and matures June 30, 2016. There were no outstanding advances on the line at June 30, 2016.

6. NOTE PAYABLE

Note payable consists of a note from Puget Sound Development Commission, payable in monthly installments of $1,328, including interest at 3%, through April 2016; secured by land and building.

	2016	2015
Total note payable	$92,842	$105,779
Less current portion	$13,336	$12,935
Long-term portion	$79,206	$92,844

Future scheduled maturities of note payable are as follows:

For the year ending June 30, 2010	$13,336
2011	$13,737
2012	$14,154
2013	$14,586
2014	$15,027
Thereafter	$22,002
Total	**$92,842**

7. CONTINGENCIES

Amounts received or receivable from various contracting agencies are subject to audit and potential adjustment by the contracting agencies. Any disallowed claims, including amounts already collected, would become a liability of the Organization if so determined in the future. It is management's belief that no significant amounts received or receivable will be required to be returned in the future.

8. RETIREMENT PLAN

Effective September 1, 2005, the Organization adopted a SIMPLE IRA plan that is available to all employees. Participants are eligible for an employer match of their contribution up to 3% of their gross wages. The percentage is established annually by the Board of Directors. The matching percentage established by the Board was 3% in calendar year 2016 and 1% in calendar year 2015. Employees may contribute the maximum amount allowed by IRS regulations. The Organization's contribution to the Plan totaled $13,927 for the year ended June 30, 2016 and $21,008 for the year ended June 30, 2015.

9. BOARD DESIGNATED NET ASSETS

During the year ended June 30, 2005, a board-designated endowment fund was established in the name of Rick Rhoades. The principal of the endowment will be held in perpetuity and income earned will be available for youth programs. Changes in endowment net assets are as follows:

	2016	2015
Balance at beginning of year	$37,537	$41,882
Investment income	$6	$205
Expenditures for programs	$(6)	$(4,550)
Balance at end of year	**$37,537**	**$37,537**

The Organization annually appropriates all income earned of the endowment fund and uses it to support youth programs.

The Organization has adopted an investment policy with the primary objective to preserve the principal value of the assets. The secondary objective is to grow the principal value of the assets. Investment risk is measured in terms of the total endowment fund; investment assets and allocation between asset classes and strategies are managed to not expose the fund to unacceptable levels of risk.

10. TEMPORARILY RESTRICTED NET ASSETS

Temporarily restricted net assets at June 30, 2016 and 2015, consist of contributions received restricted for programs.

11. SPECIAL EVENTS

Special event revenue is reflected net of contributions and direct costs of donor benefits as follows for the years ended June 30, 2016 and 2015:

	2016	2015
Gross Revenue	$208,043	$203,806
Less contributions	$(195,124)	$(173,312)
Less direct costs of donor benefits	$12,919	$30,494

Contributions from special events are included with "Contributions" on the statement of activities.

12. RELATED PARTY DISCLOSURE

During the year ended June 30, 2016, the Organization purchased electrical services of approximately $24,000 for the construction of the Advocacy Center from a business owned by a board member's family.

13. FINANCIAL INSTRUMENTS WITH CONCENTRATIONS OF CREDIT RISK

Financial instruments that potentially subject the Organization to concentrations of credit risk consist primarily of cash balances and pledges and accounts receivable. To limit credit risk, the Organization places its cash and cash equivalents with high credit quality financial institutions. The balances in each financial institution are insured by the Federal Deposit Insurance Corporation (FDIC) up to $250,000. The balances, at times, may exceed the federally insured limit.

The Organization's pledges and accounts receivable are unsecured and are from individuals, corporations, and governmental institutions located within the same geographic region.

14. FAIR VALUE MEASUREMENTS

Assets and liabilities recorded at fair value in the statement of financial position are categorized based upon the level of judgment associated with the inputs used to measure their fair value. Level inputs are defined as follows:

Level 1: Unadjusted quoted prices in active markets for identical assets and liabilities.

Level 2: Observable inputs other than those included in Level 1, such as quoted market prices for similar assets or liabilities in active markets, or quoted market prices for identical assets or liabilities in inactive markets.

Level 3: Unobservable inputs reflecting management's own assumptions about the inputs used in pricing the asset or liability. Level 3 assets and liabilities include financial instruments whose value is determined using pricing models, discounted cash flow methodologies, or similar techniques, as well as instruments for which the determination of fair values requires significant management judgment or estimation.

At June 30, 2009, assets measured on a recurring basis include certificates of deposit totaling $634,740. Fair value of certificates of deposit is determined using level 2 inputs based on amounts as reported by the financial institutions which hold the funds.

CHAPTER 4.

TRANSACTION ANALYSIS

TRANSACTION ANALYSIS: GETTING TO THE NUMBERS

Information from financial statements helps managers answer many crucial strategic questions:

- How have this organization's past decisions about fundraising, investing in new buildings, and launching of new programs shaped its current financial position?

- How might the timing of a key management decision – such as selling a building or hiring a new staff member – affect this organization's financial position?

- How do accounting policy choices regarding depreciation methods, allowances for uncollectables, and expense recognition, among other areas affect this organization's financial position?

- Why is a government's government-wide financial position different from the position in its governmental funds? Or its enterprise funds?

- Should this organization consider recognizing in-kind contributions of volunteer time and other services?

- Why are this organization's long-term liabilities portrayed differently in its financial statements compared to its budget?

The City of Rochester, NY is like most classic "Rust Belt" cities. It was once a global center of skilled manufacturing, but since the mid-1980s it has shed thousands of manufacturing jobs. Tax revenues have lagged, and the City's overall financial position has slowly eroded. Throughout the past two decades the mayor and other local leaders have invested substantial public resources in local programs to promote economic and community development.

Communities like Rochester face a financial dilemma. Some local leaders believe the City should do much more to promote economic and community development. Despite its financial problems Rochester does have one key financial strength: a comparatively low debt burden ($775/capita). Unlike many of its peers it has not issued a lot of bonds or other long-term debt that it will need to repay over time. Some leaders believe it could borrow money to invest in infrastructure projects that would spur economic growth, grow the local tax base and, in effect, pay for themselves. Or at least that's the theory.

Others disagree. They concur that the City has carefully managed its borrowing and does not owe investors much money. However, they point out that Rochester's has an enormous amount ($3,927/capita) of "other" long-term debts. Principal among them is "other post-employment benefits" or OPEB. Rochester, like many of its peers, allows its retired city workers to remain on its health insurance plan. Moreover, it pays most of the insurance premiums for those retirees and for their families. Many thousands of retired City workers are expected to take advantage of this benefit for many years to come.

Under governmental accounting rules, the money Rochester expects to spend on OPEB benefits over the next 30 years must be recognized as a long-term liability. Those rules follow from the idea that employees earn OPEB benefits as part of their salary. Once earned, those benefits become a long-term liability that appears on the City's balance sheet. Rochester can change those benefits any time, but until they do, they constitute a major long-term liability.

This anecdote highlights one of the key points of this chapter: How we account for – or "recognize" – financial activity can have a major impact on how an organization perceives its own financial strengths and weaknesses, and how it might choose to manage its finances in response. That's why all public managers must know how to analyze financial statements, and know the origins of the numbers that appear in those statements. In other words, they need to know a bit of accounting. That's the focus of this chapter.

Learning Objectives

After reading this chapter you should be able to:

- Identify an organization's assets and liabilities.

- Understand how typical financial transactions affect the fundamental equation of accounting.

- Contrast an organization's assets and liabilities with its revenues and expenses.

- Recognize revenues and expenses on the accrual basis of accounting.

- Contrast the recognition concepts in accrual accounting with cash accounting and fund accounting.

- Understand how routine financial transactions shape an organization's basic financial statements.

- Prepare rudimentary versions of the three basic financial financial statements.

CORE CONCEPTS OF ACCOUNTING

Now that we've toured the basic financial statements, let's take a step back and go over how we produce those statements. Financial statements are useful because they're prepared according to generally accepted accounting principles (GAAP). To understand financial statements you must know a few of those principles, and you must know how typical financial transactions shape the numbers you see in those statements. This section covers both these topics.

THE ACCRUAL CONCEPT

Most of us organize our personal finances around the *cash basis* of accounting. When we pay for something, we reduce our bank account balance by that amount. When we receive a paycheck, we increase our bank account balance by that amount. In other words, we recognize financial activity when we receive or spend cash.

Many small organizations also use cash basis accounting. Many small non-profits and small governmental entities like irrigation districts and mosquito abatement districts, for instance, keep separate checkbooks to track the taxes they collect and to account for their payroll and other operating expenses.

But for larger and more complex organizations, cash basis accounting tells an incomplete story. For instance, imagine that Treehouse (the organization in our previous examples) is planning to purchase $20,000 of furniture for its main office. Treehouse will purchase that equipment *on credit*. That is, they will order the equipment, the manufacturer will deliver that equipment and send an *invoice* requesting payment, and a few weeks later Treehouse will write the manufacturer a check and pay off that invoice.

This transaction will have a big impact on Treehouse's balance sheet. It will draw down its cash, and it will bring in a large capital item that will stay with on the balance sheet for several years. Treehouse's stakeholders should know about this transaction sooner than later.

But on the cash basis those stakeholders won't know about this transaction until Treehouse pays off the invoice. That might be several weeks away. If it's toward the end of the fiscal year – and many large purchases happen toward the end of the fiscal year – that transaction might not appear on Treehouse's financial statements until the following year. That's a problem.

That's why most public organizations use the *accrual basis* of accounting. On the accrual basis, an organization records an expense when it receives a good or service, whether or not cash changes hands. In this case, as soon as Treehouse signs the purchase order to receive the equipment, that equipment will appear as a $20,000 increase in non-current assets on its balance sheet. It will also record – or *recognize*, in accounting speak – an account payable for $20,000. On the accrual basis we can see how this transaction will affect Treehouse's financial position now and in the future.

Keep in mind also that accrual accounting assumes the organization is a *going concern*. That is, it assumes the organization will continue to deliver services indefinitely. If we're not willing to make that assumption, then accrual accounting does not add value. In some rare cases the audit report will suggest that the auditor believes the organization is not a going concern. In other words, the auditor believes the organization's financial position is so tenuous, that it might cease operations before the close of the next fiscal year.

We can apply a similar logic on the revenue side. Imagine that Treehouse staff run a day-long outreach program at a local school. This program was designed to sensitize public school teachers about the unique challenges faced by children in the foster care system. They typically charge $2,500 for this type of event. Assume that Treehouse staff deliver the program and then send the school district a bill for their services. Treehouse used a lot of staff time, supplies, travel, and other expenses to produce this program, but they might not get paid for the program for several weeks.

On the cash basis it will be several weeks before we know those expenses had been incurred and that Treehouse had earned $2,500 in revenue. But on the accrual basis, Treehouse would recognize both those expenses and the expected revenue immediately after delivering the program.

These two simple transactions illustrate a key point: If the goal of accounting and financial reporting is to help stakeholders understand an organization's ability to achieve its mission, then accrual accounting is far better than cash accounting. That's why the accrual concept is a central principle of GAAP. From this point forward we'll focus exclusively on how to apply accrual accounting to public organizations.

RECOGNITION AND THE FUNDAMENTAL EQUATION

Accountants spend much of their time on revenue and expense *recognition*. When accountants recognize a transaction, they identify how that transaction affects the organization's financial position. We'll recognize transactions relative to the fundamental equation of accounting. Recall that equation is:

$$\text{ASSETS} = \text{LIABILITIES} + \text{NET ASSETS}$$

One of accounting's central concepts is that the fundamental equation must always balance. In other words, the net effect of any transaction on the fundamental equation must be zero. This is also known as *double-entry bookkeeping*.

The General Ledger and Chart of Accounts

A chart of accounts is a listing of all the organization's financial accounts, along with definitions that make clear how to classify or place financial activity within those accounts. When accountants record a transaction they record it in the organization's *general ledger*. The general ledger is a listing of all the organization's financial accounts. When the organization produces its financial statements, it combines its general ledger into aggregated account categories. At the moment, the GAAP produced by the FASB and GASB do not specify a *uniform chart of accounts*, so account titles and definitions will vary across organizations. Some state governments require non-profits and governments to follow such a chart, but for the most part, public organizations are free to define their chart of accounts on their own.

Consider the previous example:

Transaction 1: Treehouse signs a purchase agreement with Furniture Superstores, Inc. for $20,000 in office furniture. It agrees to pay later.

Assets		= Liabilities		+ Net Assets
Furniture	+ $20,000	Accounts Payable	+ $20,000	

Here we recognize – or "book" – the equipment on the asset side of the equation. Because Treehouse paid on credit, we book an equivalent amount as an account payable on the liability side. Note that the equipment is a non-current asset because Treehouse expects to use it for several years. The account payable, however, is a current liability because Treehouse can expect to pay it off within the fiscal year. This transaction adds to both sides of the fundamental equation, and the net effect on the equation is zero.

What happens three weeks later when Treehouse pays for the equipment?

Transaction 2: Treehouse pays the invoice for audiology equipment received in Transaction 1.

Assets		=	Liabilities		+	Net Assets
Cash	– $20,000		Accounts Payable	– $20,000		

This transaction decreases both sides of the equation. Cash decreases, but so does accounts payable.

Public organizations execute many different types of transactions in their day-to-day operations. For most of those transactions you can identify the correct accounting recognition by asking a few simple questions:

1. Did the organization deliver a good or service?
2. Did the organization receive a good or service?
3. Did the organization make a payment?
4. Did the organization receive a payment?

If the organization delivered a service or received a service, then the transaction probably affects revenues and expenses. Note that revenues increase net assets and expenses decrease net assets. If the organization delivered or received a good, then the transaction likely affects assets, revenues, and expenses. Whether or not the transaction affects a liability has to do with whether a payment was made or received for those goods or services.

Debits and Credits

You've probably heard accountants talk about *debits* and *credits*. They are the basis for a system of accounting shorthand. In this system every transaction has a debit and a credit. A debit increases an asset or expense account, or decreases a liability or net assets account. Debits are always on the left of the account entry. A credit increases a liability or net assets account, or decreases an asset or expense account. Credits are always on the right of the account entry. Debits and credits must always balance.

To illustrate, let's say Treehouse delivers a service for $1,000 and is paid in cash. Here we would debit cash and credit services revenue. That entry is as follows:

Note that in this shorthand we don't include dollar signs.

	Debit	Credit
Cash	1,000	
Services Revenue		1,000

For another illustration, imagine that Treehouse receives $500 cash in payment of an account receivable. That entry is:

	Debit	Credit
Cash	500	
Accounts Receivable		500

If Treehouse purchased $750 of supplies on credit, we would debit supplies and credit accounts payable:

	Debit	Credit
Supplies	750	
Accounts Payable		750

This system is popular because it's fast, easy to present, and appeals to our desire for symmetry. However, it also assumes you're familiar with the fundamental equation and how different types of transactions affect it. If you're new to accounting, this can be a big conceptual leap. That's why throughout this text we present transactions relative to the fundamental equation of accounting rather than as debits and credits. We encourage you to try out debits and credits as you work the practice problems throughout this text.

The chart below presents these concepts as a flow chart. Take *Transaction 1* as an example. Recall that in this transaction Treehouse agreed to purchase audiology equipment and pay for it later. Has it received a good or service? Yes, it has received a good. To reference the flow chart, this transaction therefore starts on the bottom left corner of the chart at "Receive a Good – Received." Has it made a payment for that good? No. That's why we follow the "Payment Not Delivered" line of the chart, and we see we would recognize this transaction as an increase in equipment (in this case office furniture) along with an increase in accounts payable, since Treehouse will pay for this equipment later.

With this simple framework we can do the accounting recognition for most of the basic types of transactions a typical public organization will encounter. That said, this framework does cover certain types of transactions, and sometimes different types of non-profit and governmental transactions have unique rules that apply just in those contexts. We'll cover those more nuanced accounting rules in the lectures on non-profit financial management and government financial management.

TRANSACTIONS THAT AFFECT THE BALANCE SHEET

Transaction 1 and *Transaction 2* are good examples of financial activity that affect the balance sheet. You should be aware of a few others.

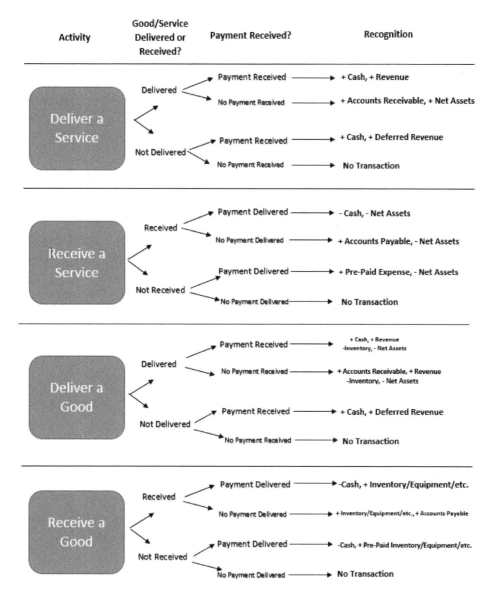

Activity	Good/Service Delivered or Received?	Payment Received?	Recognition

Deliver a Service
- Delivered
  - Payment Received → + Cash, + Revenue
  - No Payment Received → + Accounts Receivable, + Net Assets
- Not Delivered
  - Payment Received → + Cash, + Deferred Revenue
  - No Payment Received → No Transaction

Receive a Service
- Received
  - Payment Delivered → - Cash, - Net Assets
  - No Payment Delivered → + Accounts Payable, - Net Assets
- Not Received
  - Payment Delivered → + Pre-Paid Expense, - Net Assets
  - No Payment Delivered → No Transaction

Deliver a Good
- Delivered
  - Payment Received → + Cash, + Revenue -Inventory, - Net Assets
  - No Payment Received → + Accounts Receivable, + Revenue -Inventory, - Net Assets
- Not Delivered
  - Payment Received → + Cash, + Deferred Revenue
  - No Payment Received → No Transaction

Receive a Good
- Received
  - Payment Delivered → -Cash, + Inventory/Equipment/etc.
  - No Payment Delivered → + Inventory/Equipment/etc., + Accounts Payable
- Not Received
  - Payment Delivered → -Cash, + Pre-Paid Inventory/Equipment/etc.
  - No Payment Delivered → No Transaction

Some transactions affect only the asset side of the equation. For instance, imagine if Treehouse had purchased the audiology equipment with cash rather than on credit.

LIFO and FIFO

Inventory presents some unique challenges for accounting recognition. Organizations use inventory all the time, so most have to estimate the value of inventory assets at any moment. There are several ways to produce those estimates, including *First In, First Out (FIFO)* and *Last In, First Out (LIFO)*. Organizations that use a lot of inventory, small changes to inventory valuation can produce big changes to the reported value of inventory and inventory expense. That said, for most public managers, the technical aspects of inventory valuation fall squarely within the realm of "know what you don't know."

Transaction 1a: Treehouse buys $20,000 of office furniture with cash.

Assets		= Liabilities	+ Net Assets
Cash	– $20,000		
Equipment	+ $20,000		

Here Treehouse has swapped a liquid asset (cash) for a less liquid asset (equipment). Cash decreases but equipment increases, so the effect on the fundamental equation is zero. This same approach also applies to current assets like supplies and inventory.

Treehouse needs services that it purchases and then uses later. Examples include insurance, certifications, subscriptions, professional association memberships, and the like. Treehouse will purchase these services in advance, and then use or "expense" them throughout the fiscal year. These are known as *pre-paid expenses*. Conversely, this is also why assets are sometimes called "unexpired costs." For example:

Transaction 3: Treehouse pays $1,500 for three of its staff to renew their annual memberships to the National Association for Social Workers .

Assets		= Liabilities	+ Net Assets
Cash	– $1,500		
Pre-Paid Expense	+ $1,500		

Organizations like Treehouse almost always have *financial assets*. Assets like buildings and equipment are *tangible*; they have physical substance. Financial assets are *intangible assets*. They do not have physical substance, but they're valuable because they represent a contractual claim. For instance, if Treehouse owns shares of Boeing stock, they have a right to the *dividends* and other benefits that Boeing imparts on its shareholders. Treehouse can also sell its Boeing stock to another investor in exchange for cash. So even though Boeing stock is intangible, it's quite valuable.

We account for financial assets differently. If Treehouse buys $500 of supplies, it will record those supplies on its balance sheet at the $500 it cost to acquire them. In accounting, this is known as historical cost. Supplies are valuable because they help Treehouse deliver its services. They're not valuable as an investment. That is, we would not expect Treehouse to buy supplies at one price and sell them at a higher price as a way of earning revenue. That's why historical cost is the appropriate way to value most of Treehouse's assets.

Financial assets are different because they are, by definition, for investment. Treehouse invests in Boeing stock precisely because it expects the price of that stock to increase. For that reason, if we want to know if investments are adding value to Treehouse's mission, we need to see the *market value* of those investments. If those investments have become more valuable, they're contributing to the mission. If they've lost value, they're taking resources away from the mission.

That's why we record financial assets at *fair value* rather than historical cost. Financial assets are still "goods", but we account for them differently.

For most financial assets fair value means the current, observed market price. Investments the organization intends to hold less than a year that have a clear market price and can be easily liquidated are known as *marketable securities*. Investments the organization intends to hold longer than one year, or that are less liquid, are known simply as *investments*. Marketable securities are a current asset. You'll see investments classified as both a current and non-current asset.

Reliability and Fair Value Estimates

GAAP (specifically, *FASB Statement 157*) classifies investments by a three-level scheme according to availability of market prices. *Level 1 assets* have a quoted price on a public exchange. This includes stocks and money market funds, among others. *Level 2 assets* are primarily sold "over-the-counter," like corporate bonds, futures contracts, stock options, and others. Here the owner must report an estimated price based on prices of comparable assets that have traded recently. *Level 3 assets* are not bought and sold and therefore do not have a market price. This includes more exotic investments like hedge funds and private equity. For Level 2 and Level 3 assets, the owner must discount the reported asset value to account for uncertainty in that valuation.

When an organization puts money into an investment we record that investment at the purchase price. In that sense, at the time of the initial investment, fair value is not altogether different from historical cost. For example:

Transaction 4: Treehouse purchases 500 shares of Boeing stock at $145 per share.

Assets		= Liabilities	+ Net Assets
Cash	– $72,500		
Investments	+ $72,500		

If Treehouse later sells this stock before the end of the fiscal period for more than the original recorded value, the increase in value is called a *realized gain* and is recorded as an increase in net assets.

For example:

Transaction 5: Treehouse sells its 500 shares of Boeing stock at $155 per share. Recall that it originally purchased that stock at $145 per share.

Assets		= Liabilities	+ Net Assets	
Cash	+ $77,500		Realized Gain on Investments	+ $5,000
Investments	– $72,500			

Realized gains have roughly the same effect on Treehouse's financial position as a profitable program. Both increase Treehouse's overall net assets and available liquid resources. However, since Treehouse did not "earn" this realized gain by providing a good or service, we don't call that gain a revenue. The opposite is also true. If Treehouse sold its Boeing stock for less than the original purchase price, it would record a *realized loss*.

Fair value accounting is a bit more complex – and interesting! – than historical cost, because it requires organizations to *restate* the value of their financial assets at the end of every fiscal period. For Treehouse, this means they must record a new value for their Boeing stock at the end of the fiscal year, even if they don't buy or sell it. If the stock's price at the time of the re-statement is greater than the previously-recorded price, Treehouse will record an increase in investments on the balance sheet and an *unrealized gain* on the income statement. For example:

Transaction 6: At the end of the current fiscal period, Treehouse's accountant estimates and records a fair value for Boeing stock of $150 per share. Recall that during this same fiscal period Treehouse purchased 500 shares of Boeing stock at $145 per share.

Assets		= Liabilities		+ Net Assets	
Investments	+ $5,000			Unrealized Gain on Investments	+ $5,000

Unrealized gains and losses do not directly affect cash or any other resources that Treehouse has available to deliver services. That's why we euphemistically call unrealized gains *paper gains* and unrealized losses *paper losses*. But they do matter indirectly because they represent a potential gain or loss in available resources. If Treehouse's holdings of Boeing stock contribute substantial unrealized gains for several years, management might consider selling those holdings, realizing those gains, and investing in capital projects, equipment, or some other resources that directly benefit service delivery.

Of course, sometimes organizations must borrow money to purchase equipment, build a new facility, or cover other expenses. The most typical form of borrowed money is a loan from a bank. The initial accounting recognition of such a loan is simple. The borrowed money, or *loan principal*, is recognized as a liability that offsets the cash received from the loan:

Transaction 7: Treehouse borrows $30,000 from a local bank to finance the purchase of a van to transport students. The loan is for 5 years at 7% annual interest, and interest is paid on an annual basis. Treehouse purchases the van immediately after the loan closes.

Assets		= Liabilities		+ Net Assets
a) Cash	+ $20,000	Loan Payable	+20,000	
b) Capital Item: Van	+ $20,000			
Cash	- $20,000			

Public organizations can also borrow money using bonds, *notes payable, mortgages,* or *lines of credit.* Bonds typically have a longer *maturity* than loans (i.e. the organization pays them off over a longer time). Moreover, they are always paid back at a fixed rate of interest, whereas some loans, have *variable rates* or *floating rates* that fluctuate over time. Notes payable are short-term loans, usually less than 18 months. A mortgage is a loan secured by with a real estate purchase. A line of credit is an agreement between a public organization and a bank that allows that organization to borrow money on short notice, at a pre-determined interest rate. A line of credit can be especially useful if an organization has unpredictable cash flows, or if it is considering taking on a large capital project.

That said, transactions related to repaying debt present some special accounting considerations. Consider the previous example. Here the $20,000 loan principal is clearly a liability. At the same time, the interest on that loan principal is not necessarily a separate liability. Treehouse has agreed to pay interest on the loan each year the loan is active. It has not agreed in advance to pay the full amount of interest on the loan for all five years the loan might be active. So instead, interest payments on this loan, and most loans like it, is considered an expense. Treehouse pays the bank to use the bank's money. It's paying the bank for the "service" called access to credit. So to illustrate:

Transaction 8: Treehouse makes its first annual principal and interest payment on the loan described in Transaction 7.

Assets		=	Liabilities		+	Net Assets	
Cash	– $5,400		Loan Payable	– $4,000		Interest Expense	– $1,400

Since the $20,000 loan is paid off over five years, the annual payment on the principal is $4,000 or ($20,000/5 years). The interest rate was 7%, so we compute the annual interest payment as ($20,000 X 7% = $1,400). That interest payment becomes the interest expense. In year 2 the loan balance would be $16,000, so Treehouse would pay $5,120 in cash to cover a $4,000 payment on the loan principal and $1,120 of interest expense ($16,000 X 7%). If Treehouse chose to not make its interest payments, the interest expense would instead be recognized as a liability.

TRANSACTIONS THAT AFFECT THE INCOME STATEMENT

Treehouse's mission demands that it focus most of its efforts on delivering services. As a result, most of its day-to-day financial activity will involve revenues and expenses. Revenues and expenses affect the income statement.

For instance, recall from the earlier discussion that that Treehouse delivers outreach programs at local schools. When one of those programs is delivered it records a revenue.

Transaction 9: Treehouse delivers an outreach program at a local school and sends that school district an invoice for $2,500.

Assets		=	Liabilities	+	Net Assets	
Accounts Receivable	+ $2,500				Program Revenue	+ $2,500

Here Treehouse has earned revenue because it delivered a program. It recognizes those earned revenues as a "program revenue." This increases net assets. Did it receive a payment? No. Therefore, it recognizes accounts receivable on the asset side. Three weeks later, when it collects payment it will convert that receivable into cash. That transaction is as follows:

Transaction 10: Treehouse receives payment from the school district for the outreach program delivered three weeks ago.

Assets		=	Liabilities	+	Net Assets
Cash	+ $2,500				
Accounts Receivable	– $2,500				

Transaction 10 does not affect the income statement, but keep in mind that the transaction that resulted in the original accounts receivable did.

In *Transaction 9* Treehouse earned a revenue. Of course, that revenue didn't just appear. It incurred a variety of expenses – staff time, travel, supplies, etc. – to deliver that service. When should it recognize the expenses incurred to deliver that program? One of the core principles of GAAP is the *matching principle*. That is, when we recognize a revenue we try to recognize the expense that was incurred to produce that revenue. This is not always clear for services. Services are driven by personnel, and we incur personnel expenses constantly. Services also require equipment, certifications, and other assets where it's not always what it means to "use" that asset.

The matching principle is much more applicable when the transaction in question involves a good rather than a service. When an organization sells a good, it presumably knows what it cost to produce that good. Those costs, known generally as *cost of goods sold*, are immediately netted against the revenue collected from the transaction. That's why in the flow chart above you see some additional recognition related to delivering goods.

That said, public organizations do encounter a few typical transactions that account for many of their expenses. First, and most important, when Treehouse pays its staff it recognizes an expense for salaries.

Transaction 11: Treehouse recognizes and pays bi-weekly payroll of $15,000.

Assets		= Liabilities	+ Net Assets	
Cash	– $15,000		Wages and Salaries Expense	– $15,000

Payroll is critical because personnel is the largest expense for most public organizations. From the organization's perspective, payroll is an expense because the organization is receiving a service from its employees. That "service" is their day-to-day work. This is different than if the organization were to hire the one-time services of, say, a plumber from another company to fix some leaky pipes. But the accounting recognition is essentially the same.

Treehouse incurred other expenses to deliver the school outreach program. The program was held at a school 100 miles from Treehouse headquarters. The two staff members who delivered that program rode together to that off-site location in one of their personal vehicles. They will expect to be reimbursed. Many non-profits and government organizations follow the federal government's guidance and reimburse mileage at a fixed rate of 57.5 cents per mile.

Transaction 12: Treehouse pays mileage expenses of 57.5 cents/mile for a 200 mile round trip.

Assets		= Liabilities	+ Net Assets	
Cash	+ $115		Mileage expense	– $115

To deliver the outreach program staff also used up $50 of construction paper, duct tape, and other supplies. Recall that supplies are an asset. To account for the full cost of the outreach program we should also recognize that Treehouse "used up" or "expensed" these assets. For example:

Transaction 13: Treehouse expenses $50 in supplies related to its outreach program.

Recall that Treehouse also pre-pays for many of its ongoing expenses, such as insurance and

Assets		= Liabilities		+ Net Assets	
Supplies	– $50			Supplies Expense	– $50

certifications. The choice of when to expense pre-paid items is admittedly arbitrary. Most organizations have accounting policies and assumptions that state when and how this happens. Most will record those expenses monthly or quarterly. Recall that Treehouse pre-paid $1,500 for some annual professional association memberships. Assume that it expenses those memberships quarterly. At the end of the first quarter since the membership was paid, it would record:

Transaction 14: Treehouse records quarterly professional association membership expenses. Recall that annual association dues are $1,500.

Assets		= Liabilities		+ Net Assets	
Prepaid Expenses	– $375			Association Membership Expense	– $375

Keep in mind that after this first portion is expensed $1,125 in pre-paid association membership expenses remains on the balance sheet. This transaction simply expenses out one-quarter of the original $1,500 asset.

Another crucial set of accounting assumptions are around *depreciation*. Depreciation is when an organization expenses a long-term asset. To deliver its services, Treehouse must use up some portion of its building, vehicles, audiology equipment, and other capital items. Like with salaries and pre-paid expenses, it's not always clear when and how those assets are "used up." Some of that use is normal wear and tear. Some of it might happen if the asset bears a particularly heavy workload. Some capital items might be largely out of use, but they will lose value because each year that goes by, they'll become harder for Treehouse to sell should they choose to liquidate them.

In the absence of a detailed way to measure that wear and tear, accountants typically deal with depreciation through simplifying assumptions. One of the most common is to use *straight-line depreciation* also known as the *straight-line method*. Under the straight line method, when an organization purchases a new capital asset it determines the length of time it can use that asset to deliver services. This is known as the *useful life*. The organization must also determine the value of that asset once it's no longer useful for delivering services. This is the *salvage value* or *residual value* or value at *write-off*. If we subtract the salvage value from the historical cost, and divide by the useful life, we get the annual depreciation expense.

There are many other methods to calculate and allocate depreciation expenses, including the *accelerated method, declining balance, sum-of-the-years method*, and others. Different assumptions can produce rather different estimates and allocations of depreciation expenses.

For an example let's return to Treehouse's office furniture. Recall that it purchased that furniture for $20,000. Say that equipment has a useful life of 10 years. Assume also that at the end of its useful life Treehouse will be able to sell it for $2,500 to a used furniture distributor. To calculate the annual depreciation expense using the straight-line method, we take ($20,000 – $2,500)/10 = $1,750 per year. Using this assumption, we could record the following transaction:

Transaction 15: Treehouse records annual depreciation expense on its audiology equipment of $1,750.

Assets		= Liabilities	+ Net Assets	
Equipment	– $1,750		Depreciation Expense	– $1,750

After this first recording for depreciation expense, the value of the audiology equipment reflected on Treehouse's balance sheet will be $18,250, or ($20,000 – $1,750).

This same concept of spreading out the useful life also applies to intangible assets. Say, for example, Treehouse purchases some specialized case management software that allows it to safely store foster care children's school and medical records. That software requires Treehouse to purchase a five-year license. That license is an intangible asset, but it has a lot of value with respect to Treehouse's capacity to deliver services over the next five years. In this case, Treehouse would *amortize* that asset. It would use up some portion of that license – usually an equal amount, akin to straight-line depreciation – value each year in an *amortization expense*. If it purchased a five-year license for $5,000 it would record a $5,000 at the time of that purchase. Thereafter, if it amortized that license in equal annual installments, the effect on the fundamental equation is as follows:

Transaction 16: Treehouse records amortization expense on its cash management software license of $1,000.

Assets		= Liabilities	+ Net Assets	
Software License	– $1,000		Amortization Expense	– $1,000

Following this first amortization expense, the license would remain on Treehouse's balance sheet at $4,000.

Finally, we must consider what happens if Treehouse is paid for a service before it delivers that service. This is known as *deferred revenue* or *unearned revenue*. Deferred revenue is a liability because it represents a future claim on Treehouse resources. By taking payment for a service not yet delivered, Treehouse is committing future resources to deliver that service. Once it delivers that service it incurs expenses and removes that liability.

For example, imagine that Treehouse arranges another $1,500 outreach program with a different local school district. That school district is nearing the end of its fiscal year, so it agrees to pay Treehouse for the program several weeks in advance. Once it receives that payment it would recognize that transaction as follows:

Transaction 17: Treehouse takes a $1,500 payment for a school outreach program to be delivered in the future.

Assets		= Liabilities		+ Net Assets
Cash	+ $1,500	Deferred Revenue	+ $1,500	

This initial transaction does not affect the income statement. However, when Treehouse delivers the program a few weeks later, it records the following:

Transaction 18: Treehouse delivers the school outreach program for which it was paid previously.

Assets		= Liabilities		+ Net Assets	
		Deferred Revenue	– $1,500	Program Revenue	+ $1,500

The key take-away from all these income statement transactions is simple: For Treehouse to be profitable, it must take in more revenue from its programs and services than the total payroll and other expenses it incurs to deliver those programs. If those revenues do exceed those expenses, then its net assets will increase. If expenses exceed revenues, then net assets will decrease. That's why, as previously mentioned, change in net assets is the focal point for much of our analysis of an organization's financial position.

RECOGNITION CONCEPTS FOR SPECIAL CIRCUMSTANCES

PLEDGES AND DONOR REVENUES

Non-profits aren't traditionally paid for their services. In fact, large parts of the non-profit sector exist precisely to provide services to those who can't pay for those services. The homeless, foster children, endangered species, and others come to mind immediately. Non-profits depend on donations and contributions to fund those services.

At the outset, it might seem like the accrual concept breaks down here. How can a non-profit recognize a revenue if the recipients of its services don't pay for those services? In non-profit accounting, we address this problem by simply drawing a parallel between donations and payments for service. Donors who support a non-profit are, in effect, paying that non-profit to pursue its mission. Donors may not benefit directly from their contribution, but they benefit indirectly through tax benefits and a feeling of generosity. Those indirect benefits are substantial enough to support the accrual concept in this context.

Practically speaking we address this with a category of net assets called "donor revenue" and a category of assets called "pledges receivable." For example:

Transaction 19: Treehouse received pledges of gifts in the amount of $2,500 to be used as its Board of Directors considers appropriate.

Assets		= Liabilities	+ Net Assets	
Pledges Receivable	+ $2,500		Donor Revenue	+ $2,500

Most donor revenues happen through the two-step process suggested here. A donor pledges to donate and that pledge is recognized as pledges receivable. GAAP stipulates that a signed donor card or other documented promise to give constitutes a pledge that can be recognized. Once the donor writes Treehouse a check for the pledged amount, Treehouse would book the following:

Transaction 20: Treehouse collects the $2,500 pledge recognized in Transaction 19.

Assets		= Liabilities	+ Net Assets
Cash	+ $2,500		
Pledges Receivable	– $2,500		

One of the big financial questions for any non-profit is how much control does it have over where its money comes from and where its money goes? In a perfect world, non-profit managers would fund all their operations through unrestricted program revenues and donations. It's much easier to manage an organization when there are no strings attached to its money.

Most non-profit managers aren't so lucky. Virtually all non-profits have some sort of restrictions on when and how their organization can spend money. Donors who want to ensure the organization accomplishes specific goals will restrict how and when their donation can be spent. Governments do the same with restricted grants or loans. Some resources, namely endowments, can't ever be spent.

Restricted resources usually appear as restricted net assets. There are two types: *temporarily restricted net assets*, and *permanently restricted net assets*. Temporarily restricted net assets are restricted with respect to purpose and/or timing. Permanently restricted net assets can never be spent or converted to cash. Consider this example:

Transaction 21: Treehouse receives a cash donation of $5,000. That gift was accompanied by a letter from the donor to Treehouse's executive director requesting that the donation be used for staff development.

Assets		= Liabilities	+ Net Assets	
Cash	+ 5,000		Donor Revenue (temporarily restricted)	+ $5,000

This is a typical temporarily restricted contribution. The donor has specified how Treehouse will use these donated resources. We'd see a similar restriction if the donor had specified that the donation could not be spent for some period of time.

Our accounting recognition for net asset restrictions is not unlike other transactions that affect the income statement. The main difference is that with restricted net assets we have to take the additional step of "undoing" the restriction once the donor's conditions have been satisfied. For instance:

Transaction 22: Treehouse staff attend a national training conference. Travel, lodging, and conference registration expenses were $3,990. Staff are reimbursed from the resources donated in Transaction 21.

Assets		= Liabilities	+ Net Assets	
a)			Donor Revenue (temporarily restricted)	– $3,990
			Donor Revenue (unrestricted)	+ $3,990
b) Cash	– $3,990		Professional Development Expense	– $3,990

The first part of this transaction converts the temporarily restricted donor revenue to unrestricted revenue. Treehouse is able to do this conversion because it has met the donor's condition: staff attended a professional development conference. Once that restriction is satisfied, the second part of the transaction recognizes the professional development expenses. After this transaction, $1,010 of the original temporarily restricted net assets remain on Treehouse's balance sheet and income statement.

We often think of temporarily restricted net assets in terms of restricted donor contributions. But keep in mind that long-term assets like equipment donated for a specific programmatic goal also tend to appear as temporarily restricted net assets. The same applies to donated buildings, equipment, furniture, or other long-term assets where the donor requires that the recipient organization not sell the asset for some period of time.

Permanently restricted net assets most often appear as endowments. An endowment is a pool of resources, usually investments, that exists to generate other assets to support the organization's mission. By definition, the donation that comprises the original endowment – also known as the *corpus* – cannot be spent. In practice, the accounting recognition for the formation of an endowment looks like this:

Transaction 23: An anonymous benefactor donates to Treehouse 3,500 shares of Vanguard's Global Equity Investor Fund (a mutual fund). The gift stipulates that the annual investment proceeds from that stock support general operations, and that Treehouse cannot under any circumstances liquidate the endowment. At the time of the gift, the investment had a fair market value of $100,000.

Assets =	Liabilities +	Net Assets
Endowment Investments $100,000		Donor Revenue (permanently restricted) + $100,000

Once the endowment is established it generates investment earnings that become unrestricted net assets. These unrestricted net assets are usually recorded as a "distribution from endowment," or "endowment revenue."

Transaction 24: At the end of the Endowment's first fiscal year, Treehouse receives a dividend check from Vanguard (the mutual fund manager) for $4,500.

Assets =	Liabilities +	Net Assets
Cash $4,500		Distribution from Endowment (unrestricted) + $4,500

Note that endowment earnings do not always immediately become unrestricted net assets. In fact, many non-proft boards prefer to reinvest endowment earnings back into the endowment. This allows the permanently restricted net assets to grow and produce more unrestricted net assets later. Also note that some endowments are structured so that the investment proceeds fund specific programmatic needs. In those cases the investment proceeds are temporarily restricted net assets, not unrestricted net assets.

IN-KIND CONTRIBUTIONS

In addition to donated revenue, non-profits also depend on donations of goods and services. These are called in-kind contributions. According to GAAP, a non-profit can record as an in-kind contribution specialized services that it would otherwise purchase. In most cases this means professional services like attorneys, counselors, accountants, or professional development coaches. We recognize in-kind services once they've been received, and all the recognition happens in the net assets part of the fundamental equation. For instance:

Transaction 25: A local attorney agrees to represent Treehouse "pro bono" in a lawsuit filed by the family of a former student. The attorney's regular rate is $500/hour, and the case requires 10 billable hours. Without these pro bono services Treehouse would have had to hire outside counsel.

Assets	= Liabilities	+ Net Assets	
		Donated Services Revenue	+ $5,000
		Donated Services Expense	– $5,000

If in-kind contributions don't result in a net increase or decrease in net assets, then why do we bother recognizing them? Because recognizing them helps us understand the organization's capacity to deliver its services. If it had to pay for otherwise donated goods and services, those purchases would certainly affect its financial position and its service-delivery capacity.

Some in-kind contributions produce both an in-kind contribution and a donated asset. This is especially important for services like carpentry or plumbing. For example:

Transaction 26: A local contractor agrees to donate the labor and materials to construct a new playground at Treehouse. Total labor expenses for the project were $3,000, and the contractor purchased the new playground equipment for $8,000.

Assets		= Liabilities	+ Net Assets	
			Donated Services Revenue	+ $3,000
			Donated Services Expense	– $3,000
Equipment	+ $8,000		Donated Equipment	+ $8,000

BAD DEBT

Unfortunately, pledges don't always materialize into contributions. Sometimes the donors' financial situation changes after making a pledge. Sometimes they have a bit too much wine at a gala event and promise more than they can give. Sometimes they simply change their mind. For these and many other reasons, non-profits rarely collect 100% of their pledged revenues.

Most non-profits re-evaluate at regular intervals, usually quarterly or semi-annually, the likelihood they'll collect their pledges receivable. Once they determine a pledge cannot or will not be collected, the amount of pledges receivable is adjusted accordingly. The accounting mechanism to make this happen is an expense called "bad debt." Bad debt is specific type of reconciliation entry known as a *contra-account*. Like with depreciation, amortization, and other reconciliations, entries in contra-accounts do not affect cash flows. They are simply "write-off" transactions to offset the reduction of an asset, in this case pledges receivable. Consider this example:

Transaction 27: Treehouse determines it will not be able to collect $3,000 of pledges made earlier in the fiscal year.

Assets		= Liabilities	+ Net Assets	
Pledges Receivable	– $3,000		Bad Debt Expense	– $3,000

When is a pledge deemed uncollectable? That depends on the organization's policies. GAAP rules only state that an organization must have a policy that dictates how it will determine collectability. Non-profits' policies to that effect state that a pledge is uncollectable after a certain number of days past the close of the fiscal year, or if the donor provides documentation that the pledge is cancelled.

Pledges receivable among non-profits is the most common type of asset to be offset by bad debt expense. However, be aware that bad debt is not unique to non-profits or to pledges receivable. For-profits and governments can and often do record bad debt expenses, and those expenses can apply to any receivable, including accounts receivable for goods services previously delivered, or grants receivable from a donor or a government.

FOR GOVERNMENTS – RECOGNITION CONCEPTS FOR MODIFIED ACCRUAL ACCOUNTING

Governmental funds and the modified accrual basis of accounting on which they are prepared, focus on expendable financial resources. Taxpayers want to know their government used its current financial resources to meet its current financial needs. This is, once again, a core part of how accountants think about inter-period equity. If a government pushes costs into future fiscal periods, then future taxpayers will have to either pay more taxes or expect less in services.

For this reason, when thinking about the fund financial statements, we need to re-think how we recognize certain revenues. Instead of focusing recognition on when a government "earns" a revenue, we focus instead on whether that revenue is or will be available to cover costs during that same fiscal period. Specifically, GAAP for governments requires that for a revenue to be recognized in the current fiscal period is must be *measurable* and *available*.

- Measurable means the government can reasonably estimate how much it will collect. For taxes like property taxes, this is easy. They're measurable because the government determines what a taxpayer owes and then sends a bill. But for sales taxes, income taxes, or other revenues measurable might require some reasonable estimates.

- According to GAAP, available means a revenue is recognized during the fiscal period for which it's intended to pay liabilities or up to 60 days after the close of that fiscal period. Again, this is not always clear. For instance, when does an intergovernmental grant become available if it requires the government to perform certain services or incur certain expenditures?

To address this problem, government GAAP establishes a few basic types of revenues and a set of recognition concepts that applies to each. Here's a few hypothetical transactions to illustrate those concepts. We'll recognize all these transactions in the fund financial statements, and thus, on the modified accrual basis. If we recognized these transactions in the government-wide statements the normal accrual concepts would apply. To simplify, we restate the fundamental equation as Assets = Liabilities + Fund Balance.

In Chapter 1 we said the property tax is the local revenue workhorse. So let's start there[1].

Let's assume Overland Park sends out its annual property tax bills in January. Those bills are based on the City's assessed value, property tax rates, and any applicable tax preferences. After running these

---

1. Many of the transactions presented here are based on Granof (2001)

calculations OP determines it will send out $515 million in property tax bills. From past experience, it also knows it won't collect a certain portion of those bills.

Property taxes are *imposed non-exchange* revenues, meaning they are not related to a specific transaction. As such, they become measurable and available when the government imposes them. As soon as they're imposed, OP has a legal claim to them. In this case, to impose them means to levy them, or to send out property tax bills.

Transaction 28: In January 2015 Overland Park levies property taxes of $515 million for the year. It estimates $15 million will be uncollectible.

Assets =	Liabilities	+	Fund Balance
Property Taxes Receivable +$515	Deferred Property Tax Revenue $500	+	
			Allowance for Uncollectible Property Taxes + $15

This recognition records OP's property tax levy. What happens then when OP collects these property taxes?

Transaction 29: Throughout 2015 Overland Park collects $410 million of property taxes. It collects $30 million of the remaining 2015 taxes during each of the first three months of 2016 and estimates that the $15 million balance will be uncollectible.

Assets =	Liabilities	+	Fund Balance
a) Cash +$470			
Property Taxes Receivable -$470			
b)	Deferred Property Tax Revenue -$410		Property Tax Revenue +$410
c)	Deferred Property Tax Revenue -$60		Property Tax Revenue +$60
d) Property Taxes Receivable -$15			Property Taxes Receivable – Delinquent $-15

We recognize these collections in four different parts. Part a) recognizes the collections of property taxes during 2015 and during the first two months of 2016. OP collected $30 million in each of the first three months, but according to GAAP, only the first 60 days are available. Part b) converts deferred revenues into property tax revenues for the taxes collected during 2015. Part c) does the same for the taxes collected during the first two months of 2016. Part d) recognizes a write-down of the uncollectible property taxes.

Note that this recognition approach would also apply to the other main type of imposed non-exchange revenues: fines and fees. Those revenues are also recognized when they are levied or imposed.

Sales and income taxes are the most common type of derived taxes, meaning the taxes collected are derived from some other transaction. For derived taxes, the revenues become measurable and available when the underlying transaction takes place. For sales taxes, those transactions are taxable retail sales. For income taxes, it's a bit more abstract. There the "transaction" in question is when an employer pays wages to an employee, and that transaction denotes the earnings on which the income tax is based.

Let's look at a hypothetical sales tax recognition in OP:

Transaction 30: In December 2015 merchants in Overland Park collect $20 million in local sales taxes; $12 million are collected prior to December 15 and must be remitted by February 15, 2016; the remaining $8 million must be remitted by March 15, 2016. How should OP recognize these December 2015 sales?

Assets	=	Liabilities	+	Fund Balance
Sales Taxes Receivable +$20				Sales Tax Revenue +$12
				Deferred Sales Tax Revenue + $8

According to GAAP, OP should recognize the assets from derived revenues during the period when the underlying transaction takes place. That's why it records all $20 million as sales taxes receivable. At the same time, it will only collect $12 million within 60 days of the end of the fiscal year, so only that portion is considered available and should be recognized now. The remaining $8 million will become available later, so for now, it's considered deferred revenue. We would see a similar pattern with income taxes and other derived revenues.

A government recognizes an inter-governmental grant when it has satisfied all the eligibility requirements. Only then are grants considered measurable and available.

Transaction 31: In October 2015 Overland Park is notified that it will receive a $15 million grant from the state's Clean Water Revolving Fund. The funds, transmitted by the state in December 2015, must be used for stormwater infrastructure upgrades, but may be spent at any time.

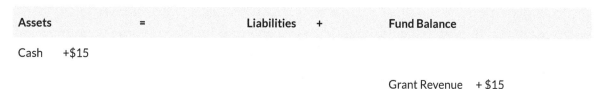

Assets	=	Liabilities	+	Fund Balance
Cash +$15				
				Grant Revenue + $15

The State has placed a purpose restriction on this grant. Purpose restrictions do not affect the measurability or availability of the grant revenues. That said, because they are subject to a purpose restriction, OP should recognize these revenues in a special revenue fund.

Many intergovernmental grants take the form of reimbursements. In this case, the revenues are not available until the government incurs the *allowable costs* stipulated by the grant.

Transaction 32: In December 2015 Overland Park is awarded a grant of $400,000 to train community police officers. During the year it spends $300,000 in allowable costs, for which it is reimbursed $250,000. It expects to be reimbursed for the $50,000 balance in January 2016 and to expend, and be reimbursed, for the remaining $100,000 of its grant throughout 2016. It must incur allowable costs to remain eligible for the grant.

Assets	=	Liabilities	+	Fund Balance	
a) CashBalance -$300,000				Expenditures to train police officers -$300,000	
b) Cash +$250,000				Grant revenue +$300,000	
Grants Receivable +$50,000					

For this grant OP must first incur the requisite expenditures before it recognizes the grant revenues. In part a) it incurs those expenditures. In part b) it recognizes that it was reimbursed $250,000 cash, it records grants receivable for the portion it expects to collect within 60 days of the end of the fiscal year, and records the $300,000 in grant revenue.

And finally, let's look at another unique revenue recognition treatment: sales of fixed assets. It's not uncommon for governments to sell buildings and other fixed assets. In the fund financial statements the value of such a sale is equal to the sale proceeds. This seems simple, but it's quite different from the government-wide statements, where we'd recognize the difference between the sale proceeds and historical cost plus accumulated depreciation.

Transaction 33: On December 31, 2015 Overland Park purchases a new police car for $40,000. On January 2, 2016 the vehicle is damaged in an accident. The City is able to sell the nearly demolished vehicle for $5,000.

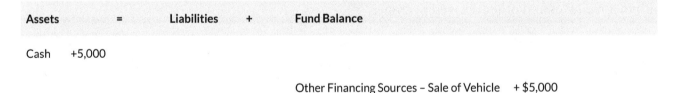

Assets	=	Liabilities	+	Fund Balance	
Cash +5,000					
				Other Financing Sources – Sale of Vehicle + $5,000	

It might seem strange that $35,000 worth of a $40,000 vehicle was lost, but the only impact on OP's governmental funds financial statements is an increase in cash. And yet, that's precisely how we would recognize this transaction on the modified accrual basis. Why? Because we do not recognize fixed assets in the governmental fund statements, because those funds are focused on near-term financial resources. Fixed assets are, of course, a long-term financial resource. Fortunately for the readers of OP's financial statements, on its Statement of Net Position OP would recognize the lost $35,000 of asset value as an asset "write off" or similar expense.

Expenditure Recognition Concepts

An expenditures in the governmental funds is, according to GAAP, a decrease in the net financial resources. An expense is, on the accrual basis, a reduction of overall net assets. How are they different? Or, to put it more practically, when are expenses not expenditures?

Most of governments' major expense items result are expenditures because they result in a reduction of financial resources. When a government pays salaries it has less cash and, in turn, less current financial resources to apply elsewhere. So practically speaking, expenditures and expenses are not that different.

There are, however a few instances where expenses are not expenditures. If a government agrees to pay a legal settlement, it will recognize an expenditure only if that settlement is paid out of current financial resources. If that payment is paid by the government's insurance company, or is paid out of long-term financial reserves, then no expenditure is recognized. Another is repayments of long-term debt. Here a government reports an expenditure as payments are made, but unlike on the accrual basis, interest on the debt is not accrued. This also applies to other occasional transactions in areas like inventory and pre-paid items. But in general, most expenditures are recognized much the same as expenses. For a full treatment of expenditure recognition concepts consult one of the many fine textbooks on governmental accounting.

Practice Problems

1. The Museum of Contemporary Art (MCA) is the recipient of a $1,000,000 cash gift from Mr. and Mrs. Carter. The donors have asked the museum to create an endowment in their name in the amount of $750,000 and use all other funds to curate a collection of contemporary music. The donors expect MCA to put up the contemporary music collection in summer 2017. What impact, if any, would this transaction have on MCA's assets, liabilities, and/or net assets. Be sure to identify whether they are affected negatively (-) or positively (+).

2. The Evans Schools of Public Policy and Governance held its annual Fellowship Dinner on October 29, 2015. The event raised $560,000 in pledges and cash contributions. As of November 30th, the school had received $350,000 of the $560,000.

   - The Director of Finance and Administration projects 5 percent of all pledges would not be collected. How much should the Evans School report in pledges receivable?

   - Following a successful fundraiser event, Dean Archibald awarded current and incoming students $450,000 in financial aid and support beginning July 2016. What impact, if any, would this transaction have on the School's assets, liabilities, and/or net assets. Be sure to identify whether they are affected negatively (-) or positively (+).

3. Dorchester Home Health Services (DHHS) is a private, nonprofit home health agency founded in 1992

by four retired nurses. At the start of FY 2015, DHHS reported $593,298 in fixed assets (net of depreciation). The nonprofit purchased four vehicles, in cash, at cost of $75,000. Assuming that these vehicles have a useful life of four years and a salvage value of $10,000, how much should DHHS report in fixed assets (net of depreciation) at the end of year if depreciation expense on the existing fixed assets was expected to be $33,450.

4. The Museum of Contemporary Art (MCA) operates a gift shop and coffee bar. The gift shop reported $1,249,066 in revenues (all cash sales). Payroll expenses for the year were $210,235. The Museum purchased $328,805 in inventory (for the gift shop) and $140,707 in supplies (for the coffee bar) and reported a balance of $44,380 in inventory and $7,035 in supplies. Assuming all purchases and expenses had been paid in full, how much did the gift shop report in profits or losses in its gift shop operaitons for FY 2015.

5. The National Breast Cancer Foundation (NBCF) has over the years assigned 2/3rds of its assets to investments (mutual funds, equities, bonds etc.). At the start of FY 2015, NBCF reported $4,759,863 in investments. Over the next 12 months, NBCF transferred $607,938 from cash to investments. It also received $144,057 in investment income (i.e., dividend and interest). At the end of the year, the investment manager reported realized gains of $75,452 and unrealized gains of $257,345. The investment manager also invoiced NBCF for services rendered ($35,263 for the year) – these were paid in full. Assuming there were no restrictions on investment income, how much did the nonprofit report in investments and investment income (net of expenses) at the end of FY 2015.

6. The Seattle Community Foundation (herein Foundation), a nonprofit entity that supports charitable organizations in the Puget Sound area, reported the following transactions for FY 2016 (July 1, 2015 – June 30, 2016). Use this information to prepare a *Statement of Activities* for FY 2016. How much did the Foundation report as Change in Unrestricted Net Assets? Change in Total Net Assets?

   ◦ The Foundation has a large portfolio of investments. At the beginning of the year, the fair value of the portfolio was $76,850,000. In the 12-month period, the Foundation transferred $4,250,000 from cash to investments.

   ◦ The Foundation received $650,000 in interest and dividend payments. At the end of the year, investment managers reported $675,000 in realized gains and $215,000 in unrealized losses. The Foundation reports investment income (interest and dividend payments, realized gains or losses and unrealized gains or losses) as unrestricted support.

   ◦ The Foundation held its annual fundraising dinner event on March 18th, 2016. The dinner raised $1,600,000 in unrestricted support and $3,200,000 in restricted support.

   ◦ As of June 30, 2016 the Foundation had received $825,000 of the $1,600,000 in unrestricted support and $1,250,000 of the $3,200,000 in restricted support. Historically, 1.5 percent of all pledges have been uncollectible.
   The Foundation's expenses were as follows

   ◦ The Foundation made $2,100,000 in cash awards to various charitable organizations. Of the total, $1,250,000 were funded with restricted public support. The remainder were funded with unrestricted revenues.

   ◦ Foundation salaries and benefits were $420,000 for the year. Of the total, $35,000 remained unpaid at the end of the year. Fundraising and marketing costs for the year were $150,000. All fundraising and marketing expenses had been paid in full by year end. Other expenses, paid in full included rent and utilities ($144,000), equipment lease ($12,000), office supplies ($8,500), and miscellaneous expenses ($15,000).

- On June 28th, the investment manager sent the Foundation an invoice for services rendered in FY 2016 of $82,000. The Foundation expected to write a check for the full amount on July 15th, 2016.

- The Foundation purchased $21,000 in computing equipment in cash. The new equipment is expected to have a useful life of 3 years and zero salvage value. Depreciation expenses on existing equipment for FY 2016 was expected to be $32,500.

- For FY 2016, the Foundation reported $25,000 in interest expense on its long-term debt. The Foundation had also made $75,000 in principal payments for the year.

7. The City of Davidson engages in the following transactions during its fiscal year ending September 30, 2015. Show what impact, if any, each has on the city's assets, liabilities, and fund balance, assuming it prepares its fund financial statements on the modified accrual basis.

- During fiscal 2015 the City levied property taxes of $154,000, of which it collected $120,000 prior to September 2015, and $5,000 over each of the next six months. It estimated that $4,000 will be uncollectible.

- On November 20, 2015 it received $12,000 from the state for sales taxes recorded on its behalf. The payment was for sales made in September that merchants were required ti remit to the state by October 15.

- In April the city was awarded a state training grant of $400 for the period June 1, 2015 through May 31, 2016. In fiscal 2015 the city received the entire $400 but spent only $320. Although the funds were received in advance, the city would have to return to the state any amounts that were not used to cover allowable training grants.

- The city requires each vendor who sells in its "farmers market" to obtain an annual permit. The funds generated by the sale of these permits are used to maintain the market. The permits, which cover the period from June 1 through May 31, are not refundable. In May 2015 the city issued $36 of permits.

- A few years ago the City received a donation of a parcel of land, upon which it expected to build a new community center. During fiscal 2015 it opted to sell the land instead for $135. When acquired by the town, the land had a market value of $119.

Case: Promoting All Student Success (PASS)

Background

The small not-for-profit Christine Chang started in graduate school, Promoting All Students' Success (PASS), was more successful than she had imagined. She had taken an education policy course in graduate school in which she learned about the disparities in achievement gaps as a result of chronic underfunding in the public schools. Her interest in after-school tutoring was prompted by recent changes in state policy that would require students to pass a series of end-of-year exams to qualify for graduation. However, the last three years of budget deficits meant that school districts had to cut back on after-school programs and services, including after-school tutoring and test-prep courses. The state was also not willing to fund these programs arguing learning and test-prep should happen during regular school hours. This meant that students, more likely those from low-income families, that needed assistance would fail their qualifying exams if they did not have access to free or low-cost after-school tutoring sessions.

Recognizing this need, Chang enlisted a group of friends including a number of students taking courses at the School of Education and began offering free after-school tutoring services at local high schools. They began contacting schools over the summer, and by August 2013, they had more students than they could handle. It was evident to her there was an urgent need to provide after-school tutoring services – it was time for her to launch *Promoting All Students' Success* or simply *PASS!*[2]

Financial Information

In November, a local newspaper ran a story about PASS's efforts which attracted the interest of a local entrepreneur, Charles Duncan. Duncan had been a borderline student in high school and had been lucky to graduate, so he contacted Chang to discuss her program. He was impressed enough with her vision and commitment and offered her a $100,000 low-interest loan to turn PASS into a full-time venture (See Exhibit 1).

Chang was a bit daunted by Duncan's generosity but immediately went to work. She resigned from her position at a local nonprofit and rented office space, signing a one-year $2,500 per month lease, with rent due on the first of each month. Chang and Duncan met up the day before Christmas. At that meeting, she briefed Duncan on her initial thoughts for PASS's operational structure including Duncan serving as the chair of the Board of Directors. As he wrote her the check for $100,000, Duncan noted that there would be a conflict of interest, as he was the initial and sole investor in PASS. Nonetheless, he knew she needed his support and he would be able to use his networks in the business community to solicit additional financial support for PASS. Chang immediately deposited the funds in a checking account and went home to celebrate the holiday with her family, knowing she had an exciting year ahead of her.

January 5, 2015, PASS officially opened for business. Her first order of business was to invest $20,000 of the $100,000 she had received from Duncan. She wanted to make sure she could earn some interest on these funds. After conversations with a local bank manager, she decided to engage the services of a local investment manager and invest the funds in a low-risk US equities fund. She wrote a check from the checking account on the 8th of January (see Exhibit 3).

Utilities (e.g., electric, water and sewer, garbage) for the new office space were expected to average $500 per month. Payments on outstanding balances were due on the 15th of the following month. She decided to take advantage of the after Christmas sale and purchase computers, laptops, tablets, phones, and printers for $10,000 (see Exhibit 4).

Chang was initially the only employee, serving as Executive Director, sole tutor and chief fundraiser. At the initial board

---

2. Promoting All Student Success was developed by Professor Ross Rubenstein and is included here with modifications.

meeting, the board voted to pay a salary of $3,500 per month and to contribute an additional $175 per month toward her health insurance. She also presented preliminary estimates for operating expenses. Her initial thoughts were that she would need to invest $1,000 in student workbooks and other teaching supplies. She would also engage the services of a local supplier that would deliver an additional $300 in supplies per month. Chang worked out an agreement with the supplier in which they would deliver two months of supplies on the first of every other month, starting February 1, with payment due on the 15th of the month of delivery.

By March 2015, Chang and Duncan had some good fundraising success. Duncan had received commitments from his network of family, friends, and business associates. They had agreed to provide PASS with $25,000 in unrestricted public support. The donors agreed to make payments on these commitments in July ($5,500), August ($3,500), October ($4,000), and December ($5,000). He suspected a few of the donors would likely not make payments on their commitments. PASS would need to adjust for $1,000 in bad debt expense at the end of the year. The remainder of pledges would be received no later than January 2016.

Chang had also worked really hard in the initial month and submitted a grant proposal to the McNamara Foundation. After an intensive vetting process, she received the news that the Foundation would support PASS efforts in closing the achievement gap. She received a check from the foundation in April for $25,000. The foundation did not impose any restrictions on the grant.

Despite initial successes, Chang and the Board of Directors realized they would not be able to run the program strictly through grants and contributions – the school districts would have to contribute toward the cost of the program. In April, she contacted the districts she had been working with and told each that she would have to begin charging $75 per student per month. Each student would receive tutoring services in September through May. This was still well below what it would cost the districts to provide the services themselves, so two districts agreed to continue the program. Each signed up 25 students. Chang agreed to delay charging the fee until the next school year started in September 2015.

Chang spent the summer preparing to expand the program in the fall. She hired five part-time tutors at $15 per hour, for 80 hours each per month, from September 1 to May 31. To keep costs down, she decided she would continue to tutor while running the program. She also decided that the organization's most pressing need, particularly with new tutors on board, was transportation. After shopping around, she decided to purchase a minivan for $35,000. She made a $5,000 down payment and took out a five-year loan at 2.5% interest to finance the rest. Monthly payments of $532 were due at the beginning of each month, starting on September 1 (see Exhibit 2). She was also required to take out insurance on the car, with payments of $540 per quarter due in advance every three months, starting on September 1. The tutors and Chang coordinated the schedules so that the car would be available for tutoring visits. They drove quite a few miles and used an average of $100 per month in gas, starting in September.

Starting October 1, she began billing the school districts monthly for services from the previous month and gave the school districts one month to pay. In other words, if she sent a bill for September on October 1st, payment would be due no later than October 31. Even though the districts never paid early, the did make payments within the 30 day grace period.

By November, Chang was already looking ahead to next year. On the first of December, she received more good news from the McNamara Foundation: it had decided to donate an additional $25,000 to PASS. The grant had strings attached. PASS was to invest the money and use the earnings to subsidize as many participants as possible. This would allow more students to participate in the program, at no cost to the school districts. After depositing the check, she initiated a wire transfer to the low-risk US equities fund. The investment manager told her that the additional investments would not yield any substantial returns by the end of the year given that the fund transfer occurred in the last month of the fiscal year.

By Christmas 2015, Duncan was impressed enough with Chang's work and PASS's accomplishments that he agreed to forgive $40,000 of the $100,000 loan. Because the long-term obligation was to be forgiven, PASS would need to recognize the value of the forgiven loan as unrestricted revenue. Duncan expected to receive payment on the balance of the loan as agreed.

Before the end of the year, a Mrs. Hughes and four other parents came to Chang's office. They had heard about the initiative and student achievements to date. They wanted to enroll their children in the tutoring program starting January 2016. They knew they would not be able to pay the full cost of PASS's tutoring services. Nevertheless, they had raised $2,000 amongst themselves and hoped that Chang would tutor their children in the upcoming year. While the $2,000 was $500 more than what the school districts was billed for on a per student basis, Chang was not sure she could provide the service directly to the parents without the additional vetting and review processes the school districts, especially the teachers, provided her. She knew this was an issue she needed to bring to the Board first.

The Board expected to meet at the start of the new year to review to review events of the past year. Chang was excited about all PASS achievements and future. Ahead of the meeting, Duncan asked Chang for copies of PASS's financial statements so he could evaluate the organization's operating performance and financial position. Chang panicked. While she had kept good records, she had not prepared any formal financial documents. Looking back, she wished she hadn't avoided that financial management class in graduate school.

Assignment

1. Demonstrate the impact of each transaction on the organization's assets, liabilities, or net assets. You may assume at the start of the year, PASS reported $100,000 in cash and $100,000 in long-term obligations and zero in net assets. Revenues for the year can be reported as either unrestricted or restricted, that simply depends on whether the donor-imposed restrictions or whether the income is earned-income not support or contributions. All expenses are to be reported under unrestricted net assets. Additional assumptions:

   ◦ The fiscal year runs from January 1 to December 31 and all transactions are material.

   ◦ Employees are paid monthly on the 7th of the following month.

2. Use the transaction information to prepare PASS's Statement of Financial Position (or Balance Sheet), Statement of Activities (or Income Statement), and Cash Flow Statement. Provide an assessment of PASS financial performance and operating position. The templates below provide some guidance for each financial statement.

3. Reflecting on PASS's financial performance and operating position, develop a 2016 budget that would be presented to the Board together with these financial statements. Be sure to include a budget narrative that outlines PASS goals and challenges for the upcoming fiscal year.

Exhibit 1: Duncan Loan: PASS received the $100,000 proceeds from the loan on December 24th, 2016. Chang deposited the check in the PASS bank account. At the end of December 2015, and each year thereafter, PASS would be required to pay $10,000 of principal plus 3% interest on the outstanding balances for the previous year. For example, interest expense for the first year would be $3,000 or 3% of 100,000.

Exhibit 2: Auto Purchase: The car was purchased for $35,000 and has a salvage value of $7,000 and a useful life of 7 years. It is depreciated on a straight-line basis with partial year depreciation pro-rated based on the number of months in service. The payment schedule for the loan is as follows:

Car Loan	$	30,000
Annual Interest Cost		2.50%
Loan Period (Years)		5
Payment (per month)	$	532

Payment Due First of	Car Loan Payment	Interest payment	Principal Payment	Remaining balance
Sep-15	$ 532	$ 63	$ 470	$ 29,530
Oct-15	532	62	471	29,059
Nov-15	532	61	472	28,587
Dec-15	532	60	473	28,114
Jan-16	532	59	474	27,641
Feb-16	532	58	475	27,166
Mar-16	532	57	476	26,690
Apr-16	532	56	477	26,213
May-16	532	55	478	25,735
Jun-16	532	54	479	25,256
Jul-16	532	53	480	24,777
Aug-16	532	52	481	24,296
Sep-16	532	51	482	23,814
Oct-16	532	50	483	23,331
Nov-16	532	49	484	22,847
Dec-16	532	48	485	22,363

	Total Interest Payment	Total Principal Payment
2015	$ 244	$ 1,886
2016	637	5,752

Exhibit 3: Investments: In January 2016, PASS received a statement from its mutual fund company stating that, as of December 31, 2015, its mutual fund holdings were worth $47,248.

Exhibit 4: Computer Equipment: The computer equipment which was purchased for $10,000, and paid for in cash. It has a useful life of 4 years and no salvage value. Since PASS uses straight-line depreciation, the depreciation expense for the year was expected to be $2,500 (i.e., $10,000/4yrs)

Statement of Financial Position
Promoting All Students' Success
For the Year Ending Dec 31 2015

		2015		2014
Assets				
Cash			$	100,000
Investments				
Accounts receivable				
Pledges receivable				
Supplies				
Prepaid Expenses				
Fixed Assets				
(Less Depreciation)				
Net Fixed Assets		-		
Total Assets		$ -	$	**100,000**
Liabilities				
Wages payable				
Accounts payable				
Deferred Revenue				
Loan payable - current				10,000
Loan payable- long-term				90,000
Total Liabilities		$ -	$	100,000
Unrestricted				
Temporarily restricted				
Permanently restricted				
Total Net Assets		$ -	$	-
Liabilities + Net Assets		$ -	$	**100,000**

STATEMENT OF ACTIVITIES

Promoting All Students' Success
For the Period Jan 1 2015-Dec 31 2015

	Unrestricted	Temporarily Restricted	Permanently Restricted	Total
REVENUES				
Tuition Revenue				
Gain on investments				
SUPPORT				
Grants and Donations				
Total Revenues and Support	$ -		$ -	$ -
EXPENSES				
Salaries				
Supplies				
Utilities				
Gasoline				
Rent				
Insurance				
Interest				
Depreciation				
Bad Debt Expense				
Total expenses	$ -			$ -
Change in Net Assets	$ -		$ -	$ -

Statement of Cash Flows
Promoting All Students' Success
For the Year Ending Dec 31 2015

Change in Net Assets   -

Cash Flows from Operating Activities
Add back non-cash expenses
Depreciation

Other adjustments
Increase (Decrease) in Wages payable
Increase (Decrease) in Accounts payable
Increase (Decrease) in Loan Payable - Current
Increase (Decrease) in Deferred Revenue
(Increase) Decrease in Accounts Receivable
(Increase) Decrease in Pledges Receivable
(Increase) Decrease in Inventory
(Increase) Decrease in Prepaid expenses   _____
Net Cash Flows from Operating Activities   -

Cash Flows from Investing Activities
(Increase) Decrease in Investments
(Increase) Decrease in Fixed Assets   _____
Net Cash Flows from Investing Activities   -

Cash Flows from Financing Activities
Increase (Decrease) in Loan Payable -- non-Current   _____
Net Cash Flows from Financing Activities   -

Net Change in Cash & Cash Equivalents   -

Cash, Beginning of the Year   100,000
Cash, End of the Year   100,000

Even though the Yakima Valley Medical and Dental Clinic (YVMDC) was projecting a sizeable deficit for FY 2016 (-$115,157; see Exhibit 2), Tatyana Sanchez, Director of YVMDC, was optimistic about the clinic's future. Edward Lowe, the loan officer at Umpqua Bank (UB) was not. He was alarmed YVMDC was projecting a deficit in excess of 16.5 percent of net patient revenues (or 15.7 percent of total revenues). While the bank would likely continue to extend the line of credit (LOC) facility to its long-term client, Lowe thought he should have a more candid conversation with the clinic's leadership team. In his most recent conversation with Sanchez he noted "Without changes to your current business practices, I am not sure how you will turn this ship around. You have already tapped into the LOC a number of times this year alone and your current cash balances of $58,000 would not cover a month of your expenses. If you don't report positive cash flows and profits in 2017, the bank is concerned YVMDC would become insolvent and perhaps even file for bankruptcy protection".

Sanchez knew she had a lot of work ahead of her. She had to come up with proforma financial statements for FY 2017 and present these the Board at the upcoming meeting. And even though the clinic had a long-standing relationship with UB, she knew presenting proforma statements together with a cash-flow budget was central to securing a line of credit.

Background

Yakima Valley Medical and Dental Clinic (YVMDC) was founded in 2003 by two retired doctors that recognized the need for access to affordable medical and dental services for a largely rural and/or migrant population that lived and worked in Yakima Valley.

At first, YVMDC was small and operated out of a founder's existing medical practice. At that time, YVMDC employed the two founders and three assistants. It gradually grew its operations and by 2009, YVMDC desperately needed new clinic space. It purchased and renovated a small building in downtown Yakima in 2014. It also invested in vehicles and equipment and expanded staff from 6 to 16 full-time and part-time staff.

In early-2013, the board decided it needed to further expand its reach to a rural population that did not seek out medical or dental services except for emergency care. The board knew it would need to invest in a mobile medical and dental clinics, but needed a "needs assessment" to be completed before it could make that investment. At the end of 2016, the board approved the purchase of mobile clinics, after it had received a report that recommended client outreach.

Financial Information

Since YVMDC serves a rural migrant population, demand for its services is largely seasonal. Approximately two-thirds of the clinic visits are in the early spring through late summer. Exhibit 8 reports forecasted monthly revenues for FY 2017. In making these projections, Sanchez took into account the contractual adjustments with healthcare providers (including Medicare and Medicaid) and non-payment from indigent patients (i.e., charity care). While YVMDC billed for services ten days after a clinic visit, no payments were received in the month of service. In fact, YVMDC received payment on 50 percent of its monthly billings one month following service, 35 percent two months following service, 10 percent three months following service, and finally, 5 percent four months after services were provided, and only after assigning a staff member to make regular collection calls.[1] For example, if services were provided in January, payments on 50 percent of revenues would be received in February, 35 percent in March, 10 percent in April. The remaining balance would be received in May – four months later.

Even though demand for services was seasonal, YVMDC salaries and expenses were relatively steady throughout the year. The agency had a firm policy of regular employment for its employees which, according to management, enabled YVMDC maintain it's skilled and committed staff. Management also believed that its employment policy contributed significantly to the clinic's reputation for quality medical and dental care. Starting in January 2017, salaries and benefits were expected to be $54,165 a month. The substantial increase in payroll costs (i.e., from $47,100 per month) reflected the Board's decision to expand YVMDC staffing capacity to meet client needs, the new outreach program, as well as cost-of-living salary adjustments. All employees were paid on the first Monday of each month for earnings from the previous month.

The Board had committed to investing in mobile medical and dental clinics that would be delivered at the end of April. The vehicle would allow YVMDC staff not only reach more clients but eliminate existing lease agreements at satellite clinics. Having negotiated with a large recreational vehicle distributor, YVMDC would invest a total of $75,000 in vehicles and equipment. The Clinic would make four equal consecutive payments to the vendor beginning in April through July. The mobile clinics were expected to have a useful life of six years and salvage value of $15,000. Sanchez thought it would be appropriate to recognize depreciation for the vehicle upon delivery. Depreciation for existing fixed assets was estimated to be $33,000.

Throughout FY 2017 disbursements related to overheads (e.g., utilities, legal fees, insurance premiums), contract services (e.g., payroll services, vehicle maintenance), and miscellaneous expenses were estimated to be $13,360, $2,250, $1,250 respectively. Contract services and overheads were paid for in the month of service. Miscellaneous expenses were paid out of petty cash, with petty cash being drawn out of the YVMDC bank account on a monthly basis.

Staff were projected to use $3,650 in medical, dental, and office supplies per month. YVMDC maintained a first in first out (FIFO) inventory system which meant older supplies had to be used first. To ensure there were sufficient supplies, the clinic would continue to order $3,500 in supplies per month irrespective on the inventory already in stock. The vendor required payments the month following delivery.

To improve the organization's solvency position, Sanchez was committed to paying down a substantial proportion of the clinic's obligations. She would make a payment to Dr. Vargas on the $26,156 short-term interest-free loan in July. She also anticipated making payments on the third-party liability (Medicare). These payments relate to reimbursements received that exceeded reimbursable costs. The first payment of $16,750 was due in January 2017. The second payment of $17,270 was due in August. The final payment on the liability was due February 2018. The third-party liability would not have any interest cost, but had a $500 late payment fee per month for payments received after the due date.

YVMDC had borrowed $450,000 to finance the clinic's current building. UB offered the clinic a 30-year mortgage that required equal principal payments of $7,500 that were due on the loan beginning December 31st, 2014 (payments were semi-annually on June 30th and December 31st). Interest of 6 percent per annum on the unpaid balance was payable at the same time. In preparing the financial forecasts, Sanchez planned to show separately the two principal payments and the two interest payments (see Exhibit 7).

Following a discussion with the investment portfolio manager, Sanchez projected returns on the investment portfolio to be 45,720. However, because the endowment was underwater (i.e., below historical dollar value or HDV) YVMDC could not draw on the endowment including any investment income until such time the endowment was $750,000, the HDV on the gift. All investment income would be recorded under permanently restricted net assets and the YVMDC could not rely on these funds to shore up cash flows or pay for expenses.

Assignment

You have been working Ms. Sanchez at YVMDC. She has asked you to prepare a monthly cash budget for FY 2017 (see Exhibit 3, 4 and 5). At the very minimum, your cash budget should report cash inflows from receivables, cash outflows, and cash balances at the end of each month.

She has also asked you to prepare proforma financial statements including the Statement of Financial Position and a Statement of Activities (see Exhibit 1 and 2).

You expect to meet with her to discuss your estimates and related analysis. Prepare a brief memo that summarizes the clinic's operations for the year. Be sure to highlight strengths and weaknesses of YVMDC cash flows, operating performance, and financial position for FY 2017.

[1] For amounts outstanding at the end of FY 2016 –i.e., $75,800 – 50 percent of the outstanding balance will be collected in January, 35 percent would be collected in February, 10 percent in March, and 5 percent in April.

EXHIBIT I: YAKIMA VALLEY MEDICAL AND DENTAL CLINIC STATEMENT OF FINANCIAL POSITION

	December 31, 2017	December 31, 2016
Assets		
Cash		58,000
Accounts receivable		75,800
Medical Supplies Inventory		32,260
Total Current Assets		**166,060**
Property Plant and Equipment (net)		593,298
Investments (Long-term)		354,475
Total Assets		**1,113,833**
Liabilities		
Salaries Payable		47,100
Medical and Office Supplies Payable		3,175
Due to Third party (Medicare)		51,290
Note payable		26,156
Mortgage (current)		15,000
Total Current Liabilities		**142,721**
Mortgage (non-current)		412,500
Total Liabilities		**555,221**
Net Assets		
Unrestricted		190,892
Permanently Restricted		367,720
Total Net Assets		**558,612**
Liabilities + Net Assets		**1,113,833**

EXHIBIT 2: YAKIMA VALLEY MEDICAL AND DENTAL CLINIC
STATEMENT OF ACTIVITIES

	December 31, 2017	December 31, 2016
REVENUES		
Gross patient revenue		809,500
Less: Contractual allowances and uncollectible accounts		(115,450)
Net Patient Revenue		**694,050**
Investment Income (Restricted Revenue)		38,450
Total Revenues		**732,500**
EXPENSES		
Salaries and Benefits		565,200
Overhead and Administration		145,750
Use of Medical Supplies		35,040
Contract Services		21,600
Equipment Lease		15,450
Depreciation		25,300
Interest, Mortgage		25,425
Misc. Expenses		8,500
Interest, Line of Credit		4,492
Total Expenses		**846,757**
Change in Net Assets = Total Revenues - Total Expenses		**(114,257)**
Net assets at the beginning of the period		672,869
Net assets at the end of the period = Change in Net Assets + Net Assets at the beginning of the period		**558,612**

YAKIMA VALLEY MEDICAL AND DENTAL CLINIC PROJECTED CASH FLOWS (FY 2017)

		Jan-17	Feb-17	Mar-17	Apr-17	May-17	Jun-17	Jul-17	Aug-17	Sep-17	Oct-17	Nov-17	Dec-17
EXHIBIT 3: PROJECTED CASH BALANCES													
Begin Balance $		58,000											
Cash Inflows *(From Exhibit 4)*													
Cash Outflows *(From Exhibit 5)*													
End Balance = Begin Balance + Cash Inflows - Cash Outflows													

		Jan-17	Feb-17	Mar-17	Apr-17	May-17	Jun-17	Jul-17	Aug-17	Sep-17	Oct-17	Nov-17	Dec-17
EXHIBIT 4: PROJECTED CASH INFLOWS													
Net Patient Revenue		69,583	110,224	145,054	153,874	167,370	90,212	88,801	66,895	66,567	37,409	38,268	50,457
Outstanding Account Receivable	75,800												
Expected Cash Inflows from Receivables													
Payments on the outstanding balance													
Payments 1 month following service													
Payments 2 month following service													
Payments 3 month following service													
Payments 4 month following service													
TOTAL CASH INFLOWS													

	Jan-17	Feb-17	Mar-17	Apr-17	May-17	Jun-17	Jul-17	Aug-17	Sep-17	Oct-17	Nov-17	Dec-17
EXHIBIT 5: PROJECTED CASH OUTFLOWS												
Cash Payments on	Jan-17	Feb-17	Mar-17	Apr-17	May-17	Jun-17	Jul-17	Aug-17	Sep-17	Oct-17	Nov-17	Dec-17
Example: Wages and Benefits												
TOTAL CASH OUTFLOWS												

		Jan-17	Feb-17	Mar-17	Apr-17	May-17	Jun-17	Jul-17	Aug-17	Sep-17	Oct-17	Nov-17	Dec-17
EXHIBIT 6: PROJECTED ACCOUNTS RECEIVABLES													
Begin Balance $		75,800											
Net Patient Revenue		69,583	110,224	145,054	153,874	167,370	90,212	88,801	66,895	66,567	37,409	38,268	50,457
Payments on Receivables *(From Exhibit 4)*													
Ending Balance = Begin Balance + Revenue - Payments													

Exhibit 7: Yakima Valley Dental Clinic Mortgage with Umpqua Bank

Total Mortgage	$	450,000		
Loan period		30 years		
Loan payments		60		
Payment per period	$	7,500		
Annual Interest Rate		6%		

(Payment schedule for the first 5 years or 10 payments)

Payment Date	Payment #	Outstanding Balance	Principal Payment	Semi-annual Interest Cost
1-Dec-14	1	450,000.00	7,500.00	13,500.00
1-Jun-15	2	442,500.00	7,500.00	13,275.00
1-Dec-15	3	435,000.00	7,500.00	13,050.00
1-Jun-16	4	427,500.00	7,500.00	12,825.00
1-Dec-16	5	420,000.00	7,500.00	12,600.00
1-Jun-17	6	412,500.00	7,500.00	12,375.00
1-Dec-17	7	405,000.00	7,500.00	12,150.00
1-Jun-18	8	397,500.00	7,500.00	11,925.00
1-Dec-18	9	390,000.00	7,500.00	11,700.00
1-Jun-19	10	382,500.00	7,500.00	11,475.00

Exhibit 8: Estimated Monthly Revenue (FY-2017)

	Gross Patient Revenue	Net Patient Revenue
January	89,700	69,583
February	142,091	110,224
March	186,990	145,054
April	198,360	153,874
May	215,758	167,370
June	116,293	90,212
July	114,474	88,801
August	86,235	66,895
September	85,812	66,567
October	48,225	37,409
November	49,332	38,268
December	65,044	50,457
	1,398,314	1,084,716

CHAPTER 5.

COST ANALYSIS

COST ANALYSIS: WHAT DOES THIS COST?

Cost analysis is useful for addressing several key questions that managers ask:

- Will the revenue from a new grant opportunity cover the costs to expand a program?

- Will a program or service benefit from economies of scale? If not, why not?

- How much should we budget for a new staff member? To add a new shift or other group of new staff?

- How much "overhead" or "indirect costs" should we negotiate into a contract with a government?

- What price should we set for a new fee-based service?

- When will we need to add more staff, and how will adding staff affect our cost structure?

- What's the best way to share costs between departments within an organization? Between organizations? Between units of government?

In February 2016 a federal judge in Albuquerque, NM approved a $1 billion settlement between the Obama administration and nearly 700 Native American tribes. This settlement ended a decades-long class action lawsuit over how the federal Bureau of Indian Affairs (BIA) had distributed aid to tribes since the mid 1970s.

This case came about because of some disagreements over how to measure costs. For more than 150 years the BIA was directly responsible for most of the health care, education, economic development, and other core services delivered on Native American reservations. But then starting in the mid-1970s it shifted its focus from direct service provision to helping tribes become self-sufficient. Instead of managing services, it redirected its resources toward training, technical assistance, and other efforts to help tribes launch and maintain their own services.

To make that transition BIA re-classified many of its activities as "contract support costs." This change was not just semantic. Funding for direct BIA-administered services was part of a regular federal budget appropriation. That appropriation was stable and predictable. By contrast, funding for support costs on federal government contracts is quite variable and must be renegotiated often. Perhaps not surprisingly, total BIA spending declined steadily under this new capacity-building model.

Tribes across the US argued that by re-classifying many of BIA's costs, the federal government gave itself permission to slash BIA's budget without Congressional approval. The tribes' alleged this simple cost measurement maneuver allowed BIA to operate well outside its authority and to inflict substantial harm on Native Americans around the country. BIA argued that the cost reclassification was a standard accounting change that has happened across the federal government for decades. The case was ultimately settled for far less than the tribes requested, but the federal government did agree to re-classify many contract support costs as direct service costs for which federal funding is far more transparent and predictable.

This case illustrates the central point of this chapter: how we define and measure costs matters tremendously. In this case, cost measurement was not just a technical exercise; it had real impacts on the lives of hundreds of thousands of Native Americans. The same is true for virtually all public services. How we define, measure, and plan for costs affects which services we deliver and how we deliver them.

Learning Objectives

After reading this chapter you should be able to:

- Define the cost objective and relevant range for the goods and services that public organizations deliver

- Contrast fixed costs from variable costs

- Contrast direct costs from indirect costs

- Allocate costs across departments, organizations, and jurisdictions

- Determine the full cost of a good or service

- Prepare a flexible budget for a program or service

- Calculate the break-even price and break-even quantity for a good or service

- Contrast cost-based pricing with price-based costing

- Recommend management strategies and policies informed by analysis of costs "at the margin"

- Analyze budget variances, both positive and negative

WHAT IS COST ANALYSIS?

If you've ever flown on an airplane, there's a good chance you know Boeing. The Boeing Company generates around $90 billion each year from selling thousands of airplanes to commercial and military customers around the world. It employs around 200,000 people, and it's indirectly responsible for more than a million jobs through its suppliers, contractors, regulators, and others. Its main assembly line in Everett, WA is housed in the largest building in the world, a colossal facility that covers nearly a half-trillion cubic feet. Boeing is, simply put, a massive enterprise.

And yet, Boeing's managers know the exact cost of everything the company uses to produce its airplanes; every propeller, flap, seat belt, welder, computer programmer, and so forth. Moreover, they know how those costs would change if they produced more airplanes or fewer. They also know the price at which they sold that plane and the profit the company made on that sale. Boeing's executives expect their managers to know this information, in real time, if the company is to remain profitable.

Cost accounting (also known as *managerial accounting*) is the process of creating information about costs to inform management decisions. Managers need good information about costs to set prices, determine how much of a good or service to deliver, and to manage costs in ways that make their organization more likely to achieve its mission. Managers in for-profit entities like Boeing, have instant access to sophisticated cost information that would assist with those types of decisions. But managers in the public and non-profit sectors usually don't. There are many reasons for this:

- Large parts of the public sector don't produce a "product," but they do produce a service like counseling juvenile offenders, protecting the environment, or helping the homeless. Sometimes we know the "unit" of production and can measure costs relative to that unit. In the case of counseling juvenile offenders, we might think about the cost per offender to provide those services. But for services without a clear "end user," like environmental protection, this analysis is much more difficult.

- Most (usually around 80%) of the costs incurred by a typical public sector organization are related to people. A parole officer will see many different types of parolees. Some will demand a lot of attention and follow-up. Some will need next to none. Some parole officers are comfortable giving each case an equal amount of time and attention. Others are not. This type of variability in how and where people spend their time, and as a result, where labor costs are incurred, can make cost analysis quite difficult.

- Employees often work across multiple programs. A program manager at a non-profit organization might work across two different programs funded by two different grants from two different funding agencies. Unless that program manager allocates their time exactly equal across both programs – and that's unlikely – we can't know the exact cost of each program without a careful study of how and where that employee spends their time.

- Public services often share buildings, equipment, vehicles, and other costs. Without a system to track exactly which staff and programs use exactly which resources, it's difficult to know the full cost to deliver a particular service.

- Good cost analysis has no natural political constituency. Careful cost analysis requires substantial investments in information technology, staff capacity, accounting information systems, and other resources. Most taxpayers and funders would rather see that money spent on programs and services to help people in the short-term, and not on information systems to analyze and plan for future costs.

These are just a few of the many barriers that prevent public organizations from acting more like Boeing, at least with respect to cost analysis.

And yet, good cost analysis is absolutely crucial to public organizations. Public financial resources are finite, scarce, and becoming scarcer. Public managers must understand how and where they incur costs, how and where they will incur costs under different service delivery models, and whether that pattern of costs is consistent with their organization's mission and objective. In this chapter we introduce the core concepts of cost accounting, and we show how to apply those concepts to real management decisions.

At the outset it's important to draw a distinction between *full cost accounting* and *differential cost accounting*. Full cost accounting is the process of identifying the full cost of a good or service. Differential cost accounting – sometimes called *marginal cost analysis* – is the process of determining how the full cost of a good or service changes when we deliver more or less of it. Good financial management requires careful attention to both.

Let's start with a simple example. Imagine a copying machine that's shared among three departments within the Environmental Health Department of a county government. Those three departments are:

1. Food Protection. This includes inspection and licensing of restaurants and other establishments that serve food. This program is designed to prevent outbreaks of food-borne diseases like E. coli, botulism, and Hepatitis A. Staff in this division make make around 500 copies each day, mostly related to documenting restaurant inspections.
2. Animals and Pests. This includes animal control, rodent testing and control, and educational programs to promote pet safety and neutering/spaying. These programs are designed to prevent communicable diseases, including rabies, that are most often spread by vagrant animals. Staff in this division make around 250 copies each day, but that number can increase in the event of a outbreak of avian flu or other communicable disease.
3. Wastewater. The Wastewater department is responsible for treating wastewater. Staff in this division issue water discharge permits to businesses and industrial operations, and also test water quality near wastewater discharge sites. These programs are necessary to prevent waterborne communicable diseases like cryptosporidium. Wastewater division staff typically make around 100 copies each day, but make up to 1,000 per day when processing complex industrial building permits. They process around six such permits each year.

As a manager you'd want to know what it costs to operate the copier, and how those costs ought to be spread across the three departments. To put this question in the language of cost accounting, we want to know:

1. What is the *full cost* to operate the copier?
2. How should we *allocate* the costs of operating the copier across the three departments?

To answer these questions we first need to know all of the different ways the copier incurs costs. A few come to mind immediately: paper and toner to make the actual copies, a lease or rental payment to take possession of the copier, and occasional maintenance and repairs. A few might be less obvious: electricity to run the machine, space within a building to house the machine, and an office manager's time to coordinate maintenance and repairs. We can observe many of these costs, but other we'll need to estimate or impute.

Cost vs. Price It's important at the outset to draw a distinction between cost and price. *Cost* is what you give up to get something. It can include money, time, uncertainty, and most important, the opportunity to invest time or money in some other project. In public financial management, we usually talk about cost in terms of the measurable, direct and indirect financial expenses required to produce or acquire a good or service. *Price* is the market rate or "sticker price," usually in dollars, of a good or service.

Most public services are delivered "at cost," meaning they are priced to generate enough revenue to cover the full cost to deliver them, but not more. The late management guru Peter Drucker called this *cost-based pricing*. By contrast, many for-profit goods and services are sold at prices well in excess of cost. For instance, most wines are priced at 100-200% above the full cost to produce them. A box of popcorn at the movies is usually priced at 700-800% above cost. And so forth. Wine retailers and cinemas will sell these products at whatever price consumers are willing to pay, regardless of what they cost to produce. Drucker called this *price-based costing*. Virtually all highly profitable businesses design the cost structure of their products and services around what consumers will pay. The opposite is also true. For-profits often sell goods and services at prices well below cost – a so called "loss leader" – in an effort to attract customers. Most public organizations cannot routinely engage in these types of price-based costing tactics and expect to accomplish their missions and remain in good financial position.

The next question is how the departments should share these costs. Imagine, for instance, that they split those costs one-third for each department? This approach is simple, easy, and transparent. But what's wrong with it? Each department makes a different number of total copies, and each also has a different workflow related to the copier. These departments also have different potential "economies of scale" for copying. Also keep in mind that Animals and Pests needs more "emergency capacity" or "surge capacity" than the other two departments. So if an even distribution is not the most appropriate, then what is? With careful attention to cost accounting methods we can begin to address these and other questions.

FULL COST ACCOUNTING

MEASURING FULL COST: THE SIX-STEP METHOD

To answer the question "what does this service cost?" cost accountants follow a six-step process. Each step of this process is driven by policies and procedures that are defined by an organization's management:

1. Define the cost object. The *cost object* is the product or deliverable for which costs are measured. Service-oriented public organizations typically define cost objects in terms of the end user or recipient of a service. Examples include the cost to shelter a homeless person for an evening, the cost per counseling session delivered to recovering substance abusers, the cost to place a family in affordable housing, and so forth.
2. Determine cost centers. A *cost center* is a part of an organization that incurs costs. It could be a program, a unit within a department, a department, a grant, a contract, or any other entity that's clearly defined for cost accounting purposes. As a general rule, cost centers work best if they are for homogeneous groupings of activities.

3. Distinguish between direct and indirect costs. *Direct costs* are connected to a specific cost center. In fact, they're often called "traceable costs." Examples include salaries for staff who work entirely within a cost center, facilities and supplies used only by that cost center, training for cost center-specific staff, etc. Many public organizations further stipulate that a cost is direct to a cost center only if it can be controlled by that center's management. *Indirect costs* apply to more than one cost center. They include shared facilities, general administration, payroll processing services, information technology support, etc. Some managers call them *service center costs*, *internal service* costs, or *overhead costs* because they are usually for support services provided within an organization. **The full cost of any service is the direct costs plus the indirect costs.**

4. Choose allocation bases for indirect costs. One of the main goals of full cost accounting is to distribute indirect costs to cost centers. This follows from the logic that all direct costs require support from within the organization. An *allocation basis* is an observable metric we can use to measure the relationship between direct and indirect costs within a cost center. For example, a non-profit might allocate indirect costs according to the number of full-time equivalent (FTE) employees within a cost center, or the percentage of the organization's overall payroll earned by employees within that cost center.

5. Select an allocation method. There are two main methods to *allocate* or *apportion* indirect costs to cost centers. One is simply to call indirect costs their own cost centers and plan accordingly. For instance, a non-profit could choose to call the executive director its own cost center. In that case it would plan for and report the executive director's salary, benefits, and other costs as a stand-alone entity, rather than allocate those costs as an indirect cost to other direct service cost centers. A more common approach is to allocate by a denominator that's common to all the cost centers that incur a particular indirect cost (see below).

6. Attach costs to cost objects. One of big challenges for public organizations is that cost objects are usually people, and no two people are alike. For instance, a parole officer might have 30 clients, but each requires a different amount of time, attention, and counseling. When the cost per client varies a lot, the cost accounting system ought to reflect those differences, usually by applying different overhead rates or percentages to different types of clients.

Let's illustrate some of these concepts with the copier example. To begin, assume that the copier is its own cost center. Services like copying, information technology, payroll, exist to serve clients within the organization, so they're called *service centers*. One of the goals of cost accounting is to allocate service centers' costs to *mission centers* that are more directly connected to the organization's core programs and services. In this case we can assume Food Inspection, Animals and Pests, and Wastewater are mission centers that will ultimately receive costs allocated from the copier service center. Given those assumptions about cost centers, we can assume the cost object for the copier service center is the cost per copy.

With those assumptions established we can define direct and indirect costs for the copier service center. Direct costs include paper, toner, the machine rental/lease fees, and machine maintenance. These costs are incurred exclusively by the copier. Electricity, building space, and the office manager's time are indirect costs. They are incurred by the copier cost center and by other cost centers.

To illustrate, the table below lists some details on the copier's full costs for FY2015.

Annual Full Cost of Environmental Health Department Copier Cost Center, FY2015

Direct Costs

Cost Item	Number	Unit Cost	Total
Paper	500 reams	$20/ream	$10,000
Toner	30 cartridges	$90/cartridge	$2,700
Machine Rental	$500/month	12 months	$6,000
Machine Maintenance	$75/month	12 months	$900
Total Direct Costs			$19,900

Indirect Costs

Cost Item	Cost Driver/Amount	Unit Cost	Total
Electricity	1,500 kWh	.12/kWh	$180
Building Space	100 sq. ft.	$15/sq. ft.	$1,500
Office Manager Time	5 hours	$20/hour	$100
Total Indirect Costs			$1,780
Full Cost			$21,380

INDIRECT COST ALLOCATION: COST DRIVERS AND ALLOCATION BASES

To find the full cost of the copier cost center we'll need to find some way to allocate to it its share of those indirect costs. A good cost allocation scheme follows from a clear understanding of an organization's cost drivers. A *cost driver* is a factor that affect the cost of an activity. A good cost driver is a reliably observable quantity that shares a consistent relationship with the indirect cost in question. Fortunately, for the copier cost center, we have an intuitive cost driver: the number of copies.

Ideally, we can allocate indirect costs according to their key cost driver(s). An *allocation basis* is a cost driver that's common to all the cost centers that incur an indirect cost. For building space, for example, we might find the portion of the total building space that's occupied by the copier, and allocate a proportionate share of the building space costs to the copier copy center.

For example, this particular county government allocates electricity costs to different cost centers per kilowatt hour (kWh). Sometimes it's feasible to measure electricity use with this level of precision, and sometimes it's not. Assume that the copier in question has an individualized meter that measures its electricity use.

This government allocates building space costs per square foot. This assumes it has a reasonably sophisticated way to measure how much space each cost center uses. Allocations by space can be contentious because not every unit uses space in quite the same way to accomplish its mission. For instance, most of the Food Protection staff spend most of their time out in the field inspecting restaurants. They report to the office at the beginning and end of the day, but infrequently during the day. This is quite different from the Animals and Pets center, where most of the staff spend most of their time in the office.

More on Cost Drivers

One of the big challenges in cost accounting is identifying appropriate cost drivers and allocation bases. Each indirect cost item is a bit different and requires a slightly different concept to support an allocation basis. In fact, many public organizations do not allocate indirect costs precisely because they cannot agree on allocation bases that make sense across an entire organization. That said, many of the most common indirect costs can be allocated using simple metrics that can be computed with existing administrative data. Here's a few examples:

Cost Item	Potential Cost Driver/Allocation Basis
Accounting	Number of transactions processed
Auditing	Direct audit hours
Data Processing	System usage
Depreciation	Hours that equipment is used
Insurance	Dollar value of insurance premiums
Legal services	Direct hours/Billable hours
Mail	Number of documents handled
Motor Pool	Miles driven and/or days used
Office machines	Square feet of office space occupied
Management	Number of employees; total payroll
Procurement	Number of transactions processed

These figures also assume the government allocates the office manager's time to individual cost centers. The office manager can do this if he or she tracks the amount of time they spend on work related to each cost center. Some public organizations have such systems, and those systems are often based on a *billable hours* concept, similar to that used by other professionals like lawyers or accountants. Many do not.

Also note that the copier cost center does not itself receive overhead from other service centers. We don't see, for example, that the copier center receives a portion of the county administrator's salary, insurance expenses, or other organization-wide indirect costs. This is a policy choice. Some public organizations do not require service centers to receive overhead costs, mostly to keep down the rates they must charge their internal clients. Many state and local governments have budgeting rules that state programs that are *independently financed,* or paid for with specific fees or charges rather than general fund resources, do not need to allocate their indirect costs or receive an indirect cost allocation.

That said, many public organizations do allocate overhead to internal cost centers. In fact, when they do they typically use the *step-down method* of allocating indirect costs. That is, they allocate organization-wide indirect costs to all cost centers first, then allocate service center costs, including their portion of the organization-wide indirect costs, to the mission centers. With those assumptions in place, recall that:

- Food Protection mission center averages 500 copies each day. Assuming 260 work days/year, that's (500 copies X 260 days) or 130,000 copies. In this case 130,000 copies is the *relevant range*, or the amount of activity upon which our cost analysis is based. If we assumed the Food Protection mission center would require twice as many copies, our per unit costs and cost allocations would look quite different. Good cost analysis follows from clear, defensible assumptions about the relevant range of activity that will drive costs.

- Animals and Pests mission center makes 250 copies each day, but makes many more in the event of a communicable disease outbreak. Assuming no outbreak, that's (250 copies X 260 days) or 65,000 copies.

- Wastewater division makes 100 copies/day, but up to 1,000 copies/day around six times per year when processing complex permits. Let's assume a typical surge in copies for a complex permit will last for five days. That would mean 240 typical days and 30 "surge days" (i.e. six permits X 5 days/permit). So total copies for typical days are (100 copies X 230 days = 23,000 copies) and surge days are (1,000 copies X 30 days = 30,000 copies), for an annual total of 53,000 copies.

From these figures we can determine the copier will make (130,000 copies + 65,000 copies + 53,000 copies) or 248,000 copies each year. If we divide the full annual cost of the copier by the number of copiers ($21,380/248,000 copies) we arrive at *unit cost* for 248,000 copies of $.086/copy (i.e. 8.6 cents per copy).

With those full costs established, we must then ask how should the Environmental Health department allocate the full costs of the copier cost center across the three mission center departments? Fortunately, this is easy to do because the copier cost center has a clear cost object (cost per copy) and each department/cost center measures the number of copies it makes. As a result, each department would be assigned copier center indirect costs at a rate of 8.6 cents/copy. Food protection would be assigned (130,000 copies X $.086/copy) = $11,180. Animals and Pests would be assigned (65,000 copies X .086/copy) = $5,590. And Wastewater would be assigned (53,000 copies X $.086/copy) = $4,558. With the right allocation basis it's possible to allocate any indirect costs in a similar way.

This copier example also shows why the cost center and cost object are so important. For instance, imagine that the copier was defined not as one cost center but as separate cost centers for large copying jobs (say, more than 500 copies) and small copying jobs, or for color copies vs. black and white copies. This would also require different cost objects, such as the "cost per black and white copy" or cost per color copy." The cost per black and white copy would presumably be less than the cost per color copy, and the cost per copy for large print jobs would presumably be less than the cost per copy for small jobs. Different cost centers, cost objects, and allocation methods can mean substantially different answers to the question "what does copying cost?"

One potential drawback of the step-down method is that it allows "double counting" or *"cross-allocation"* of service center costs to service centers that are already allocated to mission centers. For example, recall that the annual full cost of the copier service center was $21,380. That full cost incorporated the indirect costs of the office manager's time to manage the copier. Under the step-down method, the cost of the office manager's time is allocated to the copier cost center, and the copier cost center costs are then allocated across the mission centers. But what happens if the office manager makes copies? Under this indirect cost allocation scheme the office manager's copies would not be reflected in the total volume of copies made, and the office manager would not receive any of the copy center's costs. As a result, the mission centers subsidize the office manager's copying by absorbing a larger share of the copy center's costs.

In this particular example those subsidies are probably a negligible amount. But in many other scenarios cross-allocation of service center costs can have a major impact on the full cost of a good or service. For instance, imagine a non-profit organization with three mission centers, a service center for the executive director, and a human resources service center. The human resources service center spends most of its time interacting with the executive director, as is often the case in small non-profits. If this organization uses the typical step-down approach, and it first allocates the executive director's costs to the other service centers, then the full costs of the three mission centers will include a sizable subsidy for the costs of the executive director-human resource center's interactions.

To address this problem many public organizations instead use the *double-step-down method*. After each service center/department's costs have been allocated once, each center/department's cost not included in the original allocation are totaled and allocated again. To illustrate, let's return to the copy center-office manager example above. If this allocation were done with the double-step-down method the office manager's copies would be included in the total copy figure. The copy center's would first allocate its costs, excluding the office manager's copies, to the mission centers. Then in a second step, the office manager's share of the copying costs would be allocated to the mission centers in a separate allocation. This double-step method minimizes cross-allocation of service center costs.[1]

The Gap in Cost Accounting Standards

Keep in mind that there are no national or international standards for how public organizations measure and define their cost structures, also known as their cost accounting practices. Governments employ a variety of state and local-specific cost accounting methods. Non-profits tend to follow the cost accounting conventions prescribed by federal and state grants or major foundations, but those conventions do not equate to national standards. By contrast, financial accounting – or accounting designed to report financial results to outside stakeholders – is dictated by GAAP. That's why it's possible to compare a government's financial statements to that of another government, and a non-profit's financial statements to that of another non-profit, but not necessarily possible to compare different organizations' budgets or internal cost accounting systems.

INDIRECT COST ALLOCATION: INDIRECT COST RATES

Cost drivers and allocation bases work well when the service in question has a clear cost objective and a measurable unit of service. Most public organizations, as described above, don't have this luxury. Many don't deliver a service with a measurable outcome. Most public organizations' costs are related to personnel, and personnel costs are not distributed evenly across clients or cases. Moreover,

---

1. For more on cost allocation methods for governments see several chapters in Zach Mohr, ed. (2016), *Cost Accounting in Government: Theory and Applications* (New York: Routeledge); also see the chapter "Cost Accounting and Indirect Costs" in Dittenhoffer and Stepnick, eds. (2007), *Applying Government Accounting Principles* (Lexis-Nexus Publishing).

a growing number of public services today are delivered through partnerships and collaborations where it's often not clear how costs are incurred, and murkier yet how those costs ought to be allocated across the partner organizations. For these and many other reasons, traditional cost allocation methods often don't work in the public sector. And yet, it's still critically important to measure and properly account for full costs, including and especially indirect costs that can be difficult to measure.

To address these problems many public organizations rely on indirect cost rates. An *indirect cost rate* is a ratio of indirect costs to direct costs. For instance, a city police department might determine that its indirect cost rate is 15%. That means that for every dollar of direct costs like police officer salaries and squad cars, it will incur 15 cents of payroll processing, insurance, procurement expenses, and other indirect costs.

Taking Stock of Costs

Public organizations rarely have the kinds of sophisticated cost tracking and measurement systems that you might find at Boeing or other manufacturers, logistics companies like FedEx, or retail entities like Amazon. So how do budgeting and finance staff begin to understand what a public organization's services cost? There are three basic methods.

- "Time in Motion." Public organizations will occasionally send analysts to see where and how employees spend their time. For instance, a city planning department might allow analysts into their office to watch how much time staff spend on different types of permits, appeals, and other activities. After observing the department's activities for a sample of days over a period of weeks or months, cost analysts can estimate how much time staff spend on each of their different activities, and can then build out cost estimates.

- Self-reported Allocations. Some organizations ask staff to keep track of their own time, much like the billable hours method used by attorneys, accountants, and other professionals. Some of these tracking schemes are quite detailed, requiring time reported in 15 minute intervals. Others are much more general and allow for estimates on much larger intervals like days or weeks.

- Statistical Analysis. Cost accountants occasionally use regression analysis and other statistical tools to estimate the relationship between costs and services delivered. One of the most common is to determine the linear trend, if any, between total expenses and volume of service delivered over time. Variation around that trend (i.e. the residuals from the regression analysis) suggest a potential pattern of variable costs.

Let's illustrate this with a more detailed example. Surveys show that many local public health departments would like to offer more services related to hypertension outreach and management. Chronic health conditions like heart disease and diabetes are known to be related to high blood pressure, so better management of high blood pressure can affect public health in a substantial, positive way. But many citizens, especially those without health insurance, do not have access to regular blood pressure screening and other services needed to identify and manage hypertension.

Say, for example that Cheng County and Duncombe County would like to launch a new, shared hypertension prevention and management (HPM) program. Neither currently has a formal program in this area, but both offer some of the services through a patchwork of partnerships with local non-profits. Cheng County has roughly twice the population of Duncombe County, and Duncombe County's per capita income and property values are 30-40% higher than Cheng's.

What does it cost to deliver this service? As with most public health programs the main costs will be related to personnel, namely public health nurses, outreach counselors, and nutritionists. The program will also require space and other overhead costs. The outreach and education components will require advertising, travel, and other costs. For a service sharing arrangement to work, the two Counties must decide how to share these costs.

Suppose also the counties agree in advance to share the full costs evenly. This approach is simple and straightforward. However, it ignores many of the program's underlying cost drivers. Cheng has a much larger population than Duncombe, so more of the participants will probably come from County A. Simply splitting these costs "50-50" means Duncombe will likely subsidize Cheng, an arrangement Duncombe's leaders might find unacceptable.

So what's the alternative? Cheng could bill Duncombe for each Duncombe resident who participates in the program. They could use an allocation basis like population or assessed property values. A more cutting-edge scheme might be to share the costs according to the incidence of the chronic diseases the HPM program is designed to prevent. Each of these strategies demands a trade-off. Some are simpler, but at the expense of fairness. Some require cost measurement that might be expensive or infeasible. Others are more feasible, but might place costs disproportionately on the population the program is designed to serve.

To begin, let's assume Cheng will structure the new HPM as a cost center within the Health Behaviors division of its Public Health department. Let's also assume also that since HPM's main "deliverable" will be blood pressure screening, it will define its unit cost as the cost per blood pressure screening performed.

Given those assumptions, Cheng County's budget analysts estimate that for the first year of operations, the HPM program will serve 400 clients, and its cost will include:

- Direct Labor. This includes seven full-time and one half-time licensed nurse practitioners who can administer blood pressure screening. Annual salaries for these nurses is $67,108. The program will also employ a health counselor who will guide clients on how to manage hypertension through healthier eating and fitness. The counselor's annual salary is $73,815.

- Direct Non-Labor. Nurses and the counselor will need to travel to visit clients and deliver outreach programs. Staff estimate total travel of 20,120 miles of travel at $.325/mile. The HPM program will also require medical supplies, office supplies, and a few capital items. Budget staff estimate $6,142 of annual direct non-labor costs for each nurse, and $7,566 of direct non-labor costs for the counselor. This difference is due to a heavier expected travel schedule for the counselor. The program will also execute an annual contract, valued at $14,939, with a communications consultant who will develop and deliver a healthy eating outreach marketing effort in both counties. Even though most of these costs are related to labor, here they're considered non-labor "contractual" costs.

- Indirect Labor. Cheng County's Health Behaviors Manager will supervise the HPM staff, and Cheng County's Executive will provide policy direction and other leadership. A portion of both administrators' salaries are allocated to HPM as indirect labor costs. HPM staff will also incur indirect labor costs like payroll support, accounting and auditing services, and procurement support. Budget staff estimate $10,456 of annual indirect labor costs for each nurse, and $8,519 of direct non-labor costs for the counselor.

- Indirect Non-Labor. HPM staff must also have access to office space, liability insurance, association memberships, and other indirect non-labor costs. Budget staff estimates annual indirect non-labor costs of $4,799 for each nurse and counselor.

With that information and a few additional assumptions, we can begin to detail HPM's cost structure and compute some indirect costs rates. See the table below.

Is it Allowable?

One of the key questions when computing indirect cost rates is which indirect costs are *allowable* or *reasonable*? For example, in some cases it's unclear whether staff who contribute marginally to a program's operations – such as development directors, general outreach coordinators, and others – should be included as an indirect cost. Certain types of training might be helpful, but not essential for staff to understand their jobs and deliver the service. And of course, there's always reason to define indirect costs as broadly as possible, especially if you can recover those costs through some external funding source.

There are no national standards, per se, for what constitutes a relevant indirect cost. Each project, program, and funder is a bit different. That said, the federal government has guidelines on what types of indirect costs it will reimburse. Many states and local governments also use these standards or some adaptation of these standards for their internal cost accounting. You can find more information on those guidelines at OMB Circular a-87: Cost Principles for State, Local, and Indian Tribal Governments. This publication is available at http://www.whitehouse.gov/omb/circulars_a087_2004.

The first section of this table lists HPM's direct, "observable" costs. We know the program will employ nurses and counselors, and we know it will demand mileage and the communications contract as direct, non-labor costs. These "observable" direct costs total $598,603, or $1,496/client given the estimated 400 clients.

But the much more important question is how do we account for the indirect costs, and for the direct costs that are more difficult to observe? The lower part of this table outlines those costs. When we include the indirect labor and indirect non-labor costs we see the full cost of the program increase to $758,487, or $1,896/client. Or, put differently, the full cost of the program increases by more than

Total Annual Cost of Cheng-Duncombe County Hypertension Prevention and Management (HPM) Program

Direct, "Observed" Costs

	"Units"	Cost/Unit	Total
Nurses Salaries	7.5	$67,108	$503,310
Counselor Salaries	1	$73,815	$73,815
Mileage	20,120	.325	$6,539
Outreach			$14,939
Total Direct, Observed HPM Program Costs			$598,603

Full Cost, by Main Direct Labor Inputs

Nurses		Annual Cost	Percent of Total Input Costs
Direct Labor		$67,108	76%
Direct Non-labor		$6,142	7%
Indirect Labor		$10,456	12%
Indirect Non-labor		$4,799	5%
Total Cost Per Nurse		$88,505	100%
Full Cost of Nurses	7.5 X $88,505		$663,788

Counselor		Annual Cost	Percent of Total Input Costs
Direct Labor		$73,815	78%
Direct Non-labor		$7,566	8%
Indirect Labor		$8,519	9%
Indirect Non-labor		$4,799	5%
Total Cost Per Counselor		$94,699	100%
Full Cost of Counselors	$94,699 X 1		$94,699
Full Cost of HPM Program			$758,487

26% if we include all the indirect costs in our estimate of the full costs. Recall that Cheng County plans to bill Duncombe County for Duncombe's share of the program costs. If Cheng bills only for the direct costs, it "undercharges" Duncombe by nearly 26%. That's why it's critically important to measure full costs, especially when pricing services or requesting reimbursements for expenses incurred.

What about potential indirect cost rates? According to these figures, 76% of the full cost to employ a nurse is direct labor costs and 7% is direct non-labor costs. It follows that the remaining 17% is indirect costs related in a predictable way to those direct costs. Each nurse and the counselor will be insured, will have their payroll processed by the payroll office, will occupy space in an office within a County building, and so on. If those figures are predictable, we can assume the current indirect cost rate for nurses is 17%. For counselors the direct costs are a bit higher at 86%, for an indirect cost rate of 14%. In practice, this means that in future budgets the HPM program could simply assume that for every dollar it will spend on nurses salaries, it can expect to incur 17 cents of indirect costs, and for every dollar its will spend on counselor's salaries it can expect to incur 14 cents of indirect costs. Some organizations compute indirect cost rates based only on direct labor costs.

In that case the rate for nurses would be the indirect costs divided by just the direct labor costs, or (($10,456+$4,799)/$67,108, or just under 23%.

We can also think about an indirect cost rate for the entire HPM program. For that we simply compare the total indirect costs to the total direct costs. Total indirect costs for the nurses are (($10,456 + $4,799) X 7.5) = $114,413 and for the counselors are (($8,519 + $4,799) X 1) = $13,318, for total indirect costs of $127,731. Total direct costs for the nurses are (($67,108 + $6,142) X 7.5) = $549,375 and for the counselor are (($73,815 + $7,566) X 1) = $81,318, for total direct costs of $630,756. So the overall indirect cost rate is $127,731/$630,756, or 20%. Again, all these figures assume the HPM program serves 400 clients.

Information about indirect cost rates is relevant to many types of decisions. For instance:

- HPM staff might compare their indirect cost rate to the rates of other programs within Cheng County government. If its rates are noticeably higher or lower, it might more carefully review its cost structure and how it manages its costs. If its rates seem grossly out of line with other units it might request an additional review by Cheng County's budget staff.

- The counties might use these rates when applying for federal or state grants, or for support from philanthropic foundations, to support the HPM program.

- The counties might eventually decide to contract out some or all of HPM's operations to a non-profit health care provider. In that case these rates would be a focal point for negotiating the per client rate at which the counties would reimburse a prospective contractor.

- Other governments might review these rates as an initial indicator of whether they can afford their own HPM program.

Easy as ABC?

Some governments, and many private sector organizations, try to address this problem through *activity-based costing* (ABC). ABC identifies the full cost of different activities within organizations that drive costs, regardless of the original cost center to which those costs were assigned. It then allocates those full costs according to changes in those underlying cost drivers.

In the HPM example, for instance, if Cheng County followed an ABC model the information services staff might have identified the unit costs of different types of information services requests. More complex activities, like the information-gathering about Duncombe County residents, would incur costs at a different rate than simpler activities. To the earlier point, this sort of small discrepancy could easily dissuade Cheng from continuing to participate in this sharing arrangement. A better alternative might have been to measure the number of hours or percentage of total time on this project attributable to gathering information specifically on Duncombe residents. And yet, the additional time and effort to gather that information might far outweigh the benefit of more precise cost allocation. This is a small scale example but it illustrates that every cost allocation basis comes with trade-offs that all the parties involved must understand and agree to up front.

Traditional cost allocation works best when it's possible to observe where and when and where all the costs are incurred. When that information is not available, as is often the case for partnership arrangements that span multiple organizations, there are several alternative other ways to organize a cost allocation plan. To illustrate, assume the full annual cost of HPM was $800,000, and that Cheng County must bill Duncombe County for Duncombe County's share of those costs.

- *Equal share.* Total costs are divided equally across all participating partners. This is more typical for informal and arrangements. It's also common for preventative services and other activities where it's not clear who "receives" or "uses" the service, or to observe all the relevant indirect costs in a predictable and consistent way. That said, in equal share approaches one partner often subsidizes the other, sometimes unknowingly. In the HPM example, Cheng would keep $400,000 of the costs and bill Duncombe its equal share of $400,000.

- *Per capita.* Total costs are divided by the proportion of the population that resides in each partner jurisdiction. This approach is good for services without an observable "client" or discrete individual services. It's less useful when population size is not the best cost driver, or when the populations involved are different on some key characteristic that might affect utilization of the service in question. Per capita sharing is often the most transparent way to share costs. In the HPM case, recall that Cheng's population is 240,000 and Duncombe's population is 160,000. In other words, 60% of the population served resides in Cheng and 40% resides in Duncombe. Under a per capita model, Cheng would bill Duncombe $320,000.

- *Cost Plus Fixed Fee.* Personnel costs are often step-fixed cost, and it can be quite challenging to know when those costs will "step up" a higher levels of service delivery. To account for that uncertainty, some cost allocation strategies call for non-weighted cost sharing plus some fixed periodic fee. The fee part of the plan is designed to buffer the sharing arrangement against the uncertainty that surrounds step-fixed costs (more on this below). For HPM, one potential application of this method would be for the counties to share costs per capita, but for Cheng to receive an annual payment of $35,000 at the start of its fiscal year to compensate in advance should it need to hire an additional nurse during the year. The cost plus fixed fee model also can be used in an arrangement where the overhead for having the service – space, utilities, administration, accounting, etc. – would be shared one way, such as equally, and incremental costs, such as those for lab work or medical supplies, are charged based on volume.

- *Ability to Pay.* Some cost allocation arrangements are designed to make a service available where citizens and clients are otherwise not able to pay for it. In these cases it makes sense to allocate costs according to ability to pay. We can measure ability to pay through assessed property values, median household income, or some other measure of relative wealth. In the HPM example, consider the following scenario: Duncombe's median household income is $50,000 and Cheng's is $40,000. Duncombe has a smaller population but is wealthier. In this case, the ratio of Duncombe's median household income to Cheng's is 1.25 ($50,000/$40,000). This is commonly known as a *wealth factor.* Recall that an equal share allocation is $400,000 for each jurisdiction. If that equal share is adjusted by the wealth factor, then Duncombe's share is $400,000 X 1.25, or $500,000, and Cheng's is $300,000.

- *Prevalence.* In this method, the parties share costs according to the prevalence of the public health problem the service is designed to address. In the HPM example, the partners could share the total program costs according to observed instances of diabetes or heart disease. The logic here is simple: diabetes and heart disease tell us something about the expected number of people with hypertension. If the prevalence of the disease is not known, the partners can use a proxy, like socioeconomic status, to project the anticipated need for services in each population. In the HPM example, Duncombe's higher overall wealth suggests its residents are at lower risk for hypertension compared to Cheng residents. Sharing by prevalence adds substantial complexity because cost sharing is now based on data from a series of measurements not directly related to costs. In this case, those measurements are the incidence of disease or an indicator of socioeconomic status, which can be difficult to measure reliably, and other health related behaviors like smoking or medication adherence. That said, this approach is especially good where population, property values, income, and other measures vary too much among sharing jurisdictions to offer meaningful comparisons. To apply it in his example, assume that Cheng will have an estimated 12,740 cases of type 2 diabetes during the coming year, and Duncombe County will have an estimated 5,460 cases. This strategy considers each county's share of the total incidence across both counties. According to that logic, 70 percent of the total cases will be found in Cheng, and 30 percent in Duncombe. Allocating costs this way leads to a share of $560,000 for Cheng and $240,000 for Duncombe. Some versions of prevalence also incorporate a moving average so that one community does not incur huge costs in a single year, and costs are instead recovered over time.

- *Weighted formula.* This plan addresses some of the big problems with the per capita sharing approach. For example, in a weighted formula approach, the participants might agree to share total costs according to a combination of population, median household income, usage, and other factors. By incorporating these other factors, the cost apportionment method will better reflect differences in fixed costs in urban vs. rural areas, differences in travel distances within each county, and other factors that affect service delivery costs. For HPM, assume that Cheng and Duncombe decide to share HPM costs according to a three-factor formula that incorporates population, ability to pay, and prevalence of type 2 diabetes. This formula reflects both counties' shared understanding of the cost structure and cost drivers of the HPM program. The counties, realizing the difference in the prevalence of type 2 diabetes, agree to more heavily weight that difference in prevalence in the cost sharing formula. They agree to a three-factor formula where population accounts for 25 percent, prevalence is 50 percent, and ability to pay is 25 percent of the total costs allocated to each county. Recall that Cheng accounts for 60 percent of the population served by HPM, and Duncombe accounts for 40 percent. At the same time, Cheng accounts for 70 percent of the prevalence factor and Duncombe for 30 percent. We would apply that formula as:

  ○ Cheng County: $800,000 X ((.6 X .25) + (.7 X .5) + (.44 X .25)) = $488,000;

  ○ Duncombe County: $800,000 − $488,000 = $312,000

DIFFERENTIAL COST ACCOUNTING

In the previous section we explained how to measure the full cost of a public service. Those techniques assume we're measuring the cost of the service for a given level or volume of the service. Until now, for instance, we've assumed our hypothetical HPM program will serve 400 clients a year. But sometimes the more interesting question is: How do a program's costs change if we deliver more or less of it? For instance, how does HPM's cost per client change if we expanded it to 500 clients? Or restricted it to 300 clients? These questions sound simple, but they require careful attention to a different set of concepts. When we want to know how costs change in space and time, we turn to *differential cost accounting*. Differential cost accounting is, simply put, comparing how full costs change at different levels of output.

COST BEHAVIOR

We know that what a service costs depends in large part on how much of it we deliver. This is broadly known as *cost behavior*. Every type of cost falls into one of three different cost behavior categories:

- *Fixed costs* do not change in response to the amount of service provided. In the HPM case the main fixed cost is the nurses' salaries. They are paid the same regardless of the number of blood pressure screenings or other outputs they "produce." Same for the counselor. They are paid the same salary regardless of the number of counseling sessions performed. Cheng County owns some of its own blood pressure screening equipment, so the costs of acquiring equipment costs won't change even if the HPM program delivers a lot more blood pressure screenings. And so forth.

- *Variable costs* change directly in response to the amount of service provided. For the HPM program this might include copies and other office supplies needed to process physician referrals, or mileage required to travel to outreach sessions, among others.

- *Step-Fixed* or *Mixed Costs* have both a fixed and a variable component. In most cases a step-fixed cost is fixed over some range of output and then increases or "steps up" at some higher level of service volume. For example, if the HPM program grows substantially it might need to add additional nurses and counselors. If that happens the nurses' and health counselor's direct labor costs could be step-fixed costs. For instance, if the program grows enough to require an additional counselor, these salary and benefit costs will "step up" at a given level of program enrollment.

Fixed Costs Defined Differently
"Fixed Cost" can mean different things in different settings. For our purposes, it means a cost that does not change in response to the volume of service delivered. By contrast, cost accountants sometimes use fixed cost to describe a cost that does not change during a given time period. This is an important difference.

The figure below illustrates the these cost behavior concepts for a generic, hypothetical service. The horizontal axis is the quantity of service provided, and the vertical axis is total cost. The line at $50, represents a fixed cost. It does not change, regardless of the level of service provided. The triangle-marked line identifies a variable cost. Here we see each additional unit of service increases the total cost by $10, and that change is constant from 0 to 3 units of service. The line marked with squares shows a step-fixed cost. Here the cost is fixed at $20 from 0 to 30 units of service. Once we reach 4 units of service that total cost steps up to $40, where it stays fixed until seven units of service.

It's useful to think about a program or service with reference to these main cost behaviors. In fact, we can place most programs/services/organization units into one of six cost behavior categories. Those

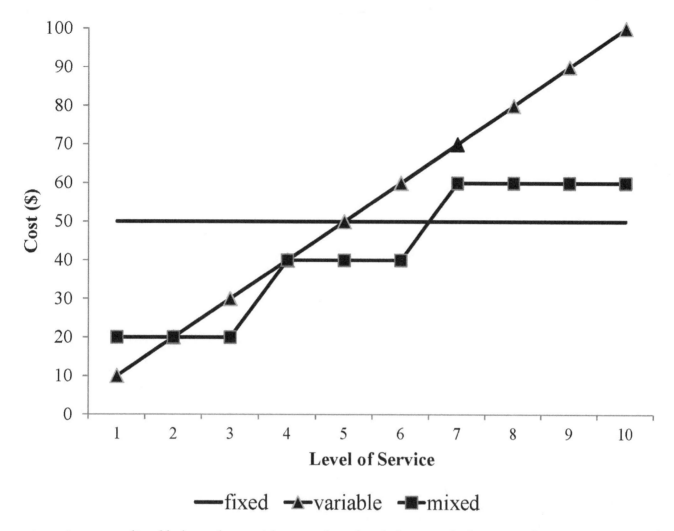

—fixed ▲variable ■mixed

categories are outlined below, along with examples of each from typical non-profit organizations and government programs.

It's immensely helpful to think about cost behavior when we have to make decisions about how to design and fund programs. Consider this simple example based on the previously-mentioned HPM program.

HPM staff have some rough budget projections for FY2017. Their program is expected to incur fixed costs of $800,000 and variable costs of $400 per client. The program has expanded a lot since it launched, and it now expects to serve 550 clients, but could serve up to 600 with current staffing levels. Meanwhile, nearby Matkin County has offered to pay $750/client to expand the program to include an additional 50 Matkin County residents. Should Cheng and Duncombe counties agree to partner with Matkin County on these terms?

HPM's cost behavior is outlined in the table below. Given its projected fixed and variable costs, at 550 clients the average per client cost is $1,855. If HPM scales up to serve 600 clients, its average cost will decrease to $1,734/client. However, that average cost of $1,734 is still much higher than the $750/ client that Matkin county offering. On the basis of "average" unit costs, this proposal is a definite "no go" for Cheng and Duncombe.

Cost Structures with Illustrations

	Direct	Indirect
Fixed	Typical cost items: Salaried program staff; Program-specific facilities Programs with this cost structure tend to: • Have mostly salaried staff that work across a few programs • Have low or no overhead Example program: Drop-in center for homeless youth	Typical cost items: payroll services, facilities maintenance Programs with this cost structure tend to: • Have mostly salaried staff that serve multiple programs/units • Allocate their costs to other units on a "billable hours" or similar allocation basis Example program: Development/fundraising staff at a large non-profit
Variable	Typical cost items: Program-specific inventory, equipment, or goods used by specific program participants Programs with this cost structure tend to: • Focus on "inventory management" • Focus on "surge capacity" Example programs: Food banks, county prosecutor home detention programs (i.e. "ankle monitors")	Typical cost items: inventory, equipment, commodities Programs with this cost structure tend to: • Allocate their costs to other units by outputs • Focus on inventory management Example program: Procurement staff within a non-profit hospital
Step-Fixed	Typical cost items: Hourly program staff, shared facilities or equipment Programs with this cost structure tend to: • Focus on participant-to-staff ratios • Focus on enrollment caps, waitlists, other enrollment management strategies Example program: Non-profit after school daycare program	Typical cost items: liability insurance, shared facilities Programs with this cost structure tend to: • Allocate their costs to other units according to "jobs" or "engagements" • Market their services outside their home organization Example program: Employee assistance program at a non-profit hospital

HPM Program Cost Calculations

# of Clients	Fixed Costs	Variable Costs	Total Costs	Average Cost/Client
500	$800,000	$200,000	$1,000,000	$2,000
550	$800,000	$220,000	$1,020,000	$1,855
600	$800,000	$240,000	$1,040,000	$1,734

However, keep in mind the relationship between fixed and variable costs. Recall that HPM staff have said they can add 50 more clients without taking on additional fixed costs. If that's true then the new cost to add a client is only the additional variable cost. Put differently, the average cost of each client is $1,734, but the *marginal cost*, or the cost of a new client, is $400. If HPM is reimbursed $750/client, the additional "profit" is $350. If HPM makes this decision "at the margin," or with reference only to the marginal cost, it should take the deal with Matkin County. This is a good example of a service with a positive *economies of scale*; the marginal cost of each unit of service decreases as the volume of service delivered increases.

Of course, there are trade-offs here. At 600 clients the HPM program will operate at full capacity. HPM staff will almost certainly have to spend less time with clients. This could lead to a decline in the service quality, and could even increase staff burnout and turnover. But if we look just at the marginal cost, it makes sense for Matkin County to join the program.

This example also illustrates the key concept of *sunk costs*. Many fixed costs are for capital items like equipment, land, and buildings that can be bought and sold. A public health department can, in concept at least, recover some of those costs by selling those capital items. However, HPM's spending on employee salaries, training, insurance, and many other costs cannot be recovered. Those costs are sunk.

Some economists argue that sunk costs ought to be irrelevant to future decisions. In other words, at the margin, all that matters is the future, measurable, variable costs. Of course, this is difficult in practice. In the HPM case, scaling up to full capacity will mean additional stress on staff, and perhaps more important, it would mean giving up the opportunity to take on additional clients without taking on additional fixed costs. These costs are much harder to measure, but they are key components of decisions about cost sharing. The key takeaway here is that when considering a service sharing arrangement, be sure to consider both the marginal costs, and the opportunity costs.

COST-VOLUME-PROFIT ANALYSIS

So far we've reviewed how public managers can identify the full cost of their services, and how that full cost changes as they deliver more or less of a service. Those are crucial questions that all good managers can answer.

However, public managers must often confront a different question: What should we charge for this service? They're also routinely asked a corollary question: What volume of service should we deliver, given that service's cost structure?

To answer these questions we turn to a particular set of concepts within differential cost accounting, known as *cost-volume-profit* analysis (CVP). CVP is how an organization determines the volume of activity needed to achieve its profit or mission goal, the price it needs to charge to achieve its profit or mission goal, or the cost limits that it must manage within to achieve its profit or mission goal.

CVP analysis is usually done for a particular program or service within an organization. The basic equation is:

$$\text{Profit} = \text{Total revenue} - \text{Total costs}$$

From this discussion so far we also know that total costs = Fixed costs + Variable costs. And since fixed costs are fixed, we can represent the cost equation as:

$$TC = a + bx$$

Where TC = total costs, a = fixed costs, and b = variable costs. We also know that total revenue is simply the price of a service (p) times the volume of service delivered (v). That said, we can show the *fundamental profit equation* as:

$$\text{Profit} = px - (a + bx)$$

For any service, the *break-even volume* is the point at which total revenue (px) equals total costs (a + bx). To illustrate how we use this formula, let's go back to the Environmental Health Department's copier. Assume for the moment that the county government's leadership wants to make copying more affordable, so it caps the price of copying at 7 cents per copy. At that price, how many copies must the copier center deliver each year to break-even. In other words, what's its annual break-even volume?

We know that the copier cost center's fixed costs (a) include $6,000 for the machine rental, $900 for machine maintenance and $1,500 for its space allocation. Let's also assume electricity and the office manager's time allocation are fixed costs of $180 and $100, respectively. So total annual fixed costs are ($6,000 + $900 + $1,500 + $180 + $100) or $8,680.

Variable costs (b) are the largest cost items. Recall that last year the copier made 248,000 copies. Total paper costs were $10,000, so the per copy cost for paper is ($10,000/248,000), or $.04/copy. Total printing cartridge costs were $2,700, so the per copy cost for printing cartridges was ($2,700/248,000), or $.011/copy. These two variable costs together give us total variable costs of $.051/copy.

At break-even, profit = 0, so we can re-arrange the fundamental profit equation to px = a + bx. Since the price per copy is capped, per management's policy, at $.07, we can then express this equation as .07x = $8,680 + .051x. To solve, we first subtract .051x from both sides, so we're left with .019x = $8,680. To solve for x we divide both sides by .019, and we're left with x = 456,842. In other words, at 7 cents per copy, the copier cost center's *break-even quantity* is 456,842 copies. That's nearly twice as many copies as it produced in FY2015. Management might want to rethink this decision.

Note that we can also express break-even quantity as a/(p-b). Arranged this way, the previous quantity is $8,680/($.07 − $.051), or $8,680/$.019 = 456,842. The quantity (p-b) is the *contribution margin*, or how much price exceeds variable costs. Break-even quantity is, in some ways, finding how many units of volume we need to spread the contribution margin across to arrive at break-even.

Let's ask a different question. Assume for the moment that the copier technician says the current copier is aging and will likely break down if asked to make more than 150,000 copies per year. At that volume, how should the copier cost center adjust its prices so it continues to break even?

Here we re-arrange the formula once again, this time as p = (a/x) + b. In other words, the break-even price is the fixed costs divided by the volume, plus the variable cost per unit. For the copier cost center this is ($8,680/150,000) + $.051, or (.0579 + .051) = .1089. Put differently, if capped at 150,000 copies, the copier cost center would need to charge 10.89 cents per copy to break even. Once again, management should take a careful look before implementing this policy.

The copier cost center is a useful illustration, but it's also an outlier because most of its costs are variable costs. This is typical in for-profit manufacturing, logistics, and other industries, but atypical among public organizations. For a more common public organization example let's return to the HPM program.

Recall from earlier that HPM has estimated fixed costs (a) of $800,000 and variable costs (b) of $400/client. Say HPM's management wants to keep the program relatively small to ensure a quality service, so it decides to limit its enrollment to 400 clients. At that volume (x), its break-even price is ($800,000/400) + $400, or $2,400/client. If management is willing to expand enrollment to 500 clients, the break even price becomes ($800,000/500) + $400, or $2,000/client.

In another CVP scenario, management reports that governments and philanthropies will pay a maximum of $1,800/client to participate in the HPM program. At that price, what is HPM's break-even quantity? Once again, the formula is a/(p-b), or $800,000/($1,800-$400), or 571 clients. To break even at that comparatively low price and contribution margin ($1,800-$400, or $1,400) the program will need to serve substantially more clients than it has served recently.

The table below summarizes these various cost-volume-profit calculations.

Calculation	Formula	Question the Calculation Answers
Break-Even Price	(a/x) + b	At a given level of service, at what price per unit does total revenue equal total costs?
Break-Even Quantity	a/(p-b)	How many units do we need to sell at a given price to ensure that revenue equals total costs?
Contribution Margin	p-b	By how much does price exceed variable costs?

Note: For all formulas p = price, x = quantity, a = fixed costs, b = variable costs

CVP is a powerful tool that can directly illuminate many important management decisions. Most CVP today is done in spreadsheets to allow for maximum flexibility when exploring alternative cost scenarios, especially when analyzing services with step-fixed costs. That said, it's still important to understand the basic concepts.

COST ANALYSIS AND FLEXIBLE BUDGETING

Once we've identified a program or service's cost structure, we can take our first steps toward preparing its budget. A *budget* is simply a plan for what an organization wants to accomplish, and the resources it will use to accomplish it. Public organizations' budgets are particularly important. For state and local governments, the budget is the law. It describes the taxes and other resources the government intends to collect, and since taxpayers must pay those taxes, it follows that the government must spend those resources in accordance with the budget. Recall from the earlier discussion that the budget is one of citizen's most important tools to hold their government accountable. That's why. Non-profits' budgets don't have the force of law, but they're also critically important. Why? Because if a non-profit deviates substantially from its budget, its funders and donors will question its ability to make good on its promises and accomplish its mission.

Budgets are made and organized many different ways (see the next chapter). But regardless of an organization's overall budget process, effective cost accounting is paramount to effective budgeting and management, particularly at the program or service level. Public managers must know what portion of the costs for which they're responsible are fixed, variable, and step-fixed. They must also understand how different cost items connect to service delivery outputs, and how their cost center is assigned indirect costs. And perhaps most important, they must understand how their program's cost structure and cost behavior will change under different performance scenarios. That's why the best budgets are flexible budgets. A *flexible budget* allows a manager to quickly and easily perform sensitivity analysis to explore how changes in key cost assumptions affect a program's unit costs, total costs, and service-delivery volume.

Flexible budgeting follows a basic four step process:

1. Identify types of output or activity. Sometimes those levels of activity correspond to cost centers. Sometimes they're related to programs or "lines of business" within cost centers. Sometimes they correspond to entire departments or divisions, especially if that department or division delivers a single good or service.
2. Collect cost and price data. For most budget-making the best source of data on costs and prices is last year's budget. Unless you're tasked with developing a budget for a new service (and some day you will!), pay careful attention to past budget trends. There are two basic types of costs reflected in most public organizations' budgets: operating costs and capital costs. Operating costs are costs incurred through the organization's regular, year-to-year activities like salaries, benefits, and training. Capital costs are related to capital assets like property, equipment, and buildings. Recall that the portion of a capital asset that's "used up" each year is reflected in the organization's depreciation expense.
3. Classify inputs. Every organization classifies its cost inputs a bit differently. For a simple budget it's appropriate to classify the spending inputs in broad *objects of expenditure* like "salaries" or "commodities," and to call the revenue inputs "service revenues," "fees," or some other appropriate broad label. Some organizations prepare budgets using the same chart of accounts used to prepare the basic financial statements. Others have much more detailed *budget item codes* to identify specific types of budget inputs. The key to a classification scheme is that it's consistent as possible. Once you make a budget with it, make every budget with it.
4. Develop a *cost rate* or *unit cost* for each key budget input. A *cost rate* is a measure, usually expressed as a unit of time, of the resources needed to staff a service. A *unit cost* is the cost to acquire or produce a unit of a good or service.

For most public organizations personnel costs are the largest and most visible budget inputs. That's why effective budgeting for public organizations starts, and often ends, with careful attention to budgeting for personnel. So let's illustrate this four step process with a personnel budgeting example.

Oz County just elected a county executive who ran on a "tough on crime" platform. On his first day in office the new executive asks his budgeting staff to figure out what it will cost to add three new sheriff patrols. From past budgets the staff can make a few assumptions:

- Patrols are for 24 hours/day, 365 days/year.

- The Sheriff's union contract species that each patrol must have 2 officers per patrol car, and that officers will work 8 hours per day, 5 days per week. All sheriffs also receive three weeks of vacation and 1 week of sick leave per year.

- Also assume that cars will be staffed with two officers.

- The average patrol officer salary is $31,472, and benefits account for an additional 30% of each officer's salary.

These figures suggest that, like with most personnel budgeting, we ought to think about a cost rate as a unit of staff time required to deliver the services. Many personnel budgeting scenarios are based on hours of staff time. In this particular scenario let's go with the number of patrol hours needed to staff a complete shift. From there, we can determine how many officers we need, and how much to budget for those officers.

Those calculations are as follows, based on the assumptions outlined above:

- Three shifts per patrol X 3 patrols per day X 2 officers per car X 365 days = 6,570 shifts per year
- 6,570 shifts per year X 8 hours = 52,560 patrol hours per year
  We then determine the number of hours or shifts one patrol officer can provide:
  - 52 weeks per year X 5 days per week = 260 potential shifts
  - 4 weeks per year X 5 days per week = 20 vacation/sick leave days per year
  - 260 days – 20 non-work days = 240 labor days X 8 hours = 1,920 hours per year
- Calculate the required number of full-time officers = 52,560 additional hours/1,920 hours per officer per year = 27.38 officers; round up to 28 officers

To budget for these new officers we can assume:

- Salary costs: 28 officers X $31,472 = $881,216
- Benefit costs: $881,216 X .3 = $264,365
- Total costs = $1,145,581

In other words, this budget analysis suggests Oz County will need to hire 28 additional officers to staff the executive's desired three new shifts, and those 28 officers will require $1,145,581 in new budgeted spending. Ideally, you'd prepare this analysis in a flexible, spreadsheet-based, budget that allows you to quickly explore new scenarios from different assumptions.

What about a scenario where most of the key input items are variable costs? Here we'd use the unit cost method. The steps for that method are as follows:

1. Project the demand for the service
2. Estimate the resources consumed per unit of output
3. Determine the average cost per unit of output
4. Multiply these three items together to determine the appropriate budgeted amounts

To illustrate, let's return to the HPM program and focus on the counselor's travel costs. Recall that the counselor travels to deliver outreach programs on healthy eating and active lifestyles, all designed to prevent hypertension among Cheng and Duncombe County residents. Let's assume that for the coming fiscal year the number of programs will be a bit lower than in previous years, but robust nonetheless:

- HPM staff project 175 outreach programs
- The average mileage per outreach program is 75 miles, and the rate per mile is $.325
- 175 programs X 75 miles per program X $.33/mile = $4,331

In this case, the unit cost" and the object of expenditure" are the same thing – individual outreach programs. And once again, we'd ideally set this analysis up as a flexible, spreadsheet-based budget.

Budget Variance

The difference between actual results and budgeted results is known as a budget variance. Effective public managers understand when, where, and why variances happen. They also use insights from variances to identify inefficiencies and other current management concerns, and how they make future budgets.

The simplest variance analysis approach is to compare budgeted expenses to its actual expenses. For example, suppose the HPM program budgeted $759,000 for FY15, but actual spending for the year was $789,000. This would be a *total variance* of ($759,000/$789,000) = .962, or 96.2%. In other words, budgeted spending was only 96.2% of actual spending. This is a *negative variance* or *unfavorable variance* of 3.8%, and it directs HPM's management toward a few important questions about HPM's operations. Did HPM serve more clients than expected? Did it spend more than expected on variable costs like mileage or supplies? Was the contract for communications and outreach properly structured? Are its indirect cost allocations fair and consistent with its actual operations? To address these questions, of course, it would help to compute variances on individual line items (known as *line item variances*). Larger organizations often compute *department variances*.

Revenue-side variances demand a different type of interpretation. Imagine, for instance, that HPM budgeted for revenues of $800,000 but collected $750,000. The variance here would be ($800,000/$750,000) = 1.0667, for a negative variance of 6.667%. Here Cheng County's HPM's management should ask a different set questions. For instance, is HPM collecting all of its revenues? Is Duncombe County slow in reimbursing Cheng County?

Positive variances beg a different set of questions. For example, say HPM's total spending was just $700,000, compared to its budgeted spending of $759,000. This variance is ($759,000/$700,000) = 1.084, for a positive variance of 8.4%. But what does positive mean here? Was management able to drive down costs and deliver the expected volume of service at lower overall costs? Or did it not deliver as much of the service as expected?

COST STRUCTURE AND MANAGEMENT STRATEGY

By now it should be clear that the principles of cost behavior, differential cost analysis, and cost sharing suggest a variety of management strategies. For instance, for organizations with mostly fixed costs one of the best approaches to manage costs and bolster profitability is to "scale up." Since fixed costs are fixed, one way to manage them is to spread them across the largest possible volume of service. However, for organizations with mostly variable costs, scaling up will simply increase variable costs. The better approach in that circumstance is to invest in new technology, procurement processes, or other strategies that can drive down variable costs. With the core principles of cost analysis established, it becomes clear how a public organization's cost behavior might be most effectively managed.

It's also essential to consider how an organization's financial management strategy is contingent on the parts of its cost structure it can control. Or in other words, how much of its costs are direct and under the control of its management, and how much of its costs are indirect and assigned to it by management? For example, organizations with mostly direct costs often find themselves "scrubbing expenses" (see the previous chapter) because they have the authority and ability to affect those costs. However, organizations with mostly indirect costs are more likely to partner with other organizations as a way to leverage economies of scale, diversify their potential customer/client base, or access new technologies or processes they might not have the authority to pursue on their own.

When we consider these two main parts of an organization's cost structure – direct vs. indirect, and fixed vs. variable vs. step-fixed – we begin to see a set of attenuated management strategies. The table below lists some of those strategies.

Main Cost Behaviors	Direct	Indirect
Fixed	1. Scrub expenses 2. Scale up 3. Add value with volunteers 4. Explore shared facilities/offices/capital equipment	1. Scale up 2. Diversify the client base 3. "Re-centralize" services 4. Consider partnering/outsourcing non-core competencies
Variable	1. Scrub expenses 2. Leverage new technology to drive down unit costs 3. Encourage cash over in-kind contributions	1. Leverage new technology to drive down unit costs 2. Re-centralize or decentralize services as necessary 3. Consider group purchasing 4. Improve workflow planning and efficiency
Step-Fixed	1. Increase "staffing ratios" 2. Set enrollment caps 3. Employ waitlists/enrollment caps/staggered enrollments	1. Diversify the client base 2. Employ waitlists/enrollment caps/staggered enrollments 3. Consider narrowing or limiting the scope of services 4. Leverage technology to "move the step" on certain costs

For example, in the bottom left section we see financial management strategies commonly employed by organizations with primarily direct, step-fixed costs. For these organizations, the key is managing work flow. As their volume increases, so do their fixed costs. In turn, many organizations of this type work to spread their fixed costs within whichever step their fixed costs currently stand. That means maximizing staff to client ratios at all times, including queuing up clients with waiting lists or staggered enrollments before hiring new staff. Since most of those costs are direct, organizations of this sort have the latitude to employ these strategies.

By contrast, organizations with mostly indirect costs may not have the ability to enact new enrollment management policies. They must also "manage the step," but for them the better strategy is to narrow or limit the scope of services, or to find new clients that can lead to more predictable enrollment patterns. In short, managing direct, step-fixed costs is quite different from managing indirect, step-fixed costs.

This table is by no means a comprehensive list of strategies, but it does orient you toward the interesting and nuanced relationship between cost structure and financial management strategy.

1. Re-review the financial statements for the Safehouse from Chapter 3. Identify two examples of each of the following types of costs for Safehouse's Transitional Housing Services program:

   ◦ Direct, fixed

   ◦ Direct, variable

   ◦ Direct, step-fixed

   ◦ Indirect, fixed

   ◦ Indirect, variable

   ◦ Indirect, step-fixed

2. The fixed costs of running a fund-raising gala for the Wenatchee Symphony are $10,000 and the variable costs are $75 per attendee. The facility where the event is being held can accommodate 400 people. What is the minimum amount the Wenatchee Symphony can charge for a ticket and still break even? Assuming 400 people attend the gala, how much does the Wenatchee Symphony have to charge for each ticket for the Symphony to earn $20,000? If the Symphony received a donation of $2,000 its break-even ticket price for the gala would increase, decrease, or stay the same?

3. The Pacific Northwest Ballet has $5,000 in fixed costs per performance, plus an additional $10 per attendee on ticket and program printing and other supplies. The normal auditorium can seat 300 people, and if more than 300 attend they must use the expansion seating area for an additional cost of $500. Suppose the program sets its break-even price based on expected ticket sales of 200 attendees per performance. What is their break-even price?

4. The Feed-A-Child Foundation wants to start a new program which will have $30 in variable costs per child and fixed costs of soliciting donations to fund the program of $10,000. If each donor were to give FAC $50, and each donor feeds one child, how many donors would FAC need to break even?

5. The housing director for the City of Coho, WA is working on a new affordable housing project. The Fixed Costs are $300,000 for the project, and Variable Costs are $250 each time a family moves into an apartment at the facility. The Coho project now has 2,500 move-ins per year. A new federal government subsidy would pay $300 for each of 500 move-ins if the project expand to 3,000 units. Should Coho take the additional tenants? Why or why not?

6. The Iron River Transportation Agency (IRTA) has two service departments (maintenance and administration) and two mission departments (rapid transit and para-transit). Rapid transit uses high-speed trains and is highly equipment-intensive, while Para-Transit uses mopeds and is far more labor intensive. Management has decided to allocate maintenance costs on the basis of depreciation dollars in each department, and administration costs on the basis of labor hours worked by the employees in each department. The following data (dollar amounts in thousands) appear in the agency's records for the current period. Allocate the service center costs to production centers using the step-down method, and determine the relevant total costs. Begin with the maintenance department. To what use would you put this information?

	Service Centers		Mission Centers		
	Maintenance	Administration	Rapid Transit	Para-Transit	Total Costs
Direct plus distributed costs	$1,160	$2,400	$8,000	$4,000	$15,560
Depreciation dollars	$200	$2,000	$3,000	$800	$6,000
Labor hours	$20,000	$10,000	$10,000	$40,000	

7. Given its cost structure, identify three near-term and one long-term financial strategy Safehouse should pursue to improve its financial position. Give a brief rationale for each proposed strategy.

8. Re-review the financial statements for the Jonas Community Center from Chapter 3. Given its cost structure, identify three near-term and one long-term financial strategy JCC should pursue to improve its financial position. Give a brief rationale for each proposed strategy.

Case: Summer School

An independent summer school has been created by a local school district to provide remedial education. Summer school will serve students from the three regular high schools within the district, and will run for 3 months, from June 1 to August 31. Each high school has about 400 students (1,200 total). Each high school is expected to send 10% of their students to summer school, but of those sent, 1 out of 4 is expected to drop out of the program each month.

The state mandates that remedial summer school can have no more than a 15:1 student to teacher ratio. The school must also have one full-time administrator and 3 full-time office staff. Full-time means 8 hours per day, 20 days per month. The going wage rates are as follows: teachers make $25 per hour, administrators make $50 per hour, and each staff member makes $10 per hour. The school must provide a desk (at $200 each) for each student, teacher, administrator and staff member, and books at $100 per student. The school receives a $300 per month allowance for each student from the district, and a $5,000 one-time grant from a local philanthropic foundation.

Questions:

1. Prepare a monthly, flexible budget for the Summer School for June, July, and August. What is the estimated surplus or deficit? What is the break-even price given your assumptions about expenses?

2. Adjust your budget to account for two new assumptions: 1) You've learned that once hired, teachers cannot be let go for the summer; 2) change the drop out rate from 25% to 15%. How do these adjustments affect the estimated surplus or deficit?

The (fictional) City of Coho (population 48,000) is a commercial and residential hub in the central region of the State of Washington. It has experienced steady population growth over the past ten years and is expected to add 8,000 new residents in the next two decades.

Many of Coho's long-time residents have retired or are near retirement age. Coho's current Mayor, Nevena Bailey, sees this trend as a strategic opportunity. She believes many young, talented people will soon have to care for elderly family members and friends. Building a high-quality "aging infrastructure" will, in her view, help attract new residents to Coho.

Bailey crafts a plan for the creation of Coho Adult Day Services, Inc. (CADS). Under the adult day services (ADS) model seniors live at home but spend a portion of each day at an ADS facility with relevant services like supervised recreation, educational programming, on-site nursing staff, and preventative health care. This model allows seniors to enjoy the benefits of independence but with a lesser burden on his or her caretaker(s). A few local non-profits provide these services but not on the scale Bailey has in mind.

To get the initiative moving Bailey persuades the city commission to subsidize CADS at an annual rate of $30,000. This annual payment will come from the City's general fund. She also convinces Coho Memorial Hospital to donate a recently vacated outpatient clinic to house CADS. A construction manager who serves on the city planning commission says the facility can open immediately, but will require at least $80,000 in renovations during the first three years of operations to bring the building in compliance with regulatory codes. The renovated facility could accommodate 85 attendees, in his estimation.

The city commission also asks the City of Coho Finance Department staff to gather information needed to prepare an operating budget for CADS' first year.

Staff collects the following information about the basic legal and financial requirements for operating an adult day services center. Federal and state regulations require one licensed nurse practitioner on the premises at all times and one licensed practical nurse (LPN) for every 10 attendees. Comparable facilities also have one certified staff assistant for every 20 attendees. These assistants do custodial work, assist with group activities, and handle other day-to-day tasks. The market wage for LPNs is $31.75/hour, and the wage for staff assistants is $12.50/hour. At most facilities the nurse practitioner also handles staffing, budgeting, and other administrative duties. A typical annual salary for this practitioner/administrator position is $86,000. Most facilities also employ a recreation coordinator at an annual salary of approximately $36,500. The recreation coordinator plans in-house activities, field trips, and other programs. On average, these additional activities cost $12.50 per attendee per day (including food, materials, transportation, and other costs).

The Coho City Commission stipulates that since the City is subsidizng the service, CADS employees should be included in the City's health care and retirement plan (even though they will not be City employees). The average premium for City employees' health insurance – regardless of the type of coverage, co-pays, and other differences – is $850/month. The City contributes $680/month, or 80% of the total cost, toward each employee's premium. Employees pay the rest. The City must also contribute 6.5 percent of the wages for the practitioner/administrator, recreation coordinator, and LPN's toward pensions and other post-employment benefits (OPEB). All employees receive two weeks paid vacation and three personal days.

The facility must be certified by the National Adult Day Services Association at a cost of $5,000/year. The practitioner/administrator and LPNs must also earn 50 continuing education units (CEUs) to maintain their individual certifications, and the staff assistants must earn 20. On average, LPN CEUs cost $25/credit and staff assistant CEUs are $15/credit.

The facility must also carry $5,000,000 in hazard insurance coverage. Local insurance brokers offer that coverage for $2,500/month. Individual employees must be trained and re-certified at an annual cost of $500 per employee. Water, electricity, wastewater, stormwater, trash collection, telephone, and other utilities are expected to cost $1,750 month.

The service will open in January 2017. Expected initial enrollment is 15 seniors. Enrollment is expected to grow 3.5% – compounding monthly – each month thereafter. The service will be available Monday through Friday from 8:30am-4:30pm.

Prepare the 2017 monthly operating budget for CADS and answer the following **questions:**

1. What should CADS charge each attendee per month for the service to break even?
2. How does the break-even fee change if enrollment grows instead at 1.5% per month? At 5% per month?
3. Identify three strategies to reduce the monthly break-even fee (based on assumed monthly enrollment growth of 3.5%) by 15%. Explain the potential impacts of these strategies on the quality and effectiveness of CADS' services.
4. Many adult day service centers operate "extended day" programs for families that need care for additional hours in the afternoon. Design an extended day program for CADS that would provide care for 10% of CADS attendees from 4:30pm to 6pm. Prepare a program budget that separates the full-day program from the extended day program, and allocates relevant indirect costs to each. Based on your design and analysis, should CADS offer an extended day program?

Case: Snow Removal

Frank Lennard, supervisor of the snow removal department for the City of Hamtrammack, stared at the memo he had just received from the director of public works. The opening paragraphs were anything but reassuring:

"As you know, I have instituted a new responsibility accounting system. From now on you will receive quarterly reports that compare the cost of operating your department with your budget. The reports will highlight the variance so that you can easily zero in on any departures from your budget. Responsibility accounting means you are to keep the costs in your department within your budget. The variances will help you identify those costs that are out of line, and the sizes of the variances will indicate the most important cost items to address. Your first report accompanies this memo. Your report indicates that several of your costs are significantly above your quarterly budget. You need to pay particular attention to the salaries of your snowplow drivers. Please get back to me by the end of next week with a plan for making the needed reductions."

Frank knew he needed a plan, yet midwinter was the busiest time of the year for snow removal, and a big storm had been predicted for the weekend.

Frank had been with the City for more than 20 years. previously, cost data had been presented to department heads only infrequently, but the new director was certain that more frequent information would provide greater incentives for his department heads to keep their costs under control. The new director had also prepared a budget for each department for the current fiscal year, and had computed quarterly budgets as one-fourth of each department's annual budget. To prepare the budgets, he had analyzed the prior three years' costs, and, in doing so, had learned that almost all of them had increased each year, with more rapid increases in the last two years. his first thought had been to establish the budgeted line items at an average of the prior three years' costs, hoping that such an approach would encourage his department heads to reduce their operating costs to his level. However, in view of the rapid cost increases during the past two years, he chose instead to base the current year's budget on the prior year's costs less three percent. For the snow removal department, he also estimated the cubic miles of snow to be removed, which he set at an average of the past three years.

Lennard received the report show in Exhibit 1 in mid-January. He reflected on its content:

"Some of my costs don't change, even if there's a change in the cubic miles of snow we plow. On the other hand, drivers, supplies, fuel, and maintenance vary almost directly with changes in cubic miles. Shouldn't my budget reflect this distinction? Also, my budget didn't include my October salary increase – was I supposed to refuse it to keep my budget in balance? It's also important to note that I had to pay overtime to the drivers because of some very heavy storms we had back in mid-December. Because of this, my average hourly rate for the whole three months was $21 instead of the $18 that was in my budget. In fact, and maybe this is a little picky, the average number of minutes it took my drivers to plow a cubic mile of snow during the quarter actually dropped from 48, which was my budget target, to 47. Somehow, even though it's pretty small, I think this improvement should be taken into consideration."

City of Hamtrammack, Performance Report, Snow Removal Department, October-December				
	Budget	Actual	(Over) Under Budget	% (Over) under Budget
Snow Days (a)	10	12	(2)	(20%)
Cubic Miles of Snow (b)	1,250	1,500	(250)	(20%)
Costs:				
Drivers (c)	$18,000	$24,675	($6,675)	(37%)
Supplies (d)	1,125	1,874	(750)	(67%)
Fuel	1,750	2,500	(750)	(43%)
Maintenance (e)	1,375	2,200	(825)	(60%)
Supervisor's Salary	15,000	18,000	(3,000)	(20%)
Allocated Administrative Costs (f)	4,000	5,000	(1,000)	(25%)
Equipment Depreciation (g)	1,250	1,250	0	0
Total	$42,500	$55,500	($13,000)	(31%)

Notes:

a. Days when there was at least one inch of snow. Less than that, and no snow plowing took place.

b. Computed, for each storm, by multiplying the depth of snowfall (according to the official measure by the City Clerk) by miles of roadways to be plowed.

c. Drivers were paid hourly, not by the mile. However, the number of hours needed to clear the roadways depended to a great extent on cubic miles of snow. For example, an inch of snow from a relatively light storm would take less time to plow, than six inches of snow from a moderate storm. The amount of time needed to clear the roadways also depended on the length of the storm. For example, if a storm deposited six inches of snow in a few hours, the drivers would wait until the storm had ended, and then clear the roads with one pass of the plows. However, if a storm deposited six inches of snow over, say, a 24 hour period, two or more passes of the plows would be needed to keep the roads clear. When a driver worked more than 8 hours in a 24 hour period, he/she was paid a 50 percent overtime premium for the additional hours.

d. Mainly sand and salt. Office and other administrative supplies were part of the administrative cost allocation.

e. Was almost directly related to miles driven. Thus, a 24 hour storm, requiring several passes, would lead to more maintenance costs than a storm of only a few hours, even if the cubic miles of plowed snow were the same.

f. Based on the town's full cost accounting system. The system used different allocation bases for different city services, such as custodial work, administrative salaries and supplies, and repairs and maintenance.

g. Exclusively for snow plows. The department had no other assets to be depreciated.

Questions:

1. What is your assessment of the method the public works director used to construct the budget?
2. Prepare a flexible budget for the snow plowing department. what does it tell you?
3. Compute the appropriate variances for drivers. What do they tell you?
4. What plan should Frank present to the public works director for making cost reductions?

CHAPTER 6.

BUDGET STRATEGY

BUDGET STRATEGY: GETTING THE DEAL DONE

With a more sophisticated understanding of budget-making processes, public managers can answer a variety of questions and management concerns:

- How is "managing costs" different from "managing a budget"?

- What's the best way – financially and politically – to respond to a potential budget cut? To respond to a potential budget increase or expansion?

- How can we structure our budget process to minimize conflict and maximize employee engagement?

- How does the budget timeline, namely when new information is introduced to budget decision-makers, affect how the budget is made?

- What are budget decision-makers key concerns throughout the budget process? How do loss-aversion, incrementalism, and parochialism affect budget-making?

- How does the format and presentation of a budget document affect how staff, clients, and other stakeholders perceive it?

- Why do government's actual budget processes regularly deviate from their statutory or legal budget processes?

- What are the most and least effective ways to engage citizens and other stakeholders in the budget-making process?

In the late 1990s several dozen people died in major house fires throughout the City of Seattle. Critics blamed the Seattle Fire Department for its slow and insufficient response to those fires. The Fire Chief accepted that criticism, and urged the City's leaders to invest in a significant upgrade to the Fire Department's facilities, equipment, and training. Then-Mayor Greg Nickels proposed a new, ten year $197 million property tax levy to pay for that upgrade, and voters approved that levy in 2003. The centerpiece of that levy was a plan to rebuild or refurbish 33 fire stations.

In 2015 the City announced it had spent $306 million to date on those fire station projects. Of the 33 projects included in the plan, 32 had exceeded their original budgets. Many had cost twice their original estimate. And the program is not yet complete. The City expects to spend at least $50 million more from other resources to complete those projects over the next five years.

How did this happen? How can a major city program staffed with many sophisticated budget and finance staff over-run its budget by more than 50%?

The problem is best captured by the late, great Yogi Berra's adage that "Predictions are hard, especially about the future." Costs of basic materials and labor change all the time, so it's difficult to forecast those costs seven to ten years into the future. And indeed, basic construction costs increased by around one-third from early 2005 until late 2007. Moreover, during the ten years of the program, professional standards for fire fighters changed. Under the new standards, fire stations must now have better training and fitness facilities, better information technology, and other upgrades that added costs to the projects.

To others, the problem is politics. According to some accounts, Mayor Nickels' staff estimated the fire station program would cost around $300 million. The Mayor, however, did not believe voters would approve that large a tax increase. So instead, he proposed the highest possible levy he believed would pass, and he assumed the fire stations could be built at lower costs or that additional money for the program would come from future city budgets. Whether you believe the problem is forecasting, politics, or something else, it's clear that the legacy of the fire station levy is two-fold: better fire protection and, presumably, closer scrutiny of future long-term capital projects.

This story illustrates the central point of this chapter: How we make a budget is just as important as the revenues and spending proposed within it. Consider, for instance, how changes to the City's budget process might have produced a different outcome for the fire station levy:

- If the program had not required voter approval, Mayor Nickels might have proposed a much larger levy that better reflected the full cost of the program.

- At the same time, if the City had paid for the full cost of fire stations out of general fund resources that did not require voter approval, then those projects might have crowded out the Mayor's other high-priority projects in areas like economic development and affordable housing.

- If the City Council had better access to more sophisticated cost estimates earlier on in the approval process for the new levy, they might have supported a higher requested amount, or been willing to spend additional city resources.

- If the City Council members were elected by districts (as they are today) rather than at-large (as they were then), then specific members would have had a stronger incentive to monitor the costs and timing of fire station projects within their districts. That might have produced more substantial changes to the program at both the planning and implementation stages.

- If the City's capital budgeting process had more stringent accountability features, then the mayor might have reduced the budget for projects scheduled later in the program once it was clear that the first few projects had run over budget.

Learning Objectives

After reading this chapter, you should:

- Recognize the key components of a public organization's budget timeline/calendar and formal/legal budget process.

- Know the typical sources of conflict and compromise in the budgeting process.

- Recognize the many different ways that we define "budget balance" and implications of those various definitions.

- Recognize that budgets ensure fiscal accountability, but do not guarantee financial solvency

- Know the basic strategies managers use to expand their budget authority or respond to potential cuts.

- Acknowledge the effectiveness of "doing nothing" as a budget-cutting strategy.

- Recognize when and why an organization's budget for a service might be quite different from what that service costs.

THE BUDGET PROCESS

Public managers can't control many of the factors that affect their budgets. Managers in government can't control the broader economy. Non-profit managers can't do much to affect the financial health of the foundations that grant them money or individuals who support them through donations. Managers across the public sector can do little to affect rising costs for employee health care, new technology, wages and salaries, and a variety of other factors that drive growth in expenses. The best we can do is understand these trends, forecast them to the best of our ability, and help policymakers understand the trade-offs these trends put in play.

But public managers can control how they make their budgets, also known as the *budget process*. In fact, process is perhaps the only part of budgeting that public managers can control. In particular, you alone can answer many of the key questions surrounding each of the three main budget process concerns:

1. Who proposes the budget? Do you develop and propose your budget on your own? When developing your initial assumptions do you solicit input from program managers or other subordinates, your board/council or other policy leaders, outside funders, or other key stakeholders? Do you ask department heads or other subordinates to develop and submit their own budgets?

2. What information is introduced into the budget process, and when? Do you share the key budget assumptions with program managers, line staff, and other stakeholders? Do you connect budgeted spending with key performance targets? If so, do you make those targets available to other stakeholders? If your budget calls for cuts, do you share when and how those cuts will happen? Do you explain why you chose the cuts you chose? Do you share that information with the entire organization at once, or through meetings with individual program managers/ department heads/etc.?

3. Who decides on final budgeted revenues and spending? Do you afford program managers/ department heads/etc. the latitude to propose their own final budget? Does your council/board approve the budget in one action, or in stages? If you have the authority to make budget *amendments* or *re-appropriations?* Do you use it, and when? Does your budget include both operations and capital projects, or just operations?

Operating vs. Capital Budgeting

Most state and local government budgets include both an operating budget, or a budget for recurring spending items, and a capital budget for revenues and spending related to long-term assets like buildings, equipment, and infrastructure. Most day-to-day operations of core programs are covered in the operating budget. The capital budget is often part of a three to ten year capital improvement plan (CIP) that identifies long-term capital spending needs. In a well-designed budget process, the operating budget includes spending related to debt service, maintenance, and other near-term parts of the capital budget. Capital budgeting is challenging because it's less visible, but incredibly expensive. Consider, for instance, that 70% of infrastructure assets are underground, but that it costs $140,000/mile/year to maintain roads

---

For this and many other reasons it's important to understand some of the main features of public organizations' budget processes. This discussion is focused on governments' budget processes, mostly because those processes are most comparable and are often prescribed by state or federal law. That said, many of the basic features of those processes can also apply to non-profits. Moreover, it's important for non-profit managers to understand how government budgets are made, given the centrality of government funding to many non-profit budgets.

BASIC BUDGET TIMELINE

The budget process in public sector organizations share some common characteristics[1]. Most follow these same basic steps:

1. **Strategic and Department-Level Planning**: This process often begins five to six months prior to the start of the next fiscal year. Program directors, together with department heads and agency directors will need to develop goals and objectives. Ideally, these are connected to the organization's broader strategic plan. At the same time the executive (governor, mayor, city manager, county administrator, chief executive officer, executive director etc) will transmit his or her budget priorities, together with instructions and assumptions, to agency directors and program managers. They'll use budget instructions and assumptions to prepare their budget based on executive priorities and on their own spending needs.

2. **Revenue Forecasting:** In most instances, revenue forecasting is an ongoing process that starts two to six months prior to the fiscal year, and revised throughout the budget execution phase of the cycle. Revenue officials (treasurer, chief financial officer, finance director, development officer etc) will track economic trends and project revenues for the fiscal year. The final revenue

---

1. Portions of the following discussion are quoted and adopted from the *Governing Guide to Financial Literacy, Volume 1*

forecast is usually the basis for budgeted revenues. Most states and large local governments have a consensus revenue forecast group comprising executive and legislative staff. Others hire consulting firms that prepare, present, and revise multi-year revenue forecasts.

3. **Executive Preparation:** Once budgets are submitted to the executive office, budget staff will review departmental and program budget requests and use these budget to prepare the *proposed* budget. That's not to say that departmental and program budget requests are adopted as is. In fact, department heads and program directors are often asked to present and defend their budgets, especially if budgets are not consistent with the executive's priorities or exceed budgeted allocations.

4. **Legislative Review and Adoption**: The legislative review process, which often integrates public hearings, begins one to two months prior to the start of the fiscal year. Legislators will review the executive's proposed budget, question department and agency heads about their spending plans, and recommend changes that would be included in the final appropriations bill or *approved* budget. A vast majority of legislative bodies in government will hold public hearings. For states, hearings are part of the regular budget legislative session. For local governments, budget hearings are typically stand-alone public meetings. For non-profits, these are often closed meetings in which the executive director, or the chair of the finance committee, presents the budget to the board of directors. Budgets are often adopted two to three weeks prior to the start of the fiscal year. Once legislators pass a budget, the governor will sign it, or use the line-item veto to change parts of the legislators' budget and have those changes approved with only a majority vote of the legislature. For city and county governments with a stand-alone mayor or executive, the approval is much like the state. In cases where the executive is appointed, the budget is passed once it is approved.

6. **Implementation:** Once the budget is approved, department heads and program managers will implement the amended/approved budget over the next twelve months. A majority of organizations anticipate changes in forecasted revenues and budgeted spending. They'll plan for mid-year adjustments, some of which may require formal changes to the adopted budget. The central budget office will closely monitor the execution processes and adjust next year's budget instructions accordingly.

7. **Audit and Evaluation:** This stage starts at the end of the fiscal year and can take many months depending on the size of the organization, complexity of the jurisdiction's chart of accounts, size and professional skills of budget staff and treasury officers, to name a few. Virtually every organization has to "close its books" and prepare financial statements ahead of a financial *audit*. They will also engage on evaluation processes on program effectiveness, especially if these were not integrated in the execution phase. The Governmental Accountability Office (GAO) is the audit and evaluation arm of the federal government. It's tasked with "auditing agency operations to determine whether federal funds are being spent efficiently and effectively" and "reporting on how well government programs and policies are meeting their objectives" to name a few.

Revenue vs. Cash flow forecasting
Forecasting has increasingly become an important fiscal planning tool. As the name suggests, to forecast

is to "predict or estimate of future events." This is often challenging in volatile economic environments. Finance officers will forecast revenues and incorporate estimates in the proposed and approved budget. For a majority of governments, revenue projections are multi-year forecasts for each unique revenue stream. The proposed or approved budget is then used to create cash flow forecasts – i.e. projections of cash inflows and cash outflows. However, unlike revenue forecasts that are multi-year projections, cash flow forecasts are on a monthly or quarterly basis. Cash flow forecasting is critical, particularly when cash flows are lumpy. For example, cash flows from sales taxes or user fees are monthly, but cash flows from property tax are on a semi-annual basis. Similarly, nonprofits will receive sizeable cash donations year end or following a campaign or special event. Moreover, grants and contracts are frequently on a reimbursement basis. Mangers therefore need to plan when and to what extent they'll draw on existing cash reserves, liquidate investments, tap their line of credit, or issue short-term notes. Conversely, they'll use the cash flow forecast to plan how they'll restore reserves, invest in safe money-market instruments, or payoff short-term debt.

THE FEDERAL GOVERNMENT "BUDGET PROCESS"

The federal government's budget process is really three processes in one. The president develops and proposes the *executive budget*, also known as the *budget request*. In Congress, the House Budget committee and the Senate budget committee pass a *budget resolution* that identifies the main spending policies and targets for the Congressional side of the budget. The budget resolution allocates *budget authority*, or the power to incur spending obligations, and *budget outlays*, or the amount of cash that will flow from the Treasury to a federal agency. Most budget authority must be re-authorized each year, even though many programs and services call for budget outlays that will span multiple years. It's not uncommon for a project to receive budget authority but not receive adequate budget outlays

The third part of the process is that the House Ways and Means committee and the Senate appropriations committee pass a series of *appropriations bills* that allow the rest of the government to spend money. Once the appropriations bills are passed, usually following a lengthy conference committee process, and the President signs them, those bills become the federal budget.

The basic timeline for the federal budget process was outlined in the *Congressional Budget Act of 1974*. That process is as follows, with the goal of passing the new budget prior to the end of the federal fiscal year on September 30:

• November/December (shortly after passage of the current fiscal year's budget): President's *Office of Management and Budget* works with executive agencies to develop their budget requests for the coming fiscal year. Executive agencies includes all the cabinet-level agencies like the Departments of State, Treasury, Justice, Education, etc., as well as the federal judiciary, independent regulatory agencies, and several other parts of the federal government.

• February: President submits the budget request, usually concurrent with the State of the Union address. House and Senate Budget committees, and House and Senate appropriation committees, working through their subcommittees, hold hearings and develop appropriation bills that provide funds for agency operations.

- March/April: Budget committees prepare a budget resolution. This resolution is an act of Congress, therefore does not require the President's signature. Because the budget resolution does not go to the President, it cannot enact spending or tax law. Instead, it sets targets for other congressional committees than can propose legislation directly providing or changing spending and taxes.

- April/May: House-Senate conference committee negotiates the final budget resolution. Congress adopts that resolution.

- May/June: House and Senate appropriations committees make their *302(b) allocations*. These allocations establish the spending cap for each of the appropriations subcommittees

- June/July: House and Senate committees prepare *reconciliation bills*. These are bills that implement changes in *authorizing legislation*, or the laws that determine spending on entitlement programs, required by the budget resolution. Most resolution measures are related to entitlement spending like Medicare or to changes in tax law, namely tax cuts. Meanwhile, the appropriations committees debate and prepare appropriations bills.

- July/August: House and Senate pass their appropriations and reconciliation bills.

- September: Conference committees resolve differences in the final appropriations and reconciliation bills. President signs those bills.

- October 1: Fiscal year begins

The Congressional Budget Act of 1974 established the formal rules of the federal budgeting game. However, in the last few decades, the formal budgeting process explains less and less of how the federal government actually spends money. Consider the following:

- If the appropriations bills are not signed into law by Oct. 1 Congress must pass a *continuing resolution*. This is a temporary measure that extends the existing appropriations bills for a short time, usually 30 to 60 days. For 16 of the past 20 years, Congress has passed at least one continuing resolution. In some years, the government operated on continuing resolutions for most of the next fiscal year.

- For most of the past 20 years Congress has not passed a budget resolution. Without a resolution, the House and Senate usually pass different substitute versions of the budget targets that would otherwise appear in the budget resolution. Those substitute or *deeming* authorization bills are advisory, rather than binding on the appropriations committees.

- At any point during the fiscal year Congress can impose a *rescission* that cancels existing budget authority. In fact, the threat of rescission, and in some cases the actual use of it, has become a way to enforce de facto budget priorities that were never written into the budget resolution or appropriations bills. The best recent example is Congress' persistent attempts to strip funding for the Affordable Care Act (ACA, more commonly referred to as "Obamacare").

- In 2011 Congress passed the Budget Control Act (BCA). This law established that unless Congress can reduce the annual budget deficit by a predetermined target, then automatic cuts in discretionary and selected entitlement – known broadly as the *sequester* – will take effect. Unless amended, BCA extends the sequester through 2021. Neither the Budget Act, nor any other piece of federal budget legislation makes mention of anything like the sequester. BCA was the latest of many *statutory budget caps* designed to automatically limit federal government spending. Those caps are not part of the existing budget process framework laid out in the Congressional Budget Act.

- Many of the federal government's most expensive activities are now paid for outside of the budget process. The best recent example is the wars in Iraq and Afghanistan. By some estimates, those engagement have cost $1-3 trillion, or somewhere between $2,000 and $10,000 for every US taxpayer. Congress appropriated around $50 billion for "The Surge" of US troops into Iraq as part of the FY2006 Defense Department Appropriations bill. But otherwise, the vast majority of the funding for that war was allocated through *supplemental appropriations* and *budget amendments*. Supplemental appropriations are an appropriations bill that adds to an existing appropriation. They are designed to provide resources for unexpected emergencies, such as disaster relief after a hurricane or earthquake. Budget amendments are changes to budget outlays to that same effect. Most of these supplemental/emergency appropriations were financed with debt.

- Since roughly 1990, Congress has used budget *reconciliation* to pass several major pieces of legislation, including the "Bush tax cuts," the Medicare prescription drug benefit ("Part D"), and the Affordable Care Act. Reconciliation is a powerful tool because by Senate rules, reconciliation bills are not subject to filibuster. A *filibuster* is when an individual Senator kills a proposed bill by "talking it to death," taking advantage of Senate rules that allow for unlimited debate. To end a filibuster, the Senate must invoke *cloture* with a two-thirds majority vote of all Senators. Given the highly partisan character of the Senate throughout the past few decades, the threat of a filibuster is always present, which imposes a de facto two-thirds majority to approve virtually every piece of legislation proposed in the Senate.

STATE AND LOCAL BUDGET PROCESS

At the state and local level much of this same basic process applies. Substitute the governor or mayor for the president, and substitute the state legislature or city council for Congress. The same basic tensions among near-term spending needs, appropriations, and budget authority apply.

A vast majority of states prepare and present an annual budget. Washington State is one of a few states that prepares a biennial budget with an annual session.[2] In other words, the states prepares and presents a budget for two years at a time and adjusts that budget at the end of the first year. Many cities, including Seattle, follow a similar model. In concept, biennial budgeting facilitates more effective long-term planning. In practice, revenue and spending estimates are often adjusted, sometimes substantially, after the end of the first year.

In January 2015 the WA legislature debated and ultimately passed a budget for the 2015-2017 *biennium* (i.e. two-year period). The basic steps to arrive at that budget were as follows:

---

2. Other states include Connecticut, Hawaii, Indiana, Kentucky, Maine, Minnesota, Nebraska, New Hampshire, North Carolina, Ohio, Oregon, Virginia, Washington, Wisconsin, and Wyoming. States with biennial budget and biennial sessions are some of the smallest in the nation -- Montana, Nevada, and North Dakota. Texas is the exception here.

- June-September 2014: State agencies prepared and submitted budget requests to the Governor. Much of that preparation process is done by the Governor's *Office of Financial Management* (OFM). OFM is the state's analog to the federal OMB, and this process is akin to how OMB gathers budget requests from all the executive agencies.

- December 2014: Governor Inslee proposed a budget to the state legislature immediately before the start of the 2015 legislative session.

- January-March 2015: Legislature debated and prepared its own legislative budget. Specific committees in both the House and Senate have specific responsibilities to prepare parts of the state legislative budget, including: Appropriations, Capital, Finance, and Transportation. Unlike the federal budget, the state budgeting process does not call for separate authorizing and appropriations processes. Legislative budget-writers include both authorizing and appropriations language in the same legislation.

- February 2015: The WA State Economic and Revenue Forecast Council met and determined the final revenue cap for the coming biennium. This is a key part of the budget debate. If the Council increases its expected revenues from its previous forecast, then state budget writers are able to work within a higher spending cap, and vice versa.

- March-April 2015: Legislature debated its legislative budget. Conference committees worked to resolve large differences between the House and Senate versions. A particularly contentious part of this debate was how to fund a $2 billion classroom size reduction measure that voters passed in 2014, an additional $1 billion in court-mandated spending on public education, and a multi-billion statewide transportation funding package. The Democrat-controlled House of Representatives proposed funding for many of these initiatives through a new statewide capital gains tax and an increase in gasoline taxes. The Republican-led Senate proposed diverting money from taxes on newly-legalized marijuana, in addition to cuts and re-appropriations.

- April 26, 2015: The regular 105 day legislative session ended without a passed budget bill.

- June 2015: The Economic and Revenue Forecast Council released its revised revenue estimates, which called for an additional 3-5\% growth in revenue collections. If the budget process is behind schedule, as was the case that year, the Forecast Council's revision can impact the final budget bill.

- June 1, 2015: Governor Inslee called the legislature back for a 30 day *special legislative session* to debate and pass a budget.

- June 15, 2015: The special session expired with no budget

- June 17, 2015: Governor Inslee called a second special legislative session.

- June 30, 2015: The second special legislative session expired without a budget; the legislature passed and Governor Inslee signed a temporary spending measure to keep government from shutting down.

- July 1, 2015: Governor Inslee called a third special legislative session.

- July 9, 2015: The legislature passed a budget.

- July 10, 2015: Governor Inslee signed a $39 billion biennial budget. This concluded the longest legislative session in state history.

- July 2015: New budget took effect.
- January-June 2016: Legislature considered and passed a *supplemental* budget to adjust the biennial budget for the remainder of the biennium. This process is essentially the same as the legislative budget process, but it is not as comprehensive.

The Importance of Fiscal Notes

One of the most important roles for state budget analysts it to prepare fiscal notes. A *fiscal note* is an analysis of how a proposed piece of legislation would affect the existing state budget. Most are prepared by staff at OFM, or by non-partisan staff for the legislature's Ways and Means Committee or other relevant committees. Budget staff in Seattle's budget office also prepare fiscal notes that pay particular attention to the implications of budget decisions for race and social justice. Specifically, they look at how potential cuts or changes in programs, or the incidence of a new tax or fee, might disproportionately affect people of color or particular neighborhoods within the City.

Cities, counties, schools, and special districts generally follow the same basic process. In Washington State, most local governments follow a January 1 fiscal year. The mayor/executive/superintendent's staff review departments' budget proposals throughout the late summer and early fall, and the mayor/executive/superintendent proposes a budget in usually in early September. The Council/Board debates the budget and revises it throughout the late fall and early winter. At the City of Seattle those proposed changes are articulated in *Green Sheets* that suggest a change to the Mayor's proposed budget. State law requires a passed budget by December 2. Most local governments do not have the same executive-legislative tensions as the state and federal government, and local budget processes are rarely as formal, but the same basic processes, institutions, and incentives are at play.

Making a Change

When spending on a capital project is expected to exceed its budget, the party responsible for the project – usually a private partner or contractor – must request a *change order*. If the government approves that change order the project budget is amended and the additional costs are incurred. Change orders happen for a variety of reasons, but most commonly for increases in commodities or other basic construction costs, and for unexpected challenges with excavation and other site preparation during the early stages of construction. An effective *capital budgeting* process includes a procedure to quickly evaluate change orders and, if necessary, require governing body approval.

BUDGETING IN THE NONPROFIT SECTOR

Budget process in the nonprofit sector are comparable to those of government, except their processes are not as protracted. For the average mid-sized nonprofit, program directors will often submit a wish-list budget to a budget or finance officer, who then scrutinizes their budget in relation to the organizations strategic plan and policy priorities. Larger nonprofits will provide program directors with specific guidance on policy priorities, budget format, and key assumptions. For a vast majority of small to medium sized nonprofits, budget preparation is generally a responsibility of the executive director. The executive director, together with the finance officer, will finalize the budget and present the proposed budget to the finance committee, a committee delegated by the board, or the full board. Adoption of a budget by the full board should make it unwavering policy. Like most governments, budgets are frequently revised to reflect changes in revenues and expenses. Board members will frequently receive monthly or annual budget reports detailing year-to-date revenues and expenses, budget variances, and key changes in programs or policies that affect the operating budget.

Budget Balance, in Theory and Practice

By definition, state and local government budgets must balance. But perhaps surprisingly, there's no uniform definition of "balanced budget." A budget can be balanced by several different definitions. Each state and locality is subject to a different mix of state and local laws that define balance. Some of the most common definitions are based on different ideas about *solvency*. For instance:

- *Cash solvency.* The budget is balanced if short-term assets cover short-term liabilities. In other words, does this government have the resources on hand to cover its short-term liabilities as those liabilities come due?

- *Budgetary solvency.* The budget is balanced if budgeted revenues are greater than budgeted expenditures. For some governments this means budgeted revenues must equal or exceed budgeted revenues when the budget is passed. This is also known as balance "at adoption." For others, it means budgeted revenues and expenditures must equal actual revenues and expenditures, also known as balance "at conclusion." In some governments budgeted revenues and expenditures must equal or exceed actual revenues and expenditures at periodic intervals throughout the fiscal year. Some balanced budget laws require these definitions be applied to just the general fund, where others apply them to all governmental funds or total government revenues and spending.

- *Long-run solvency.* The budget is balanced if total long-term assets cover total long-term liabilities. This definition is based on accrual accounting. It's designed to ensure that the government does not incur a structural deficit.

- *Service-level solvency.* Some local governments take a longer view of solvency, defining balance as when revenue-generation capacity covers expected future service obligations.

INCREMENTALISM AND BUDGET REFORMS

Budgeting is many things to public organizations. It's a mechanism to plan and develop strategy for the coming year. It's a tool to evaluate how well managers manage. It's a way to evaluate if and how an organization's resources are connected to it's priorities. It's a tool to get feedback from key stakeholders about an organization's successes and failures. For governments, the budget is a legally binding document that commits it to a spending plan for the coming year(s). But fundamentally, budgeting is a form of politics. Resources are scarce, and budgeting is the process by which organizations allocate those scarce resources. As such, budgeting is about managing conflict.

Budgeting in governments, and most large bureaucratic institutions, is an *incremental* process. That is, the focal point for each year's budget is an incremental increase or decrease over last year's budget. Put differently, there's an old adage: "most budgets are last year's budget plus three percent." Since the Great Recession most budgets have been last year minus three/five/ten percent. For budget policymakers, conflict and compromise is often around that annual percentage change, or *increment*. This assumes, of course, that last year's budget – or *base budget* – was a fair representation of the organization's goals and priorities. If this is not true, then debating incremental change will only amplify that disconnect between resources and priorities. In fact, for most public organizations, that disconnect is persistent and pervasive.

Historically, governments have prepared line-item budgets that place significant emphasis on inputs. Unfortunately, line-item budgets do not present information in a format that connect its mission to its money. A vast majority have experimented with various budgeting models designed to "reform" the line-item format and incrementalist tendency. One of the most popular reform strategies is to allocate resources not through political bargaining, but in a more mechanical or formula-driven way that's driven by priorities or goals. For roughly fifty years one of the most popular strategies to this effect is *performance budgeting*. In this format, the organization allocates resources not according to inputs or line items like salaries or supplies, but rather according to the level of overall resources, regardless of inputs needed to achieve some desired goal or outcome. Some governments extend this model into a *Price of Government* or *Priorities of Government* approach. Under this model citizens identify the levels and outcomes of government services most important to them, and the government allocates packages of resources to achieve those outcomes.

Performance budgeting and the "Priorities of Government" approach are not mutually exclusive. Cities like Redmond, WA and Somerville, MA have implemented performance-based budgeting programs that are tightly connected to strategic priorities. In the Somerville model, departments orient their budget requests around outcomes rather than budget inputs or *line items*. For example, the library system requests its budget in terms of the cost per library patron served, not just in terms of payroll, commodities, equipment, and other line items.

A few state and local governments have experimented with versions of *zero-based budgeting* (ZBB). Under ZBB the organization assumes there is no such thing as a base budget. Each year departments and programs must justify everything in their budget. Much of the money state and local government spend is "required by law" or "necessary for public safety," so a large portion of a government's budget cannot be cut through a ZBB process. Some versions of ZBB require departments/programs to connect their non-required spending to the organization's strategic goals or priorities. Proposed spending most closely connected to those goals is most likely to make its way into the final budget, and vice versa. In some ZBB models departments and programs must present decision makers with "scenarios" or "decision packages" that identify what will happen if their department/program does not receive a portion of its base budget. All these innovations are designed to remove some or all of the pure political bargaining from budgeting.

That said, the vast majority of governments and non-profit organizations continue to practice traditional, incremental, line-item budgeting.

"Creating" Budget Balance

One of the main criticisms of state and local budgets is that "balanced budgets" might actually hide structural deficits. There are two reasons for this. First, most governments prepare their budgets on a cash basis rather than an accrual basis. This masks the long-term effects of current budget decisions. Second, managers and policymakers can employ a variety of tactics to create "phantom" budget balance. They include:

- Inter-fund transfers and fund sweeps. Moving resources in and out of governmental funds just before or just after budget approval for the sole purpose of presenting a balanced budget.

- Under-estimate revenue collections. Budgeting for less revenue than you expect to collect will produce an end of year "surplus."

- Over-estimate expenditures. Budgeting for more than you intend to spend also produces an end of year "surplus."

- Shift revenue collection dates and due dates. This changes when revenues are recognized, and that can change the complexion of budget balance in a given fiscal period.

- Under or overestimate property tax delinquency. Overestimating delinquency is akin to underestimating revenue collections, and vice versa.

- Use of one-time revenues such as capital asset sales and leases, privatizations, and contract arrangements. This is why one-time revenues should never be used to fund the operating budget.

- Delay intergovernmental payments. This is a common tactic because governments have limited ability to collect revenues from each other.

- The "Magic Asterisk." This tactic was made famous by President Reagan's long-time budget director David Stockman. He would routinely budget for higher spending without an concurrent increase in revenues. Resources to cover the new spending would come from vaguely-described "projected savings" and "efficiency gains" in existing programs. Programs expected to produce those new resources were identified with an asterisk in President Reagan's budgets, hence the name the "Magic Asterisk."

BUDGET POLITICS

Within the formal budget process, there are budget politics. For most public managers the politics and strategy of making a budget are just as important, if not more important, than the formal budget process. Here we briefly discuss some of the most common budget-making strategies. Some of these strategies are more appropriate if the goals is to limit spending, while others are more appropriate if an department or agency wants to expand programs, or at the very least maintain status quo. They include:

- Cultivate a clientele. Effective public managers understand who "uses" and who "benefits" from their programs and services. They also understand that those users are the best advocates for a program. This is especially true for programs that benefit children, the disabled, and other vulnerable populations. A simple anecdote about a program from one of its clients can be exponentially more powerful than a well-done differential cost analysis.

- Make friends with legislators. Legislators are much more likely to support a program when they understand that program and who benefits from it. This is particularly true when that program benefits their constituents, and when they played a role in creating, expanding, or protecting it. Of course, this strategy comes with risks. Governors, mayors, and other executives often try to limit department heads and program managers' access to legislators to prevent staff relationships with legislators that might undermine their own budget priorities.

- "Round it Up." This is especially true on the spending side. Rounding up caseloads, spending estimates, interest expenses, and other costs will expand budget authority and, if actual spending falls short of budgeted spending, create an end of year "surplus." The risk is that persistent over-budgeting for spending can undermine a budget-maker's credibility.

- "We have a crisis." Some managers like to project that major revenue shortfalls or spending cuts are imminent, even if they aren't. Staff who believe they might face difficult budget cuts are more likely to manage their programs with careful attention to spending discipline and timely collection of revenues. Of course, this can also lead to staff burn-out and ruin a manager's credibility if said crisis never happens.

A few strategies are most effective when a manager is asked to trim their budget.

- "Across-the-Board." Some managers prefer to respond to budget cuts by cutting all their programs equally, or "across the board" (ATB). To staff, ATB cuts appear fair, transparent, and simple. Cutting all programs equally assumes those programs have identical cost structures, current staff openings, and capacity to generate revenues. That's rarely true. The result is that ATB often affects different programs and services in quite different ways, even though the intent is to bring about a uniform impact. Sometimes those differential effects can themselves be valuable to managers.

- "Do Nothing." An unchanged budget is, in effect, a budget cut. If a program is given no new resources it must find other ways to address cost inflation, growth in caseloads, staff cost of living adjustments, and other growth in spending. Sophisticated managers argue, often successfully, that a "steady state" budget (i.e. no new resources, but no cuts) is a fair way to take a budget cut.

- Lean on precedent. In a cutback environment, what happened in the past can be a powerful tool for managers. No manager wants to have to choose how to cut his or her program. But if they can say "I didn't really choose these cuts, we're just following past precedent" they're afforded some degree of political cover. Whether past precedent really dictated those cuts, or whether there even is a past precedent, are often debatable.

- "It's essential for public safety." Managers can try to position their program as vital to public health or safety. Sometimes these connections are obtuse, at best. For instance, during the Great Recession, many local libraries protested cuts to library hours by pointing out that libraries are a safe and supportive gathering place for teenagers. Unsupervised teenagers roaming the streets would create, they argued, a serious public safety concern.

- Propose a study. Public organizations can rarely predict, or so they say, exactly how a budget cut will affect their clients, staff, and overall mission. So in response to a cut, managers routinely propose to "study the issue." A study allows for more time to either identify potential cuts, or, for the political or economic environment to shift in ways that will obviate the need for a cut at all.

- "Cut the main artery." One way to respond to a requested cut is to cut the largest program that's most central to your mission (i.e. the "main artery"). Cutting that program is, in effect, threatening to cripple your program. Some policymakers will respond with a request for a smaller cut or to a cut to a program that's less mission-centric. The danger here is what happens if policymakers agree to allow a manager to cut the main artery.

- "Just take the whole thing." If a program was cut recently, managers can take the request for an additional cut as an opportunity to offer to end the program. They'll ask: "We've already been cut to the bone, so what's the point of staying open?" or something to that effect. Whether additional cuts would really harm the program is often incidental to the argument.

- "You pick." Instead of proposing cuts, offer policymakers a range of options and ask them to decide which option the program should pursue. Like with "lean on precedent," this allows managers to avoid direct responsibility for specific cuts to his or her staff and other resources. This strategy is prone to backfire when policymakers respond by saying "It's not my job to pick. You know your program better than anyone. You pick."

- "Washington Monument." In 1994 the federal government shut down after President Clinton and House Speaker Gingrich could not agree on a continuing resolution. President Clinton responded by ordering the National Park Service to close all of the key historic sites in Washington, DC. One of the first to close was the Washington Monument. As the shutdown dragged on, President Clinton was able to frame the closed Washington Monument as a symbol of Congressional intransigence. The essence of the Washington Monument strategy is to propose cuts to a small, but highly visible program.

And finally, managers often deploy a different set of strategies when attempting to expand their program's budget:

- "It pays for itself." Managers can sometimes argue that investing in a program will "pay for itself" through cost savings later. For instance, public health advocates have long argued that expanding childhood immunization programs pays for itself by reducing the incidence of communicable diseases like tuburculosis, measles, and rubuella that place enormous strain and expense on public hospitals.

- "Spend to save." Investments in technology, equipment, and infrastructure can save staff time, reduce paperwork, collect revenues faster, etc. Or, at least, that's how managers sell those investments in the budget process.

- "Foot in the Door." Many large, long-standing, popular public sector programs began small. An effective way to expand a program is to run a small pilot program, study, or demonstration project. Legislators and board members are generally willing to appropriate small amounts of money to try "innovative" approaches. With time, many of those small experiments morph into large-scale programs.

- "It's just temporary." Like "small innovations," legislators and board members are much more willing to provide temporary funding for a program or project than they are to provide permanent funding or budget authority. Crafty managers are able to convert temporary funding into either "ongoing temporary funding" or even permanent authority.

- "Finish what we started." This approach is especially popular with respect to capital projects. Many capital projects begin with an appropriation to analyze, plan, and design a capital project. With that planning in place, managers can make a compelling argument that it's necessary to appropriate more money to "finish what we started," often without regard for whether the plans are complete or whether the analysis suggests the project is even necessary.

- "Re-categorize." Sometimes shifting a program to a different part of the budget is a necessary step toward expansion. For example, public health advocates have successfully argued that many public health activities like smoking cessation or diabetes prevention are actually education or outreach programs. Within the education budget they have access to a much wider range of funding sources and constituent champions. We've seen a similar dynamic with homeland security. Many programs in areas like crime prevention and cybersecurity were once local public safety initiatives, but have since migrated to far more lucrative state and federal homeland security budgets.

Practice Questions

1. Pick three US states and compare their balanced budget requirements. How do those requirements define budget balance? Does the balance requirement apply to the enterprise funds? To the government as a whole?

2. The following are proposals legislators are considering for balancing the 2016 budget. You've been asked to identify whether the proposed strategy is appropriate (yes or no). Briefly discuss the policy implication(s) of each strategy.

   ◦ A proposal by a legislator to increase the revenue forecast provided by the staff in the comptroller office.

   ◦ A proposal to issue $10 million in bonds. Proceeds from the debt issue will be used to close the gap in the operating budget. The treasurer projects the bonds will paid off in full in FY 2030.

   ◦ A proposal to draw down on existing reserves and limit contributions to the reserve fund through FY 2020.

   ◦ A proposal that projects savings in key initiatives that could materialize in the next three to five years. The savings are based on current estimates for demand for services and improvements in technology used to deliver the services and is contingent on the programs receiving funding for the initiatives.

   ◦ A proposal to cut base funding for all programs by 5 percent.

   ◦ A proposal to limit intergovernmental transfers to local governments (e.g., county, city, school districts etc.).

   ◦ A proposal to lease out parking garages to a private vendor for a 10-year period (FY 2025). The one-time lump-sum payment from the private vendor will be used to close the current year budget gap.

- A proposal to delay improvements on public buildings and local infrastructure as well as limit purchases of new equipment through FY 2018.

- A proposal to provide competitive funding (e.g., $100,000 up to $1,000,000) to programs or department to develop projects that would streamline service, improve efficiency, and achieve cost savings.

- A proposal to privately operate highway rest stop areas. While the vendors will be expected to make regular payments to the Department of Transportation (DOT), ownership of the properties will not transfer to the private operator.

3. What are some of the potential advantages and disadvantages of a biennial budget compared to an annual budget?
4. What are some of the most popular alternatives to traditional, line-item, incremental budgeting? What are the advantages and disadvantages of those models, compared to incremental budgeting?

CPSIA information can be obtained
at www.ICGtesting.com
Printed in the USA
LVHW050420260721
693564LV00006B/51

9 781927 472590